VisualAge for Smalltalk Distributed

Developing Distributed Object Applications

The VisualAge Series

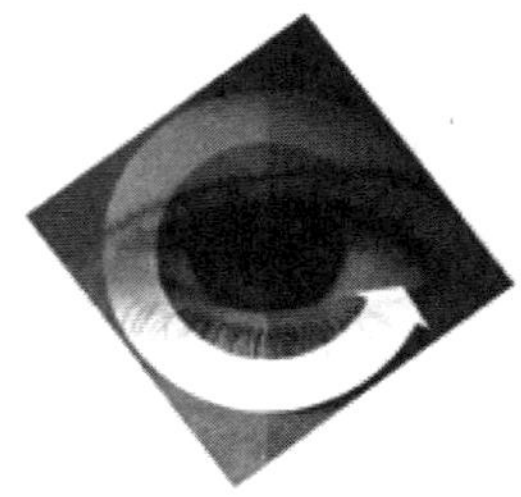

Bitterer, Brassard, Nadal, and Wong
VisualAge and Transaction Processing in a Client/Server Envir.onment

Bitterer, Hamada, Oosthuizen, Porciello, and Rambek
AS/400 Application Development with VisualAge for Smalltalk

Bitterer, Carrel-Billiard, Bianco, Bosman-Clark, Georges, and Tsang
World Wide Web Server Development with VisualAge for C++ and Smalltalk

Carrel-Billiard, Jakab, Mauny, and Vetter
Object-Oriented Application Development with VisualAge for C++ for OS/2

Fang, Chu, and Weyerhäuser
VisualAge for Smalltalk and SOMobjects: Developing Distributed Object Applications

Fang, Guyet, Haven, Vilmi, and Eckmann
VisualAge for Smalltalk Distributed: Developing Distributed Object Applications

VisualAge for Smalltalk Distributed

Developing Distributed Object Applications

Walter Fang
Sven Guyet
Randy Haven
Matti Vilmi
Eduardo Eckmann

INTERNATIONAL TECHNICAL SUPPORT ORGANIZATION
SAN JOSE, CALIFORNIA 95120

PRENTICE HALL PTR
UPPER SADDLE RIVER, NEW JERSEY 07458

This edition applies to Version 3.0 of IBM VisualAge for Smalltalk product set, and to all subsequent releases and modifications until otherwise indicated in new editions.

Comments about IBM Redbooks may be addressed to:
IBM Corporation ITSO, 471/80-E2, 650 Harry Road, San Jose, California 95120-6099

Published by Prentice Hall PTR
Prentice-Hall, Inc.
A Simon & Schuster Company
Upper Saddle River, NJ 07458

Acquisitions Editor: Michael E. Meehan
Manufacturing Manager: Alexis R. Heydt
Cover Design: Andreas Bitterer, Marc Carrel-Billiard, Design Source
Copy Editors: Laura Nystrom, Camie Goffi
Production Supervision: Patti Guerrieri

The publisher offers discounts on this book when ordered in bulk quantities. For more information, contact:
Corporate Sales Department, Prentice Hall PTR, One Lake Street, Upper Saddle River, NJ 07458
Phone: 800-382-3419; FAX: 201-236-7141; E-mail (Internet): corpsales@prenhall.com

Printed in the United States of America

10 9 8 7 6 5 4 3 2 1

ISBN 0-13-570805-2

Prentice-Hall International (UK) Limited, *London*
Prentice-Hall of Australia Pty. Limited, *Sydney*
Prentice-Hall Canada Inc., *Toronto*
Prentice-Hall Hispanoamericana, S.A., *Mexico*
Prentice-Hall of India Private Limited, *New Delhi*
Prentice-Hall of Japan, Inc., *Tokyo*
Simon & Schuster Asia Pte. Ltd., *Singapore*
Editora Prentice-Hall do Brasil, Ltda., *Rio de Janeiro*

To my wife, Susan, for taking care of everything when I am away from home (which is most of the time), and to my two daughters, Jennifer and Christine, who delight me and are my reasons for working.

Walter

To my wife, Barbara, for her patience and support.

Sven

To my beautiful wife, Sherri, who has endured many long hours and lonely dinners. To my son, Joshua, whose playful belly laugh will always turn the corners of my mouth, and baby Nicholas whose joys I am just discovering as you read on.

Randy

I want to thank my wife, Riitta, and my daughter, Emmi, for their love and support.

Matti

To my mother, Lillian, my wife, MariaPaz, my daughter, Kristine and my son, Stefan, for their love and support.

Eduardo

Contents

Figures

Tables

Special Notices

This publication is intended to help software development managers, software designers, and application developers design and develop applications with distributed objects using VisualAge and its Distributed feature. The Distributed feature provides the capability to develop client/server and peer-to-peer applications. The information in this publication is not intended as the specification of any programming interfaces that are provided by VisualAge, IBM Smalltalk, and the Distributed feature. See the PUBLICATIONS section of the IBM Programming Announcement for VisualAge, IBM Smalltalk and the Distributed feature for more information about what publications are considered to be product documentation.

References in this publication to IBM products, programs or services do not imply that IBM intends to make these available in all countries in which IBM operates. Any reference to an IBM product, program, or service is not intended to state or imply that only IBM's product, program, or service may be used. Any functionally equivalent program that does not infringe any of IBM's intellectual property rights may be used instead of the IBM product, program or service.

Information in this book was developed in conjunction with use of the equipment specified, and is limited in application to those specific hardware and software products and levels.

IBM may have patents or pending patent applications covering subject matter in this document. The furnishing of this document does not give you any license to these patents. You can send license inquiries, in writing, to the IBM Director of Licensing, IBM Corporation, 500 Columbus Avenue, Thornwood, NY 10594 USA.

The information contained in this document has not been submitted to any formal IBM test and is distributed AS IS. The information about non-IBM (VENDOR) products in this manual has been supplied by the vendor and IBM assumes no responsibility for its accuracy or completeness. The use of this information or the implementation of any of these techniques is a customer responsibility and depends on the customer's ability to evaluate and integrate them into the customer's operational environment. While each item may have been reviewed by IBM for accuracy in a specific situation, there is no guarantee that the same or similar results will be obtained elsewhere. Customers attempting to adapt these techniques to their own environments do so at their own risk.

The following terms are trademarks of the International Business Machines Corporation in the United States and/or other countries:

AIX	CICS OS/2
Common User Access	CUA
DATABASE 2	DB2
DB2/2	Distributed Relational Database Architecture
DRDA	IBM
Operating System/2	OS/2
SOMobjects	VisualAge

The following terms are trademarks of other companies:

Windows is a trademark of Microsoft Corporation.

PC Direct is a trademark of Ziff Communications Company and is used by IBM Corporation under license.

UNIX is a registered trademark in the United States and other countries licensed exclusively through X/Open Company Limited.

C-bus is a trademark of Corollary, Inc.

Other trademarks are trademarks of their respective companies.

Preface

This book describes the process of designing and building a distributed object application with the VisualAge for Smalltalk Distributed feature. It contains:

- An overview about the features and architecture of the Distributed feature.
- Sample application components with supporting documentation to illustrate design and coding.
- Recommendations for building distributed object applications with VisualAge.

Two residencies were conducted to produce this book. The first residency was run at the IBM Software Solutions, Research Triangle Park, where we worked in close collaboration with members of the VisualAge and IBM Smalltalk development departments. The second residency was run at the International Technical Support Organization, San Jose Center.

During the second residency we completed work on this book as well as on another redbook, *Developing Distributed Object Applications with VisualAge Smalltalk and SOMobjects*. You will discover that both books share common sections. The commonality is intentional. Because both books deal with developing distributed object applications using VisualAge, we did not wish to expend too much effort on "reinventing the wheel."

This document is intended for software engineers, application designers, application programmers, and software development managers.

This book also includes a diskette which contains the sample programs used throughout this book. To install this program, make VisualAge subdirectory your current directory and type:

```
C:\VISUALAG>a:\install
```

How This Document Is Organized

The document is organized as follows:

Part 1, "Introduction"

- Chapter 1, "The Need for Distributed Object Computing", provides a summary of the stages of evolution that led to the new application architecture described in this document.

- Chapter 2, “The VisualAge Distributed Feature”, introduces the Distributed feature and compares it to IBM’s CORBA-compliant DSOM implementation.
- Chapter 3, “Applications Suitable for the Distributed Feature”, describes the three different types of applications that are suitable for the Distributed feature.
- Chapter 4, “Set Up the Development Environment”, guides you through installing the Distributed feature and setting up the development environment.
- Chapter 5, “A Quick Tour Through Distributed Object Land”, provides a step-by-step example of how to develop a simple distributed application using the Distributed feature.

Part 2, “Developing Distributed Object Applications”

- Chapter 6, “The Foreign Currency Exchange Application”, introduces the Foreign Currency Exchange (FCE) application and the distributed extensions made to it.
- Chapter 7, “Planning a Distributed OO Development Project”, provides planning considerations for distributed object application projects.
- Chapter 8, “Designing Distributed Object Applications”, describes considerations for designing distributed object applications.

Part 3, “The Distributed Foreign Currency Exchange Application”

- Chapter 9, “An Approach to VisualAge Application Architecture”, introduces the base application architecture used in our project.
- Chapter 10, “Introduction to the Distributed FCE Case Study”, describes the redesign and partitioning of the distributed Foreign Currency Exchange (FCE) application extended with the active server capabilities.
- Chapter 11, “The First Iteration”, contains an overview of the distributed FCE application and describes our initial implementation.
- Chapter 12, “The Second Iteration”, describes the changes and improvements we made to the application during the second iteration.
- Chapter 13, “The Third Iteration”, describes our project’s final iteration of the performance-tuned FCE application.
- Chapter 14, “Applying the Event Services Framework”, provides ideas on how to further enhance our application.

Part 4, “Distributed Object Applications: The Rest of the Story”

- Chapter 15, “Testing Distributed Applications”, describes testing strategies for distributed VisualAge applications.

- Chapter 16, "Run-time Configuration Considerations", describes run-time configuration considerations for distributed VisualAge applications.
- Chapter 17, "Optimization and Performance Tuning" contains optimization and performance issues related to using the Distributed feature.
- Chapter 18, "Lessons Learned, Hints, and Tips", summarizes our experiences using the Distributed feature during the residency project.

Part 5, ""

- Appendix A, "Requirements Specifications", provides the requirements specifications of the Foreign Currency Exchange (FCE) application.
- Appendix B, "Database Definition", provides listings of the data definition language for the relational database tables used in this project.
- Appendix C, "Sample Code", contains sample code of the application development iterations.

Related Publications

The publications listed in this section are considered particularly suitable for a more detailed discussion of the topics covered in this document.

- *Client/Server Computing: The Design and Coding of a Business Application*, GG24-3899.
- *Object-Oriented Application Development with VisualAge in a Client/Server Environment*, GG24-4227. This publication will be replaced by:

  Visual Modeling Technique: Object Technology Using Visual Programming, by D. Tkach, W. Fang and A. So, Addison–Wesley Publishing Company, ISBN 0-8053-2574-3 (in press).
- *Developing Distributed Object Applications with VisualAge Smalltalk and SOMobjects*, SG24-4390.
- *Object Technology in Application Development*, GG24-4290.
- *VisualAge Distributed User's Guide*. It is provided in online format with VisualAge for Smalltalk, Distributed feature, Program Number 5697-233.
- *IBM Smalltalk Programmer's Reference*, SC34-4493.
- *IBM Smalltalk User's Guide*, SC34-4536.
- *VisualAge for Smalltalk, Getting Started*, SC34-4535.

- *VisualAge for Smalltalk User's Guide*, SC34-4518.
- *VisualAge for Smalltalk User's Reference*, SC34-4519.
- *VisualAge Programmer's Guide to Building Parts for Fun and Profit*, SC34-4496.

International Technical Support Organization Publications

A complete list of International Technical Support Organization publications, known as redbooks, with a brief description of each, may be found in:

> *International Technical Support Organization Bibliography of Redbooks,* GG24-3070.

To get a catalog of ITSO redbooks, VNET users may type:

```
TOOLSSENDTOWTSCPOKTOOLSREDBOOKSGET REDBOOKSCATALOG
```

A listing of all redbooks, sorted by category, may also be found on MKTTOOLS as ITSOPUB LISTALLX. This package is updated monthly.

How to Order ITSO Redbooks

IBM employees in the USA may order ITSO books and CD-ROMs using PUBORDER. Customers in the USA may order by calling 1-800-879-2755 or by faxing 1-800-445-9269. Almost all major credit cards are accepted. Outside the USA, customers should contact their local IBM office.

Customers may order hardcopy ITSO books individually or in customized sets, called GBOFs, which relate to specific functions of interest. IBM employees and customers may also order ITSO books in online format on CD-ROM collections, which contain redbooks on a variety of products.

ITSO Redbooks on the World Wide Web (WWW)

Internet users may find information about redbooks on the ITSO World Wide Web home page. To access the ITSO Web pages, point your Web browser (such as WebExplorer from the OS/2 3.0 Warp BonusPak) to the following page:

```
http://www.redbooks.ibm.com/redbooks
```

IBM employees may access LIST3820 files of redbook titles as well. Point your Web browser to the IBM redbooks home page:

```
http://w3.itsc.pok.ibm.com/redbooks/redbooks.html
```

International Technical Support Organization

The IBM International Technical Support Organization (ITSO) is a unique group within IBM, with centers located in major product development sites. These locations include:

- Austin
- Boca Raton
- Böblingen
- Poughkeepsie
- Raleigh
- Rochester
- San Jose

The ITSO mission is to provide how-to technical support for IBM products worldwide. Working closely with development organizations, each center provides support for the products developed at their location. In addition, the ITSO centers work together to provide cross-product and cross-platform support with a total system solution perspective.

Technical bulletins such as the one you're reading, commonly known as redbooks, are produced by the ITSO centers as one of their primary vehicles for delivering technical product information to customers and IBM field personnel. These redbooks are typically the result of a several month effort involving multiple IBM residents from around the world. These residents bring their technical expertise and knowledge of their customer's environment to the ITSO center and spend 6-8 weeks exercising the product and documentation. Their experiences and findings are then published in a redbook such as this one.

Redbooks are not intended to replace product documentation, but rather to supplement it with actual user experiences. The residents work with development to better understand the products and as a result, IBM development organizations better understand user requirements.

The ITSO centers also produce workshops and other deliverables designed to provide technical information to those who use and support IBM products.

We hope you find this and other ITSO redbooks to be useful and that you will make them an integral part of your systems library. Please take the time to fill out the enclosed evaluation form and let us know what you think.

Comments or questions regarding this redbook may be sent via electronic mail to:

WalterFang
ITSOSanJoseCenter
Internet:fangw@vnet.ibm.com
IBMVNET:FANGWat WTSCPOK

About the Authors

Walter Fang is a Senior Object Technology Consultant at IBM's International Technical Support Organization (ITSO) - San Jose Center. Before joining ITSO, he was an Information Technology Architect at IBM Canada Client/Server Center, where he helped customers develop object-oriented client/server architectures and solutions.

Sven Guyet graduated with honors in mathematics from the Technical University Aachen, Germany, and joined IBM in 1984. Since 1991 he has worked as a consultant in object-oriented application development projects with specialization in Smalltalk and visual programming.

Randy Haven is a member of the IBM VisualAge for Smalltalk development team. During his first 10 years with IBM, he worked as tester, developer, architect, project manager, customer liaison, educator. He has been working on Smalltalk since 1988.

Matti Vilmi holds a BS degree in Computer Techniques and is currently working as a team leader in Object Technology Group in IBM Finland.

Eduardo Eckmann graduated from the University of Lima, Peru, as an Industrial Engineer. He joined IBM in 1984. He started working with Smalltalk in 1991 and is currently a consultant on object technology in the IBM Consulting Group.

Acknowledgments

This book is the result of two residency projects conducted by the International Technical Support Organization in Raleigh and San Jose. We would like to thank our managers in our home countries: John Bailey, Andy Banaszak, Peter Pies, Osmo Tehilä, Bob Roush, and Roberto Gamio, for letting us work on the project and this book.

Thanks to Dr. Yen-Ping Shan, IBM Software Solutions, Raleigh, for the invaluable advice and guidance he provided during the project and the production of this book. Thanks also to the following people from the VisualAge for Smalltalk development and marketing departments, IBM SWS Raleigh, who contributed information, resources, and technical advice: Robert Berry, Paul Blizniak, Jim Mickelson, John De Binder, Larry Smith, Pat Huff, John Kellerman, Steve Robinson, and Skip McGaughy.

Many thanks to Jens Tiedemann, ITSO San Jose Center Manager, who provided an empowered environment that allowed the project to succeed. Special thanks to everyone at the ITSO San Jose Center, in particular Elsa Barron, Mary Comianos, Alan Tippett; Andi Bitterer for the cover design of the book and his tips on getting the book *framed*; and Maggie Cutler and Laura Nystrom for doing a great editing job. Finally, thanks to Barbara Isa, IBM Santa Teresa Lab; Mike Meehan, Patti Guerrieri and Sophie Papanikolaou at Prentice Hall; and to Lou Evart, Doris Chen, and Satkartar Khalsa at Softline International Inc. for their support. Thanks also to the many other collaborators and reviewers who contributed to improve this book.

F.W.F.
S.G.
R.H.
M.V.
E.E.

Part 1

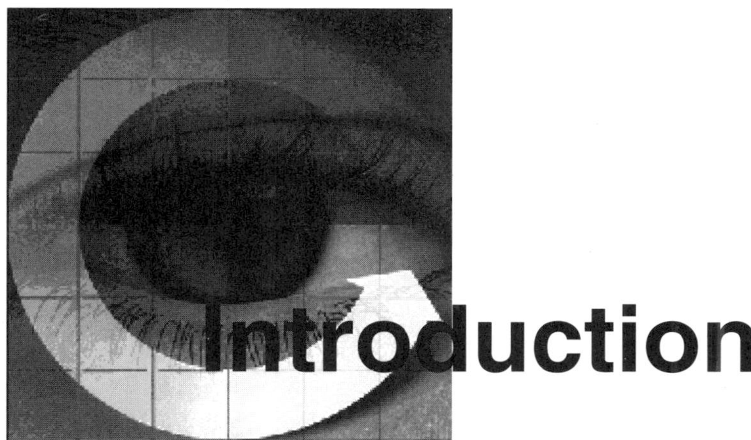

Introduction

1

The Need for Distributed Object Computing

Today's software developers face increasingly complex business requirements, including rapid change and new technology such as multimedia. Application developers must be able to develop and update their business applications quickly.

Object-Oriented (OO) concepts such as reuse and encapsulation offer many benefits to client/server application development, particularly in managing complexity and change. In theory, all the benefits of OO that apply to the client can apply equally well to the server. However, until now, these concepts have been proven to benefit only the client side. There is no intrinsic or conceptual reason for this; rather, it is a result of timing, the availability of tools, and the conservative restraints that result from the mission-critical nature of server computing.

In this chapter, we summarize the stages of evolution that led to the new application architecture described in this document:

- "From Host Computing to Client/Server Computing",
- "From Procedural Computing to Object Computing", and
- "Distributed Object Computing", discusses the next logical stage in evolution, which combines the strengths of the previous two stages.

From Host Computing to Client/Server Computing

Moving from traditional host computing to client/server computing is no longer a fashion but is deeply rooted in today's application development. According to Orfali and Harkey, the technologies and needs pushing client/server computing come from three directions [Orfali94, 12-14]:

- Downsizing
- Upsizing
- Rightsizing.

Downsizing refers to the migration of applications from larger systems to workstations. Typically, this process starts with moving the user interface functions to the clients and replacing character-oriented host screens with graphical user interfaces.

Upsizing efforts go the opposite way. For example, applications formerly residing on stand-alone systems are extended to make use of common peripheral devices provided by larger systems like LAN servers or even mainframes.

Finally, *rightsizing* means the movement of parts of an application to that platform that supports them best.* Developers must design their applications to run on networks of interconnected machines that share the processing load. Applications must make the best use of existing resources to meet the needs of the business and to achieve performance, scalability, security, usability, and maintainability objectives.

The advantages that the client/server and peer-to-peer computing models promise to provide include:

- The scalability of the necessary hardware when the application grows
- The ability to react faster to business changes and corresponding requests regarding the application.

* The decision about the " best ' platform is not always obvious. Often, it is a trade-off among factors such as autonomy from the main site, performance, reliability, and security.

Different Approaches: Fat Clients and Fat Servers

Most current client/server implementations fall into two different approaches, either the *fat client* or the *fat server*. The first approach runs most of the logic on the client side while the server provides the data shared by many clients. The second approach reduces maintenance efforts (up to now, only a few client/server implementations use real automated software distribution) and network traffic. Since the processing is done mainly by the server, only requests and final results have to be transferred between the participating systems.

Both approaches are based on two completely different application architectures, remote data access, and remote processing requests. To reflect the *rightsizing* intention discussed above, we want to move to a more balanced state. However, this movement requires great development efforts if the environments between the client and server differ. Most situations today have different operating systems, different software development techniques, and even different programming languages for the clients and servers.

We see in "Distributed Object Computing" that the distributed object computing model helps to eliminate these difficulties when adapting an application to different platforms.

From Procedural Computing to Object Computing

Object-oriented technology is radically different from traditional software development. The key benefit is reusable code and the resulting reductions in development and maintenance time.

Thanks to encapsulation, inheritance, and polymorphism, this technology has increased productivity over traditional programming techniques. Object-oriented methodologies have revolutionized every stage of the development process, from requirements analysis through actual implementation. Gaps between the different stages no longer exist. Business objects do not have to be broken down into entities, functions, processes, or data models. The object model remains stable throughout the complete development process.

Where Are We Today?

The most familiar OO implementation is in the growing number of advanced, user-friendly Graphical User Interfaces (GUIs). A major reason for the popularity of OO GUIs lies in the complex nature of GUI programming. To manage this complexity, application developers constantly search for new ways to structure and manage their programs. OO programming is useful because it allows close mapping

between the problem domain (in this case, constructing the user interface) and the solution domain (software objects representing screen elements such as buttons and windows). This has led to the success of OO GUI tools and the saturation of the OO GUI market.

OO GUIs have also contributed to the evolution of today's advanced GUI-based development environment, in which OO technology leads to the benefits of rapid application development. OO is now a pervasive force in the client application development tool market, and many power tools in this market are OO-based. The cost of entry into OO programming for the client side is low; as a tool provider, you do not have to buy an expensive host server to start your development. Experienced programmers are easier to hire because most workstation programmers move to object-oriented programming earlier than host/server programmers. In addition, Cupparo notes that inexperienced programmers are able to be productive while still learning the technology [Cupparo93].

The OO-based development environment has made it possible for more sophisticated OO client applications to appear. OO technology enables developers to deliver application prototypes in stages that include increasing levels of complexity, and OO applications are easier to debug and modify in response to user input. OO frameworks enable programmers to reuse existing designs and customize them to fit new requirements. Additionally, domain models developed with OO methodologies are fully reusable in future applications.

Distributed Object Computing

Data will be encapsulated in objects that will in some cases be able to roam to where they are most needed.

(Peter Wayner, Byte Magazine, 01/94)

As seen in "From Host Computing to Client/Server Computing", developers must contend with the trend toward reducing costs by *rightsizing*, which requires that processing be distributed. Developers must design their applications to run on networks of interconnected machines that share the processing load. Applications must make the best use of existing resources to meet business needs and performance, scalability, security, usability, and maintainability objectives.

Today's businesses are finding that the traditional client/server approach is inefficient. Typically, most application logic in a client/server environment is located on the client machines, with the servers acting as centralized databases, as discussed in "Different Approaches: Fat Clients and Fat Servers". This approach can lead to excessive network traffic and difficult maintenance. One solution to these problems is to put some of the application logic back on the server where it can access the data locally. This requires an approach much more flexible than the traditional client/server environment.

The new approach is called *distributed object computing* and it has objects on the server *and* on the client machines.

Evolution of Object-Oriented Computing

Figure 1 demonstrates the evolution of object-oriented computing. OO has moved into the client/server realm, primarily on the client side. Eventually, we will reach the situation represented by the right-most configuration, in which objects will be a common feature of client and server alike.

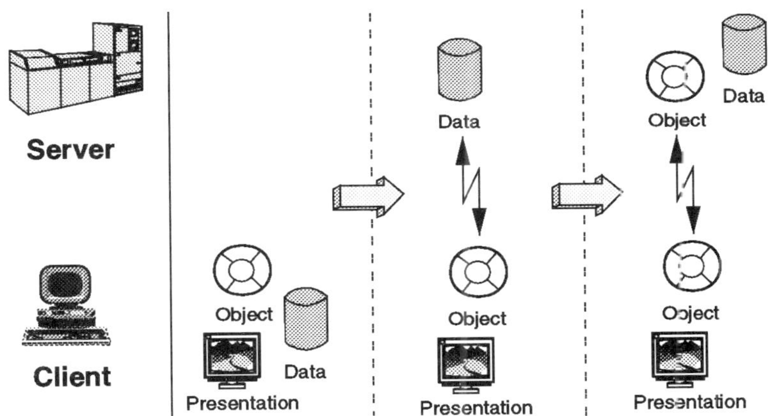

Figure 1. *Evolution of OO Implementation*

The benefits that OO has brought to client programming can apply equally well to the server side. Perhaps most important is the ability to manage complexity and change. The multiuser requirements and greatly magnified scale of the server side lend themselves to complexity, which creates a need for the encapsulation, reusability, and close mapping between the problem and solution domains that OO makes possible.

Encapsulation and reusability when using OO technology also help to manage system changes. They enable server programmers to isolate changes and minimize maintenance costs. The close mapping between the problem and solution domains allow the modeling of an enterprise and then the building of the implementation which maps directly to it. This ensures not only that changes are made quickly, but that they are also made correctly. Today's business environment creates pressure for information systems flexible enough to cope with the rapid pace of change. Such flexibility is difficult to manage on the server level, as evidenced by the pervasive IS backlogs. Benefits such as the ones offered by OO are greatly needed.

In spite of the potential advantages, to date there have been few successful OO server implementations. One reason is an old story in the industry: critical mass. An organization cannot afford to maintain an entire proprietary OO programming language or server environment just for its own use, and tool developers are hesitant to develop the needed tools until there is a proven market for them. However, as tool providers converge on architectural and language standards, costs can be spread among many users.

Standards

As with any new technology, common standards are required for OO server technology to gain widespread acceptance. The *Common Object Request Broker Architecture* (CORBA) standard has gained acceptance in recent years and has come to provide the basis for the *Object Transaction Service* (OTS) distributed object architecture defined by the *Object Management Group* (OMG). In addition, two distributed transaction standards with OO implications are widely recognized: the X/Open *Distributed Transaction Processing* (DTP) model and the ISO OSI-TP standard.

Standardization of programming languages is equally essential. In recent years, the industry has begun to converge on C++ and Smalltalk as standard industrial-strength OO languages.

Standards can help to ensure that objects developed using different vendors' tools are mutually compatible. As software vendors develop OO components that conform to these standards for the server, customer confidence will continue to grow and customers will increasingly adopt this new technology.

Benefits

Distributed object computing represents a new and exciting trend to merge two powerful technologies in the information industry, namely, client/server computing and OO technology. The architecture holds significant promise for tomorrow's distributed applications.

Objects communicate with each other through a message-passing mechanism. An object's role can change between both client and server. A given object may act as a server to some objects and, at the same time, as a client of other objects. Furthermore, these client and server objects may be on the same machine or distributed between different machines connected through a network.

Onset of Network Computing

Analysts have predicted that network computing will naturally evolve from client/server computing. Technologies such as distribution will play a key role in the development of future systems. Those systems will not only access data remotely, but will also optimize the availability of multiple processors by bringing the power of parallel processing within reach of the end user.

With increasing access to vast networks such as the Internet, applications will be free to span many processors that gather data, perform calculations, and affect transactions as though all resources were available locally.

Conclusions

In this chapter, we examined some key aspects of using OO technology on both the server and client sides. We discussed some scenarios to show the need to distribute objects between clients and servers, or even between two clients.

As Orfali and Harkey point out [Orfali94, 902], we are within the third wave of client/server technology as shown in Figure 2 on page 9.

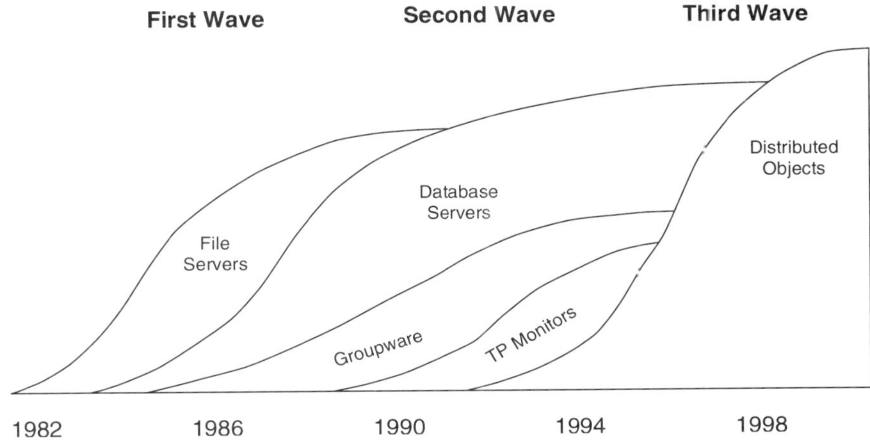

Figure 2. *Waves of Client/Server Technology*

The first wave, starting in the early 1980's, came with network operating systems that allowed applications to share files, printers, and other networked devices. The second wave began in the middle of the 1980's and introduced SQL database servers into client/server applications. Along with the second wave trend, groupware and Transaction Processing (TP) monitors such as IBM CICS OS/2 gained a solid piece of the client/server cake. The third wave is the distributed object wave.

The time is right for the server environment to benefit from OO technology. The distributed object wave is still at a moderate height, but we should start surfing now to catch that wave!

2

The VisualAge Distributed Feature

With the VisualAge for Smalltalk, *Distributed feature* customers can jump right into distributed object computing. In this chapter, we introduce the Distributed feature product and compare it to VisualAge's support for the *System Object Model* (SOM) and *Distributed System Object Model* (DSOM).

Before you try to follow any of the applications in this book or in the samples that accompany the product, we recommend that you read this chapter carefully so that you will be familiar with the Distributed feature.

This chapter consists of the following sections:

- "What Is the Distributed Feature?" introduces the Distributed feature product,
- "New Terms for Distribution" summarizes new technical terms,

- "The IBM Smalltalk Distribution Toolkit" gives an overview of the Smalltalk tools provided by the Distributed feature, and
- "SOM and DSOM and the Distributed Feature" summarizes SOM/DSOM concepts and provides a brief comparison with the Distributed feature to help in the selection of the appropriate distribution strategy or combination thereof.

What Is the Distributed Feature?

The Distributed feature provides a set of Smalltalk classes and tools that facilitate the development of distributed applications in the IBM Smalltalk Professional environment. You can install this feature on top of either the VisualAge for Smalltalk or the IBM Smalltalk products. The distributed Smalltalk technology is part of IBM's overall strategy for distributed OO development.

The Distributed feature provides:

- An easy-to-learn, high-level development paradigm with true transparency of local or remote implementation
- An industrial-strength development environment that supports large-scale application development by teams, with the distribution design and code changes kept synchronized in a central repository
- Distributed garbage collection for efficient storage management
- Integration with the VisualAge visual programming environment
- The IBM Smalltalk Distribution Toolkit that includes a set of tools to help developers and administrators design, develop, debug, optimize, and configure distributed applications
- Sample applications that help the developer to understand and use the product.

Figure 3 on page 13 shows the relationship between VisualAge, the Distributed feature, and IBM Smalltalk. This figure also shows the overall picture of IBM software products for visual application development using Smalltalk.

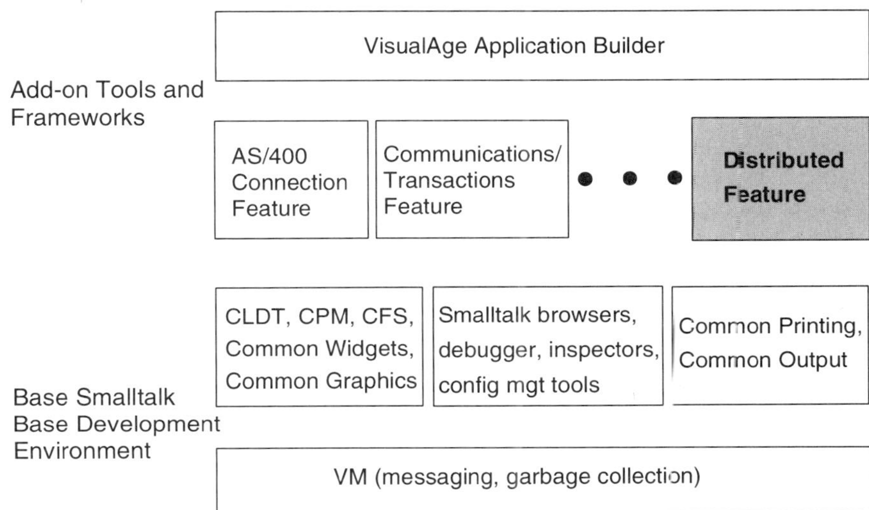

Figure 3. *Product Architecture*

The Distributed feature extends the basic Smalltalk model to support distribution of objects on different computers in a network. These objects can send standard Smalltalk messages to one another, regardless of their physical location. They can also freely send other Smalltalk objects as arguments and receive objects as results. The different parts of an application can be located on any computer in the network that is running IBM Smalltalk with the Distributed feature.

The run-time environment provides all of the support required to implement distributed execution of Smalltalk applications with true local and/or remote transparency. It provides an additional layer on top of the standard Smalltalk model as illustrated by Figure 4 on page 13.

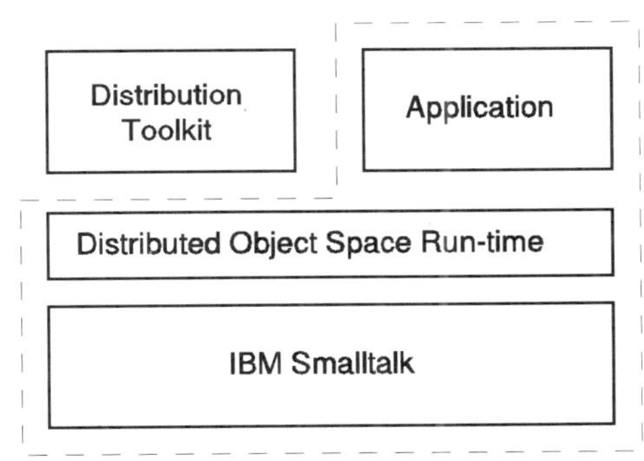

Figure 4. *Extended Smalltalk Run-Time Environment*

Using this new technology, any Smalltalk programmer can create distributed applications after learning only a few additional concepts.

The Distributed feature offers many benefits that ease the transition to distributed OO application development. They include:

- Smalltalk development model

  Using the Distributed feature, programmers can quickly develop applications that span networks without having to learn the details of network communications, distributed application programming, or specialized interfaces.

  The Distributed feature extends the familiar Smalltalk tools like browsers, inspectors, debuggers, and workspaces to the distributed environment. Applications written in Smalltalk are the first to benefit from the Distributed feature because by using the event profiler and object visualizer, developers can identify the best places to split an application.

- High-level development paradigm

  The Distributed feature enables developers to focus on solving the business needs of the enterprise, rather than the mechanics of distributed programming. The Distributed feature is based entirely on the Smalltalk model, providing a high level of programming abstraction and removing much of the distribution complexity from the task of program design.

- Flexible distribution approach

  The Distributed feature supports much more than a simple client/server approach. Applications can be "split" in many different ways, supporting both client/server and true peer-to-peer designs. The distribution of an application can be dynamically changed throughout the development cycle.

- Visual programming paradigm

  The Distributed feature includes a visual part that gives the visual programmer access to remote objects in a familiar, VisualAge variable part format.

- Security

  The Distributed feature is enabled to use the industry-standard *Generic Security Services* (GSS) API and currently supports the IBM product *Network Security Program* (NetSP), Version 1 Release 2. Used with NetSP, the Distributed feature provides transparent support for client authentication, message verification, and message encryption.

- ❑ True server programming

  The Distributed feature enables you to use Smalltalk everywhere in your client/server environment. It provides full support for true server programming, such as:

  - ➢ It is scalable to accommodate the demands of your business.
  - ➢ Its security support provides for authentication of clients and servers.
  - ➢ It supports concurrent execution of multiple client requests within a single server Smalltalk image.

New Terms for Distribution

The Distributed feature works with five fundamental objects that are new compared to the standard Smalltalk model:

- ❑ Object spaces
- ❑ Object references
- ❑ Shadow objects
- ❑ Remote objects
- ❑ Name servers.

In addition, a non-Smalltalk activator program must be running on a server machine so that authorized clients can connect to servers. The activator facilitates the connections of client object spaces to server object spaces.

This section contains a brief explanation of the new terms listed above.

Object Spaces

When all parts of a distributed application are written in Smalltalk, the Distributed feature takes advantage of this situation with a technology called the *distributed object space*. In effect, the distributed object space extends the Smalltalk model across a network.

The distributed object space is made up of multiple individual object spaces. An object space is a single instance of a running Smalltalk image that can exist on any computer attached to a network and running the Distributed feature. It is possible for a single machine to have multiple object spaces that are loaded from the same or different image files. The scope of an object space makes all objects within it local to one another. Objects in different object spaces are remote from one another. Figure 5 on page 16 depicts three object spaces, A, B, and C, in three different machines.

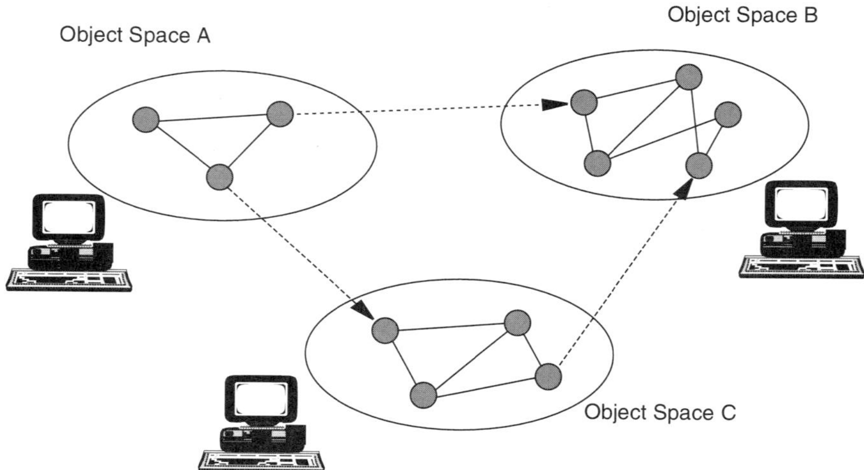

Figure 5. *Object Spaces*

With the distributed object space technology, objects can:

- ❑ Send standard Smalltalk messages to one another regardless of physical location
- ❑ Send and receive other Smalltalk objects as arguments and results, even across the network, without having to "flatten" them into serialized data
- ❑ Reside in different physical locations from one application version to the next, without any change to the Smalltalk code.

An object space is also represented by an object that can provide information about the location of the object space. Object spaces connect and disconnect when objects communicate. An object space has a location defined by a host machine identifier and object space key. The object space key is defined in an activator configuration file.

Messaging. When objects are local, they can send messages to one another using the normal Smalltalk syntax or visual connections. If objects are remote, they can send messages by using the features provided by the Distributed feature regardless of where the object spaces are physically located in the network. Once configured with the necessary location information, the Distributed feature handles the low-level task of passing Smalltalk objects across a network connection. The syntax and semantics for messages sent to remote objects are the same as for local objects.

Distributed garbage collection. The Distributed feature extends the Smalltalk garbage collection so that it is distribution-aware. Unused memory is freed when it is no longer being used by other local or remote objects. Objects that have references from other remote object spaces are candidates for garbage collection only after the last reference is removed.

Activation support. The Distributed feature provides the support to start and/or connect to any remote Smalltalk images that the application requires. If an object in one object space sends a message to an object whose image is not currently running, the Distributed feature activator automatically starts that image.

Object References

An object reference is an object that has the information required to find another object. Object references contain the address of an object. The referenced object may or may not be currently available.

Object references are used to create shadows of remote objects. See Shadow Objects on page 18 for more information about shadows.

Object references can be categorized based on the objects they reference. There are four kinds of object references:

- **Global object reference**

  This is a reference to an object that is defined in an object space's global Smalltalk dictionary, that is, a global variable. For example, all classes are global variables. See Figure 6 on page 18, arrow (a).

- **Dictionary item reference**

  This is a reference to an object that is contained in a dictionary other than the global system dictionary of an object space. The dictionary containing the object, however, must be defined in the global system dictionary. See Figure 6 on page 18, arrow (b).

- **Name server reference**

  This is a reference to a name server. See Name Servers on page 19 for more information about name servers.

- **Object space location reference**

  This is a reference to an object space. See Object Spaces on page 15 for more information about object spaces.

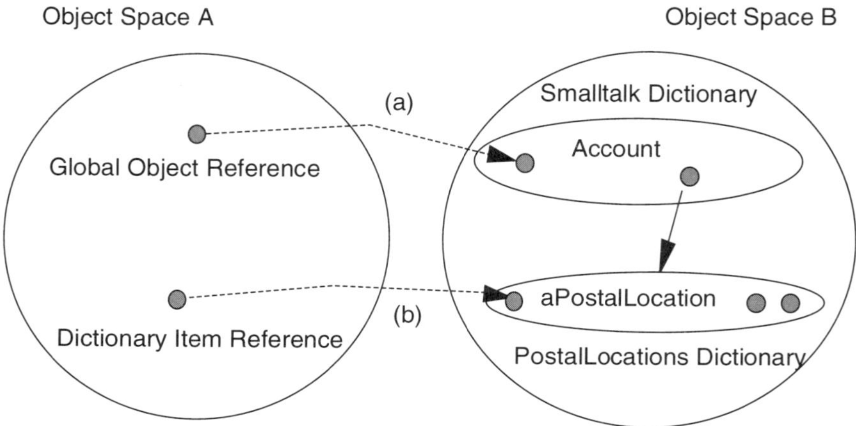

Figure 6. *Object References*

Shadow Objects

A shadow object is a local representation of an object that resides in another object space. It serves as a pointer to a remote object. A shadow object is also often called a *proxy object*.

A shadow object receives messages and interacts with other local objects in exactly the same way as if it were the real object. When a message is sent to a shadow object, it is automatically sent to the real remote object. The object space of the source and target are automatically connected or reconnected, if required. Messages sent to the shadow object are forwarded to the target object space in which the object actually resides. Anything that returns from the remote object as a result of a message's execution goes through the local shadow object.

The Distributed feature can create shadows automatically when it is necessary, without any change in the code. This only requires partitioning the application into new applications and distributing them with the distribution matrix. See The IBM Smalltalk Distribution Toolkit on page 20 for more information on this feature.

Figure 7 on page 19 shows the relationship between a global object reference and its shadow object. A local object requests a shadow from the global object reference (1). The global reference object creates the shadow object (2) and returns that shadow object to the local object (3). Finally, the local object sends a message to the shadow object (4).

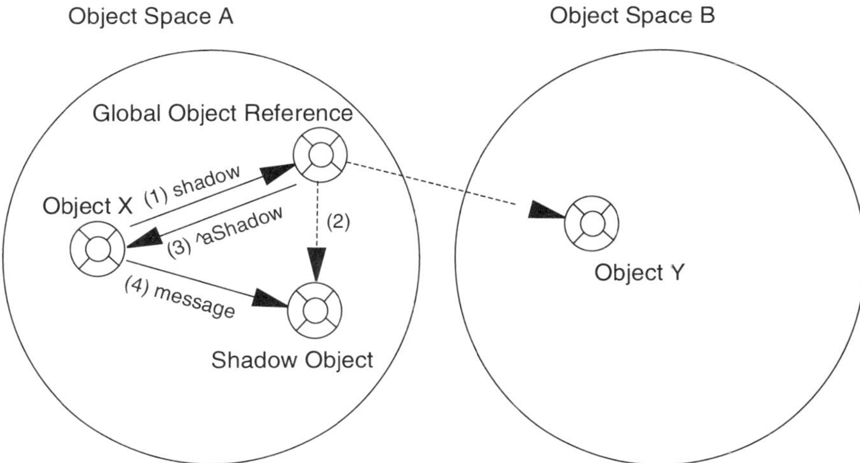

Figure 7. *Shadow Objects*

Remote Objects

Remote objects are similar to shadow objects but are not created by means of object references. Remote objects are created when a shadow or another remote object answers an object in another object space. Shadow objects and remote objects behave very similarly; that is, a message is forwarded to the object space where the object exists, and the answer is returned synchronously.

Remote objects, unlike shadow objects, do not automatically re-establish the link to their remote objects. If an object space is disconnected, on reconnection, cannot validate the state of the other object space, the state of a remote object becomes "dead" the next time a message is sent to it. This can occur when object space images are saved and restarted at different points. When object spaces reconnect and their states are validated, remote objects are still valid.

Name Servers

A name server is a specialized Smalltalk dictionary of string keys and string values. It is used as a directory of objects in a network. It stores the string representations of object references, indexed by unique string keys.

Using a name server avoids the need to "hard-code" an object's location in the application. A local object uses symbolic names to query fully-specified object references from the name server at run-time. By changing the object references in the name server, a developer can update the location information for the objects without having to change the Smalltalk code.

If the name server cannot resolve a particular object reference, it has the ability to relay the request to a second-level name server and so forth. The Distributed feature name server is designed to comply with the industry-standard OMG naming services specification. The name server is also designed to be adaptable to other naming services, such as the *Open Systems Foundation* (OSF) *Distributed Computing Environment* (DCE) directory service.

The IBM Smalltalk Distribution Toolkit

The IBM Smalltalk distribution toolkit included in the Distributed feature is a set of tools to help developers and administrators design, develop, debug, optimize, and configure distributed applications from a single physical location. Many of these tools are distributed extensions to existing IBM Smalltalk tools. They are:

- Distributed debugger
- Distribution matrix
- Event profiler
- Event services framework
- Name server browsers
- Name server distributed part
- Object visualizer
- Remote browsers
- Remote file dialog
- Remote inspector
- Remote transcript
- Remote workspace.

In this section, we summarize the development tools listed above.

Distributed Debugger

The distributed debugger is an enhanced Smalltalk debugger that shows distributed program execution as a single call stack. The distributed debugger enables you to trace the execution of an application process that spans a network just as you would with an entirely local process. You can inspect objects, code remotely, and step through code execution even as the process crosses object space boundaries. You can also make changes to remote code from within the debugger.

Distribution Matrix

The Distributed feature includes a special editor that enables you to partition and distribute the modules of an application to various object spaces on the network. Each module is a group of Smalltalk classes.*

Once you have divided a program into two or more applications, you can designate the relationship between these applications and the different object spaces. There are three different choices:

- ❑ Do not load this application into this object space (*Do not load*)
- ❑ Load this application into this object space (*Fully load*)
- ❑ Load shadows for this application in this object space (*Shadow-load*).

To visually define the relationship between applications and the object spaces, you can use the distribution matrix property of the configuration map. Figure 8 on page 21 shows a sample distribution matrix.

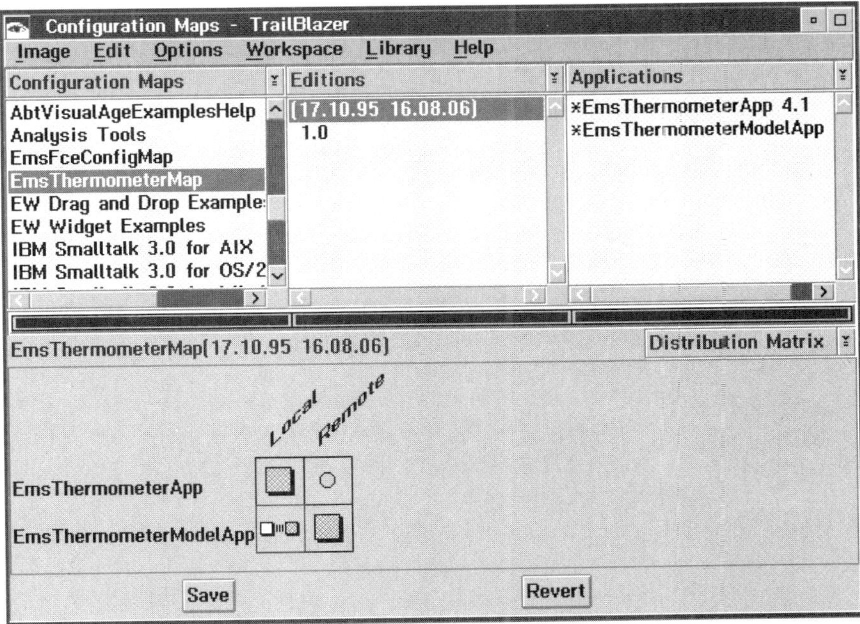

Figure 8. *Distribution Matrix*

* Each group of classes is actually called an *application* in IBM Smalltalk terms, although in fact it may be only a part of your complete application.

The distribution design of a configuration map is saved along with the name and version of each application. You can dynamically change the locations of the different modules of the distributed application to fine-tune performance.

After you have specified the location for each application, you can automatically load the appropriate modules into the remote object spaces.

Event Profiler

The event profiler helps you analyze the message traffic among the objects in an application. You can use it to record all messages sent to an instance of an object or into or out of an object space. Thus, you can figure out the best way to divide your application. For example, if there is a lot of traffic between two objects, both objects probably should be in the same object space. If, however, two objects seldom interact, they are candidates to be remote from one another.

You can create five different profiles:

- An instance profile monitors a specific instance of a class
- An all instances profile records all messages to all instances of a specific class
- An object space profile monitors all messages coming to and going out of a specific object space
- A remote object profile records all messages to a specific remote object
- An all remote objects profile records all messages to all remote objects in a single profile.

The event profiler presents information collected with the profiles browser, event list, and event tree.

The profiles browser provides a list of all event profiles that currently exist in an object space. Figure 9 on page 23 shows an example of the profiles browser.

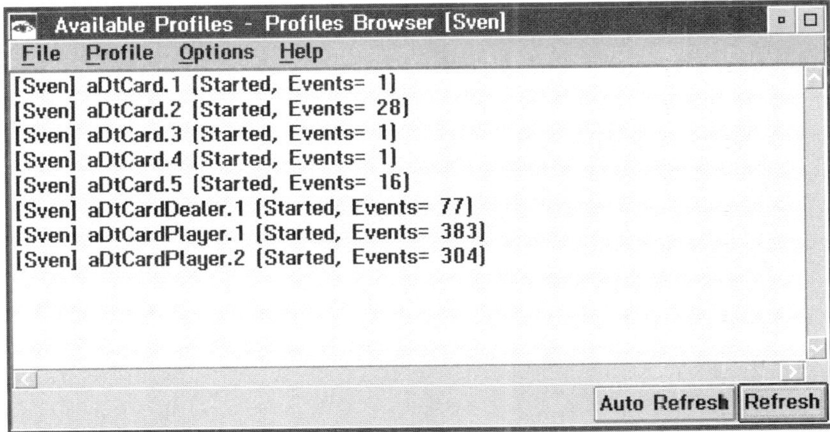

Figure 9. *Event Profiler, Profiles Browser*

The profiling activity produces a list of all messages sent to the objects profiled, as well as a copy of the call stack that led to the sending of those messages. Figure 10 on page 23 shows an example of an event list. This list can be used to easily find the number of times a message was sent to an object.

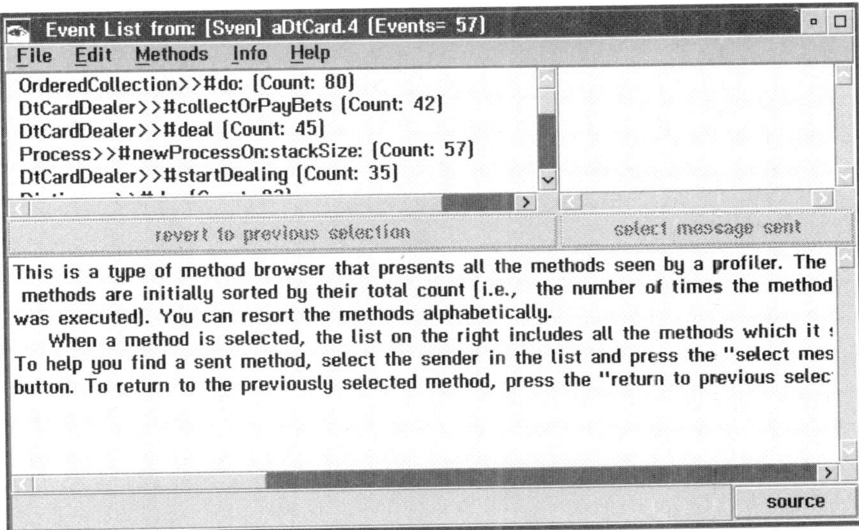

Figure 10. *Event Profiler, Event List*

The event tree is used to follow the call stack that led up to the message send. Figure 11 on page 24 shows an example of an event tree. This browser can also be used to measure the time spent processing the messages. This time includes time spent waiting for user response to modal dialogs, or message flow across the network.

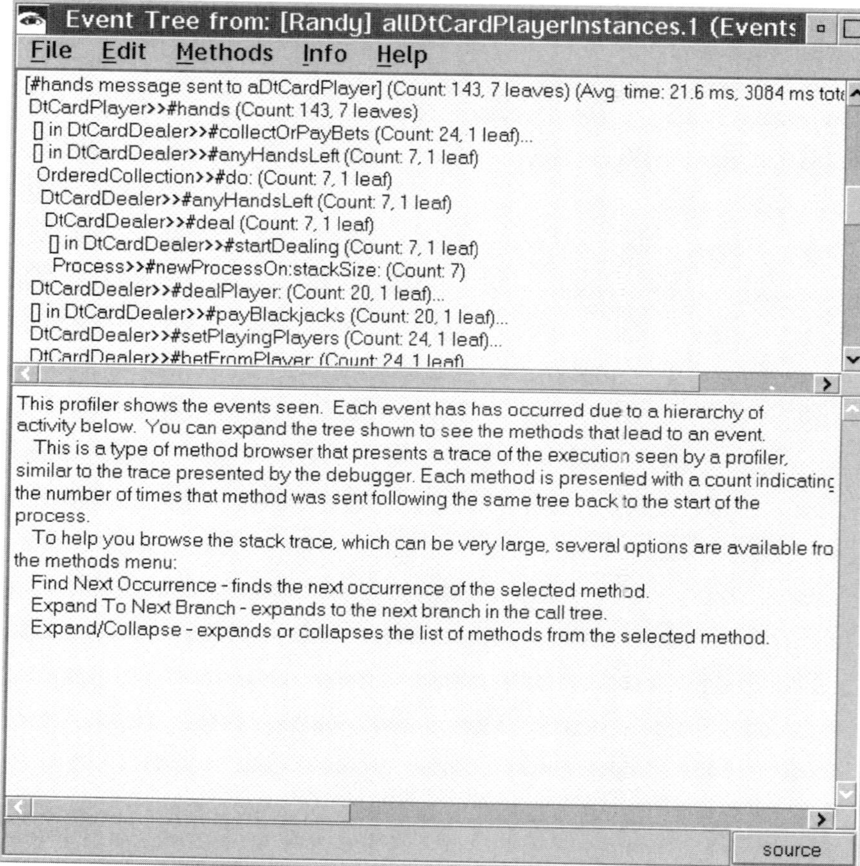

Figure 11. *Event Profiler, Event Tree*

Event Services Framework

The distributed event services framework provides a set of classes you can use to transmit events. An event is an object (of any class) that might become available at any time during application execution and must be communicated from one part of the application to another, or even from one application to another.

The event services framework provides a standard CORBA-compliant interface for event notification. In addition, it provides a set of Smalltalk wrapper classes that simplify its use in Smalltalk programs.

Name Server Browsers

Name server browsers enable you to browse and update the contents of your name servers. You can add, delete, and change object references and other named objects. The name server browsers also provide menu interfaces to start other distributed development tools.

Figure 12 on page 25 shows an example of a name server browser.

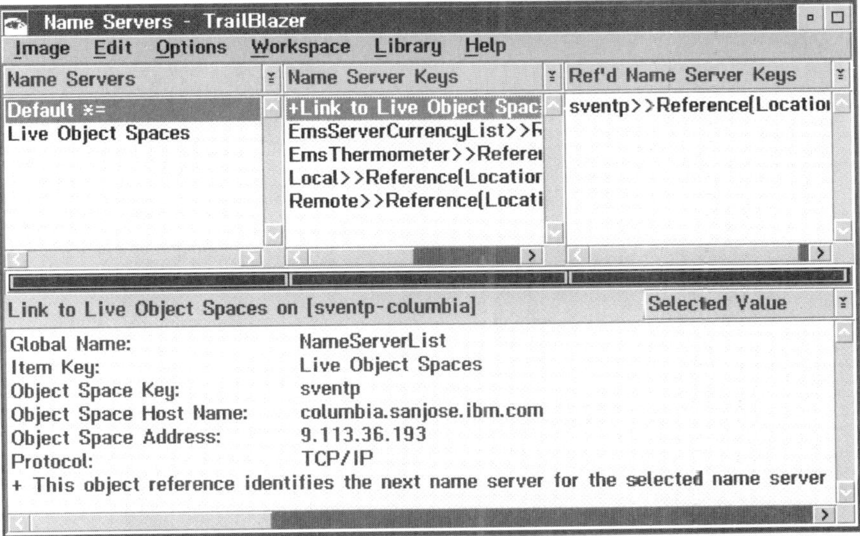

Figure 12. *Name Server Browser*

Name Server Distributed Part

The name server distributed part provides a visual interface to references defined in the name server. The distributed part is available on the TCP/IP palette of the Composition Editor. It appears and functions as a VisualAge variable allowing connections to the shadow of the object it represents.

Object Visualizer

The object visualizer enables you to visualize the static and dynamic behavior of the objects in your applications by focusing on the changing set of the objects and the interactions among them. The object visualizer depicts instances of selected classes and messages sent between the instances. Figure 13 on page 26 shows an example of the object visualizer. Message frequency and processor time spent processing these messages are encoded with a color scheme ranging from blue (cold) to red (hot).

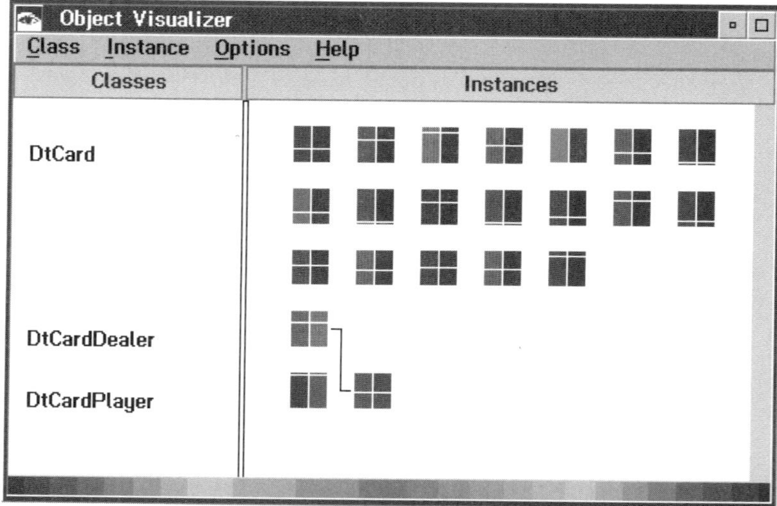

Figure 13. *Object Visualizer*

These visual representations of your program execution may also be used for debugging purposes. In many cases, the creation and destruction of objects can be difficult to detect. The object visualizer is ideal for detecting the following types of problems:

- Inadvertent creation of instances from an abstract class
- Unexpected instance creation
- Inefficient instance creation
- Failure to remove references to unused instances.

You can open several other views to further analyze program execution:

- Behavior browser
- Cluster view
- Event profiler
- State browser.

The behavior browser lists the instance methods (selectors) of a selected object, the number of invocations, and the processor time spent to process each method. The behavior browser uses the same color scheme as the object visualizer to encode message frequency and processor time.

Figure 14 on page 27 shows an example of a behavior browser for an instance of the *DtCard* class. Information within square brackets is updated dynamically during program execution.

DtCard-41 [103 messages in 8881ms]

Selectors	[Invocation / Time (ms)]
suit:	[1/2]
rank:	[1/1]
value:	[1/1]
turnUnder	[1/1]
hand:	[8/22]
deck:	[1/1]
hash	[2/3]
basicHash	[1/1]
turnUp	[7/67]
viewString	[9/56]
value	[16/77]
isAce	[19/-93]
viewStringFor:	[6/6323]
isDownFor:	[22/-13]
valueFor:	[6/2410]
clearHand	[2/22]

Figure 14. *Object Visualizer, Instance Behavior Browser*

The cluster view is illustrated in Figure 15 on page 28. While the program is executing, objects that send messages to one another most often are attracted to each other. Program errors, such as unexpected interaction with instances of a particular class, are readily visible from this view.

The view below depicts the interaction of the instances selected from the object visualizer. You can also select classes from the object visualizer to obtain a class cluster view. The class cluster view provides a summary of all message traffic between instances of the selected class.

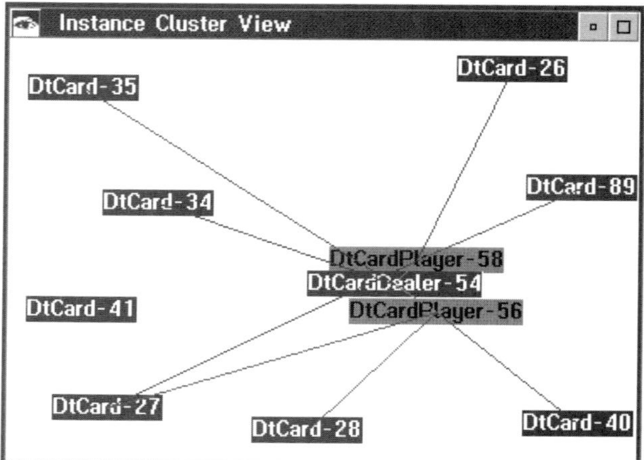

Figure 15. *Object Visualizer, Instance Cluster View*

The event profiler, introduced in Event Profiler on page 22, helps you analyze the message traffic among the objects in an application.

The state browser is like a dynamic Smalltalk inspector. It displays the values of instance variables of a selected object as they are updated. Figure 16 on page 28 shows an example of a state browser for an instance of the *DtCard* class.

DtCard-41 [103 messages]

Variables	Values
rank	'Ace'
suit	'Spades'
value	1
playerNumber	nil
hand	a DtCardBlackjackHand
state	#up
deck	a DtCardDeck

Figure 16. *Object Visualizer, Instance State Browser*

Alone or in combination with the event profiler, the object visualizer can help you determine which objects communicate with each other. Both tools help you decide how to distribute objects among object spaces to minimize the traffic between local and remote objects.

Remote Browsers

The user interface for the remote browsers is just like the user interface for the local enhanced browsers. Using these browsers, you can add, delete, or edit the classes, applications, configuration maps, and name servers that reside in other object spaces.

Remote File Dialog

A remote file dialog is a file dialog that enables you to access files that reside on a remote system. You can use a remote file dialog to open a remote text file in a workspace, make changes, and then save the file on the remote system.

Remote Inspector

A remote inspector is a standard Smalltalk inspector from which objects in a remote object space can be inspected and modified.

Remote Transcript

A remote Transcript window is the same as a normal Transcript window, except that it executes within the context of a remote object space. It mirrors the System Transcript window of that remote object space, meaning that it enables developers to interact with a remote Smalltalk image as if it were local. All updates to the System Transcript in the remote object space are reflected in connected remote Transcripts.

Remote Workspace

A remote workspace is an extension of a standard Smalltalk workspace. With it you can address objects in a remote object space. Any Smalltalk code that you execute in a remote workspace window runs in the remote object space to which the workspace window is connected, not in the local object space.

SOM and DSOM and the Distributed Feature

In this section, we summarize SOM and DSOM, IBM's implementation of CORBA. We explain their relationship with VisualAge and IBM Smalltalk and compare DSOM to the Distributed feature.

OMG's CORBA

The OMG was founded in 1989 to create standards for OO technology. It is a not for profit international trade association that has over 500 members, including IBM, Apple, AT&T, Hewlett-Packard, Borland, and SUN. The standards are focused on portability and interoperability of objects across networks of computers from multiple vendors.

In 1990, OMG published the *Object Management Architecture (OMA) Guide*. Figure 17 on page 31 shows the four most important components of this architecture:

- *Application objects* are end-user application objects. They use the Interface Definition Language (IDL) to interact with the rest of OMA's components. IDL is a standard language used to describe the interface for a class of objects.
- *Common facilities* are frameworks that help an end user do a job. Within this category we find compound documents, database access, and so on.
- *Object Request Broker* (ORB) is the middleware layer that establishes the client/server relationships between objects. It is a mechanism that lets objects transparently interact with other local or remote objects.
- *Object services* are frameworks that provide basic functions for the manipulation of objects.

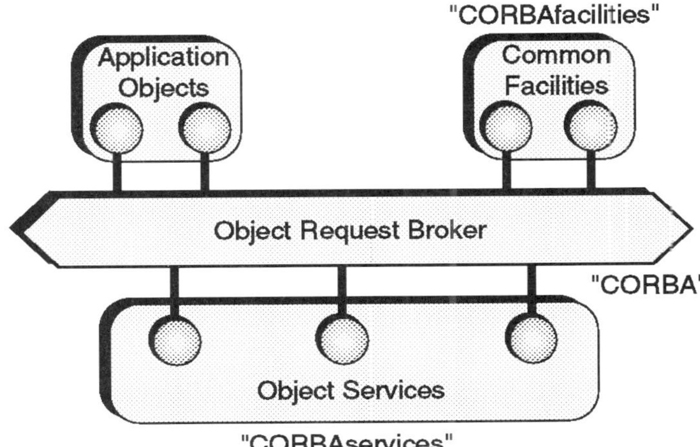

Figure 17. *Object Management Architecture*

The CORBA standard provides an object-oriented, language-neutral technology for distributed programming. SOM and DSOM are the IBM implementations of that standard. CORBA-compliant object request brokers provide facilities for object communication across a network, without regard to object location or the computer system of the sending or receiving objects.

CORBA consists of the following functions:

- ORB core

  Responsible for the communication between objects.

- IDL

  Defines the services available for an object.

- Interface repository

  Stores IDL definitions and provides information about objects and the object hierarchy.

- Dynamic invocation interface

  Enables a client object to dynamically build a request for services from a server object.

- Object adapter

  Provides an interface to ORB services. The object adapter, along with the IDL, can be used to integrate both new OO applications and older non-object-oriented systems through a technique called *wrappering*.

Figure 18 on page 32 shows the client and server components of an ORB. A more detailed explanation of this figure can be found in [Orfali94, 700-703], which is its source.

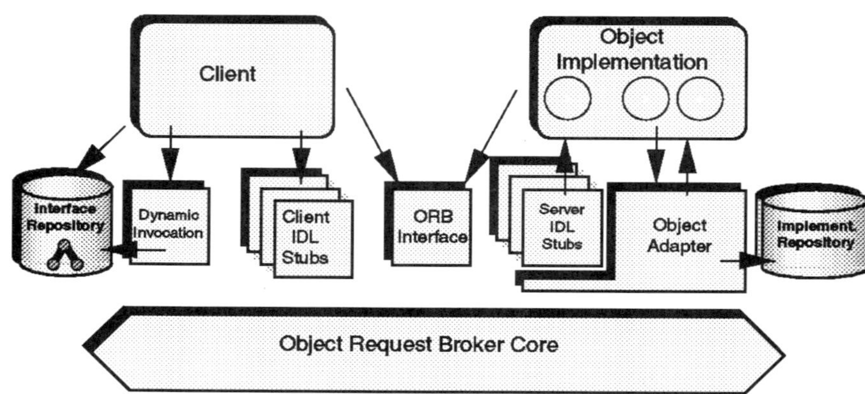

Figure 18. *Common ORB Architecture*

System Object Model (SOM)

The System Object Model (SOM) is an OO programming technology for building, packaging, and manipulating binary class libraries. It is already available on IBM OS/2, AIX, MVS, SUN Solaris, and Microsoft Windows. It will also be available on AS/400 and other platforms.

SOM is IBM's implementation of the OMG's CORBA standard. The most important benefits of SOM are:

- Language-independence

  With SOM, class implementers use the IDL to describe the interface for a class of objects. Thus they can implement methods in their preferred programming language, which can be either an OO language or a procedural language, such as C. Figure 19 on page 33 illustrates the idea of language-independence.

- Binary class libraries

  SOM allows you to ship the implementation part of your classes in executable (binary) form by separating the class interface from its implementation.

- Extensions without recompilation

  SOM allows class libraries to be extended (new methods added) without requiring the applications using these classes to be recompiled. SOM dynamically binds applications to objects at run-time.

Figure 19. *SOM's Language-independence*

Distributed System Object Model (DSOM)

The Distributed System Object Model (DSOM) is a scalable extension to SOM that provides transparent, distributed object services that are fully compliant with OMG's CORBA specification. DSOM is an object request broker and conforms to the CORBA architecture.

DSOM is a framework of classes that allow method calls on SOM objects to be made across processes. The interprocess communication is totally hidden from the programmer. The DSOM classes implement a generic sockets-based protocol that maps to a networking protocol if the processes are on different systems. A shared memory interprocess communication mechanism is utilized if the processes are in the same physical system. The protocols supported for cross-system communication are TCP/IP, NetBIOS, and IPX.

The implementation for a DSOM environment is very similar to a SOM implementation. However, the object class implementer whose classes can be used in a DSOM environment needs to keep in mind some common practices to avoid problems resulting in differences between single-process and multiple-process environments.

VisualAge SOM/DSOM Support

The VisualAge SOM support feature provides an interface through which VisualAge applications can use objects implemented under SOM. SOM objects can be developed in any language that has SOM bindings. With the VisualAge interface, applications can create instances of SOM objects and send messages to them. This capability extends to the classes that make up the SOM kernel, meaning that VisualAge applications can interact with the SOM run-time environment.

Figure 20 on page 34 illustrates how to access SOM objects from a Smalltalk environment.

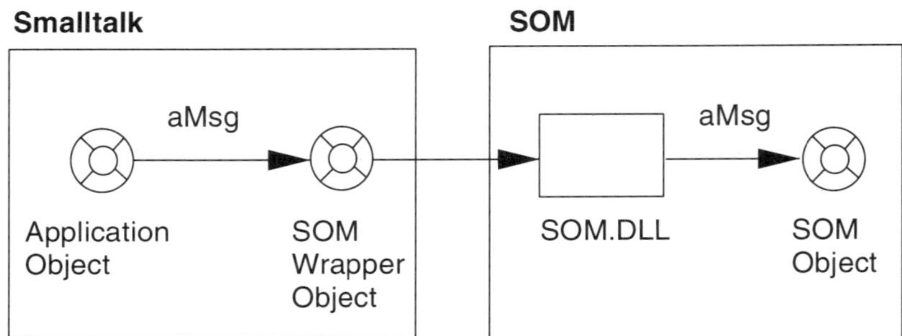

Figure 20. *VisualAge Support for SOM Objects*

SOM support is implemented through the use of Smalltalk wrapper classes that represent SOM classes. You can interact with these wrapper classes as if you were directly using the SOM classes they represent. When you create an instance of a wrapper class, you create an instance of the associated SOM class. You can then interact with the instance of the Smalltalk wrapper just as you would with any Smalltalk class. The attributes and methods of the SOM class are represented by methods of the Smalltalk class.

You can also use SOM Smalltalk wrapper classes visually in the Composition Editor. When you add a wrapper object to the Composition Editor, it appears as a nonvisual part. Attributes and actions on the part's public interface represent the attributes and methods of the SOM object.

Choosing Distributed Feature or SOM/DSOM Support

In this section we list some criteria to use when deciding whether to select the Distributed feature or VisualAge's SOM/DSOM support. This selection is not an easy task because these two features are based on quite different technologies and approaches.

Pure Smalltalk programming versus language-independence. The decision to opt for pure Smalltalk programming or language-independence depends on the specific requirements of each customer. Some customers prefer to develop OO applications in a single programming language; in this case Smalltalk would be the better choice. Other customers want to have classes written with language-independence so that they can use the classes in different languages.

Memory management. The concept of distributed object spaces enables developers to use the full power of the Smalltalk language, including high-performance messaging and efficient memory management through automatic garbage collection.

Transparency during development. Because the Distributed feature is based on Smalltalk, you can send Smalltalk objects as arguments to remote objects just as you would pass them locally, without any conversion being necessary. The Smalltalk code used to send messages to remote objects utilizes the same standard syntax used to communicate with local objects. Therefore, at development time, the programmer would not need to be concerned with the physical location of the objects in the application. In fact, throughout the development process any programmer could dynamically change the physical location of the application modules without changing the Smalltalk code.

Communication protocols. Distributed feature supports only TCP/IP. DSOM supports TCP/IP, NetBIOS, and SPX/IPX.

Distributed tools. The Distributed feature has many tools that help developers build distributed applications. Tools like the distributed debugger and the distributed event profiler help them see which messages are going through the network and what is happening in the remote machine. SOM and DSOM do not have such tools.

If you want to debug an application that uses a SOM object, you have must use the Smalltalk debugger for Smalltalk messages and the IBM Presentation Manager Debugger (IPMD) for SOM messages. If you are using a DSOM object that exists in a remote machine, you must use the IPMD in the other machine too. As you can see, debugging is much more complicated with DSOM than with the Distributed feature.

The convenience of dynamically querying object state information across object spaces is not available in a heterogeneous language environment. The remote inspector enables you to examine the values of instance variables for objects in local and remote locations.

Existing source code that is remotely located can be browsed and updated from a single workstation. Tools such as the remote browsers, remote transcript, and remote workspace provide you with a remote development environment fully integrated with your local development environment. Without these tools, you would have to physically move to each workstation to set up the appropriate configuration for each processor. As an alternative, you could write your own set of tools to invoke remote commands and capture the results. The results could then be transferred back to your local workstation. This alternative would undoubtedly add additional time and effort to the project with little impact on the expected results.

The distribution matrix greatly simplifies the task of configuring systems spanning multiple processors. Assuming the system you design requires components to reside on client and server processors, the tasks of developing, updating, and testing the individual pieces becomes quite complex. If those components are written in different languages, you will be required to maintain additional configuration management tools for the components outside of the Smalltalk development environment. Issues of component synchronization would be left to manual processes.

The expertise of the application developers would have to span multiple development environments if a multiple language solution were required. For IBM Smalltalk, a working knowledge of the IBM Smalltalk environment would be required. For additional languages, the configuration management software of choice would be required as well.

None of the other tools mentioned in The IBM Smalltalk Distribution Toolkit on page 20 is available for SOM/DSOM support.

3

Applications Suitable for the Distributed Feature

In this chapter we describe three application types that are suitable for the VisualAge Distributed feature. These types of applications raise a new set of requirements that can better be addressed with a distributed object solution than with a traditional client/server approach.

The chapter is divided into the following sections:

- "Object Server" describes applications that suffer from excessive traffic between client and database server.
- "Active Server" describes applications in which servers can initiate requests to clients.

- "Peer-to-Peer Applications" describes applications in which clients can both initiate and service requests between each other.
- "Applying the Distributed Feature" proposes the application of the Distributed feature to build the three application types.

In Scenarios for a Distributed FCE Application on page 85 we show you how to apply the three application types to extend a Foreign Currency Exchange application.

Object Server

The most common client/server implementations today use remote data access where the business logic is on the client system (so-called *fat clients*, as discussed in Different Approaches: Fat Clients and Fat Servers on page 5).

Using existing Distributed Relational Database Architecture (DRDA), client workstations can access a centralized database through the SQL interface across the network. However, this approach can lead to excessive network traffic between the clients and the relational database server, especially when many intermediate results must be retrieved from the database server to accomplish one task on a client.

In a *fat client* situation, the data server does not filter any information it retrieves from the database, normally in the form of rows of data tables, before sending it to the client. Therefore it generates unnecessary network traffic.

One way of reducing the network traffic is to use *stored procedures*, which many relational database products support. A stored procedure is a named collection of SQL statements and procedural logic that is compiled, verified, and stored in the database server. The problem with stored procedures is that there is no standard for them and they work only for local databases. Each relational database vendor has its own implementation of stored procedures. If we want to use multiple databases from multiple vendors in a single client task, we cannot use stored procedures.

To avoid excessive network traffic, we can put more processing functions in the server, in addition to its traditional data access function. The server then becomes an *object server*. Instead of using the SQL interface between the client and server, clients issue the request to the server in the form of the objects they require.

By collecting data and constructing the requested objects at the server before sending them to the client, we can reduce network traffic and improve overall application performance. Having the server perform data collection and object construction can potentially reduce the number of requests that the client must send to the server.

Figure 21 on page 39 shows the differences between a data server and object server.

A side benefit of the object server is that it is not required that the relational database software be installed in the client workstations. In an operational environment with many clients, eliminating the database license cost for client workstations could lead to substantial savings.

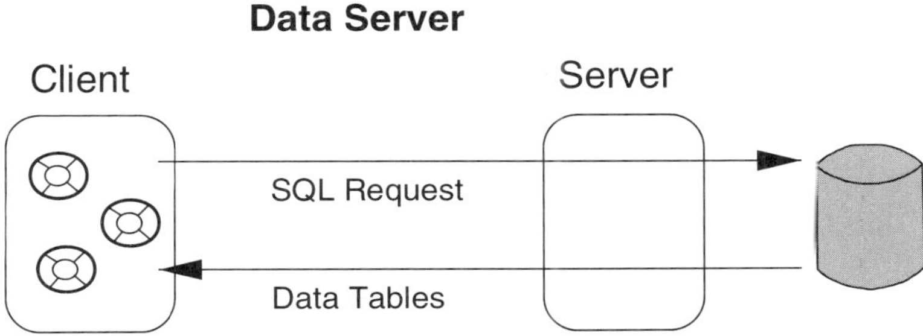

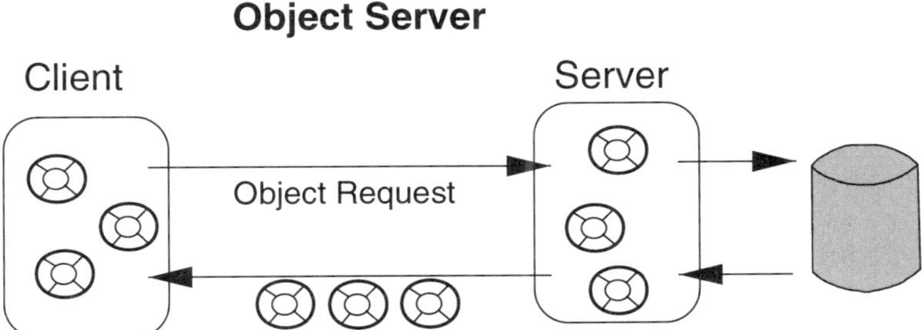

Figure 21. *Data Server and Object Server*

Active Server

In a traditional client/server computing model, the client always originates the requests. The server is *passive* in the sense that it reacts only to the client's requests. We can change the way the server behaves in the model so that the server is an active party in the system. An *active server* can process data by itself and initiate communication with clients.

Some database systems have programs that can be executed automatically. These programs are called *triggers*. Triggers are usually stored procedures that are kept on the server. They are automatically executed on the basis of data-related events. The difference between triggers and an active server is this: for the triggers to work, the events must originate from client actions. An active server can activate triggers all by itself.

Let us look at an example of an active server in a publisher-subscriber scenario. The server publishes events that it can handle, and clients can then subscribe to those events in which they are interested. Let us say that a stockbroker is interested in current prices of some specific shares. In an active server environment, the stockbroker (the client) can ask the server for the available (published) share prices and then choose (subscribe) those stocks that are needed (see Figure 22 on page 40). Whenever the price of a subscribed-to stock changes, the subscribers are notified automatically.

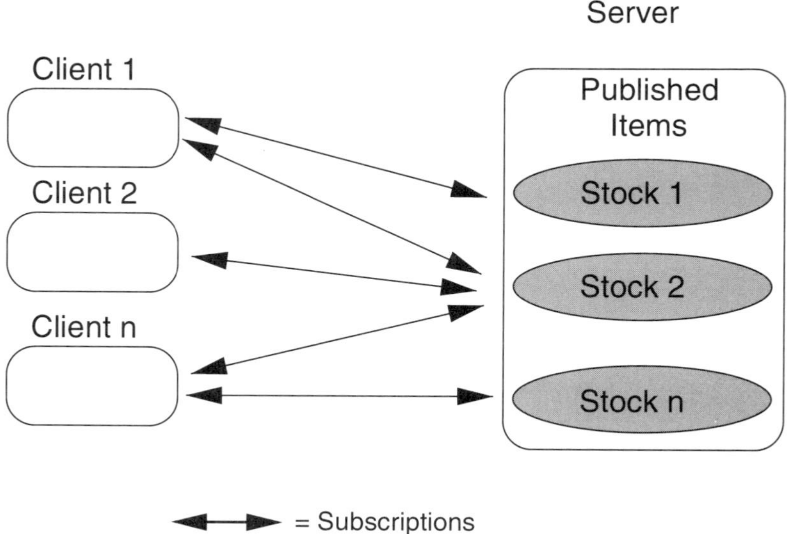

Figure 22. *Publisher-Subscriber Scenario*

Another example of an active server environment is an auction. At an auction, the auctioneer is the active server that starts the event and keeps track of the biddings. Clients can send their bid to the auctioneer active server, which holds the current, highest bid on an item and the name of the client. All clients are notified whenever the bid changes.

Peer-to-Peer Applications

In peer-to-peer applications, two client workstations communicate with each other directly, both acting as a server and a client at the same time.

In the traditional client/server computing model, where communications between two clients go through the server, we would need to establish two separate concurrent sessions between each client and the server, hence causing more overhead on the network and server. Instead, we want to have a direct communication between the two clients, as shown in Figure 23 on page 41. In this scenario, clients should be able to establish the connection whenever they want, without causing any additional stress to any other machines in the system.

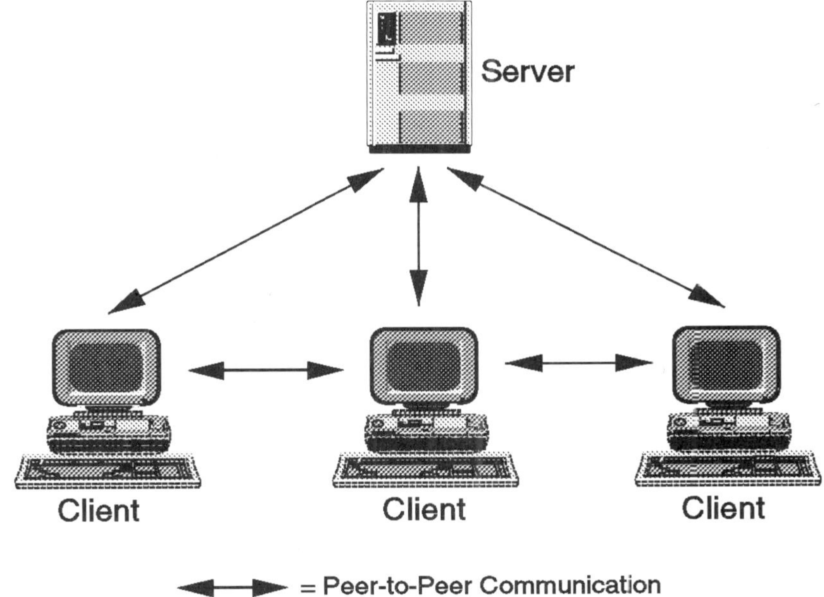

Figure 23. *Peer-to-Peer Scenario*

Peer-to-peer applications can be useful, for example, when two users on different client workstations must establish a session for consultation or negotiation on a certain subject.

Applying the Distributed Feature

We can use the Distributed feature to build the server business logic that is needed to create an object server *and* an active server. For example, we can have an active process on the server that interacts with object instances that have shadows on client machines. Whenever the state of an instance is changed in a server object space, all clients see the change automatically.

By using the Distributed feature we can split the application logic to reside both on the server and the client side. We can design our class structure, methods, and class locations so that the network traffic is minimized and the needed processing is done on the appropriate side.

We can also implement the server side of the application so that one client transaction can actually access different kinds of data sources on the server side, including relational databases. This way, a client application is not tied to any specific database system, and changing the underlying database system is much easier.

We can use the Distributed feature to easily build peer-to-peer applications. We do not have to worry about programming to some network API or know anything about the network protocol. The Distributed feature has a rich set of tools in the base distribution classes to implement peer-to-peer behavior in an application.

Any object space can act as a server if we have appropriate classes in all images. We can set up the image to start as a server object space by defining the server object space key in the startup parameters (see Server Activator File on page 51).

Summary

The three types of applications described in this chapter raise a new set of requirements that can be addressed by a distributed object solution better than by using a traditional client/server approach.

VisualAge with the Distributed feature is a versatile application development tool for developing solutions for these new breeds of applications.

4

Set Up the Development Environment

In this chapter we explain how to install the VisualAge Distributed feature for OS/2 and set up the development environment.

This chapter consists of the following sections:

- "Prerequisites" shows the required hardware and software configurations, and the setup of the TCP/IP product needed by the Distributed feature as its communication protocol.
- "Installation" describes how to install the Distributed feature. It contains the following sections:
  - "VisualAge for Smalltalk, Professional Server" describes the installation of a VisualAge for Smalltalk, Professional Server machine.

- "VisualAge for Smalltalk, Professional Client" contains the steps to be taken to install the first VisualAge for Smalltalk, Professional (Client) machine with all needed features, including the Distributed feature.
- "Additional Clients" describes how to install additional VisualAge for Smalltalk, Professional (Client) machines.
- "Server Activator File" describes how to install and configure the Distributed feature activator files to differentiate between client and server object spaces.

- "Verification" explains how to ensure that the installation and configuration steps have been completed successfully.

Prerequisites

This section presents the recommended hardware configuration, prerequisite software, and TCP/IP configuration required to install the Distributed feature.

Hardware Configuration

For the VisualAge for Smalltalk, Professional for OS/2 product, the recommended minimum hardware for the development environment is:

- Server:
  - 486 processor, 33 MHz, 24 MB RAM, 110+ MB DASD
- Client:
  - 486 processor, 33 MHz, 24 MB RAM, 35+ MB DASD.

The hard disk (DASD) recommendations cover only VisualAge and Distributed feature needs. Also, if you plan to have multiple images running on your machine, the recommended RAM amount is at least 32 MB.

Prerequisite Software

The Distributed feature is installed on top of one of the following products:

- VisualAge for Smalltalk, Professional, Version 3.0

- ❑ IBM Smalltalk, Professional, Version 3.0

It supports the client/server editions of VisualAge for Smalltalk, Professional, and IBM Smalltalk, Professional, on all supported operating system platforms, namely OS/2, AIX, and Windows. However, in this book, we refer to the VisualAge for Smalltalk, Professional for OS/2 edition.

In addition to one of the products listed above, you must have the VisualAge Communications/Transactions feature Version 3.0. Installation of the Distributed feature is similar to the installation of any other VisualAge or IBM Smalltalk feature; however, it requires a few more steps.

If you plan to install VisualAge for Smalltalk, Professional Server or IBM Smalltalk, Professional Server on OS/2, you must have OS/2 LAN Server and LAN Requester Version 3.0 (or higher) with requesters on each client. For Novell NetWare users, Version 3.11 (or higher) is required with the appropriate client software. Windows for Workgroups, Version 3.11 has the necessary network software built in, therefore, no additional software is needed either at the client or the server. For AIX, only TCP/IP is required for the communication between VisualAge for Smalltalk, Professional Server and VisualAge for Smalltalk, Professional. Refer to the installation guide for the Professional product for specific requirements.

For the Distributed feature you must also have TCP/IP. For OS/2, use IBM TCP/IP Version 2.0 or higher. For Windows, NetManage Chameleon TCP/IP for Windows Version 4.5 is recommended. For AIX, TCP/IP is already available.

To use the security services conforming to the Generic Security Services (GSS) industry standard on OS/2, you must have the IBM Network Security Program (NetSP) Version 1.2 for OS/2. The security services provide a file-based interface which may be used as an alternative solution.

The prerequisite products are listed below. In general, versions that are newer than those listed should be acceptable.

- ❑ IBM OS/2 Version 3.0 (Warp), Microsoft Windows Version 3.11 (enhanced mode), or AIX Version 4.1.3
- ❑ IBM OS/2 LAN Server and LAN Requester Version 3.0 or Novell NetWare Version 3.11 (to use the client/server edition of VisualAge or IBM Smalltalk)
- ❑ VisualAge for Smalltalk, Professional, Version 3.0 or IBM Smalltalk, Professional, Version 3.0
- ❑ VisualAge for Smalltalk, Communications/Transactions Version 3.0

- ❑ IBM TCP/IP for OS/2 Version 2.0 or, for Windows, one of the products supporting the Microsoft Windows Socket API, Version 1.1 (such as NetManage Chameleon TCP/IP for Windows Version 4.5)
- ❑ IBM NetSP Version 1.2 (for third-party authentication on OS/2 through the GSS API).

TCP/IP Configuration

You must install TCP/IP on every machine that will use the Distributed feature. If you are using OS/2, you must install the Base Kit portion of TCP/IP for OS/2. Before you start installing TCP/IP on your machine you must have the following information:

IP address

The Internet Protocol (IP) address is the unique address assigned to your workstation. The format is nnn.nnn.nnn.nnn.

Subnet mask

The subnet mask is used to separate the subnet address from the host portion of the address. The format is nnn.nnn.nnn.nnn.

Router IP address (optional)

The router IP address is the IP address of your default router. The format is nnn.nnn.nnn.nnn.

This machine's host name

The host name is the unique name assigned to your workstation. The format is 1 to 30 alphanumeric characters.

Domain name (optional)

The domain name is the name of the domain where your host resides. The domain name is part of a fully-qualified domain name that is a naming scheme for a hierarchical naming system. A fully-qualified domain name consists of a host name and domain name, separated by periods.

Domain name server address (optional)

The domain name server address is the IP address of a server in your domain that resolves domain names to IP addresses. The format is nnn.nnn.nnn.nnn.

If TCP/IP is already used in your network, you can obtain the correct configuration parameters from the system administrator. See the TCP/IP for OS/2 installation instructions for more information to install the Base Kit.

After installing the Base Kit, you can change the TCP/IP configuration. To do so, use the TCP/IP Configuration program icon in the TCP/IP folder. Table 1 shows a sample TCP/IP configuration for a server machine called *eddyhost*:

Table 1. Sample TCP/IP Configuration

Parameter	**Value**	**Comments**
	Network Page	
IP address	9.87.65.123	
Subnet mask	255.255.255.0	
	Routing Page	
Router IP address	1.23.45.67	Router IP address is optional. If you have a router in the network, enter the IP address of the router.
	Services Page	
This machine's host name	eddyhost	
Domain name	sanjose.ibm.com	If you do not use a name server, leave the domain name blank.
Domain name server address	1.23.45.68	The domain name server is optional. If you have a name server in the network, enter the IP address of the name server.

If you do not have a name server in your network you can use TCP/IP for OS/2 to resolve host names. Start the TCP/IP configuration program and select the services configuration. In the list *HOST*, add the host names for your configuration.

Installation

Figure 24 on page 48 summarizes the installation steps for the VisualAge Professional server and clients.

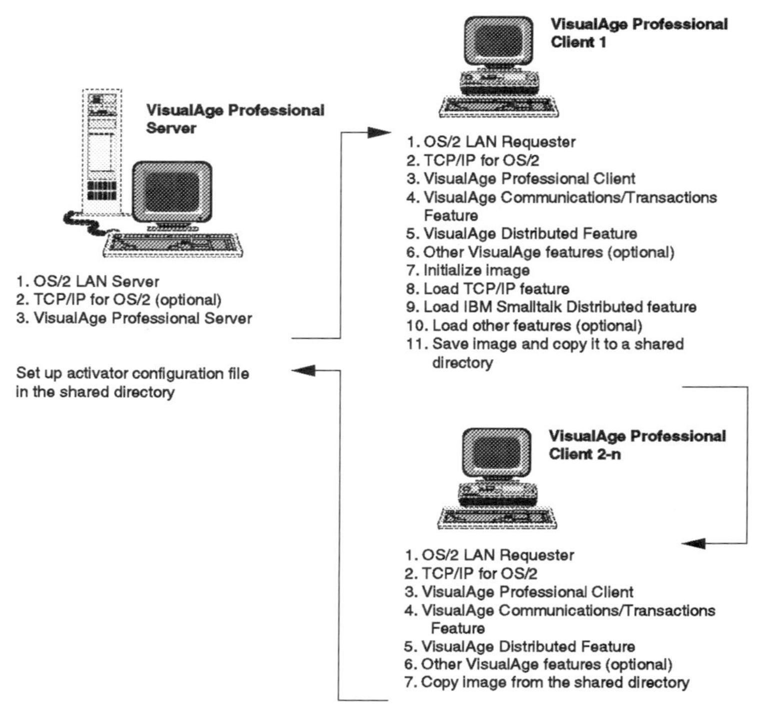

Figure 24. *Installation Steps*

VisualAge for Smalltalk, Professional Server

To create a LAN server that holds your shared VisualAge development library, follow these steps (if the VisualAge for Smalltalk, Professional Server product is already installed, skip to "VisualAge for Smalltalk, Professional Client"):

1. Install OS/2 LAN Server or Novell NetWare, using the product's installation instructions.
2. If you are going to use the LAN server machine as a client workstation using the Distributed feature, install TCP/IP for OS/2 (see its installation instructions).
3. Install VisualAge for Smalltalk, Professional Server on your LAN server. See the product's installation instructions.

VisualAge for Smalltalk, Professional Client

To create a new client workstation that accesses your VisualAge server, follow these steps (we recommend that you begin with a fresh image when you start using the Distributed feature for the first time):

1. Install OS/2 LAN Requester or Novell NetWare, using the product's installation instructions.
2. Install TCP/IP for OS/2 2.0 or higher (see its installation instructions).
3. Access your VisualAge server on a drive.

   Install VisualAge for Smalltalk, Professional (Client) on your development machine as described in the installation documentation.
4. Install the TCP/IP component of the VisualAge for Smalltalk, Professional, Communications/Transactions feature Version 3.0 on your client. (This feature also supports IBM Smalltalk, Professional.) For details, see the product's installation instructions.
5. Install the Distributed feature on your server. For details, see the product's installation instructions.
6. Install the other features that you will use in your applications.
7. Reboot your system.
8. During the installation process, a new VisualAge folder was created on your OS/2 desktop. Start the new client by clicking on the **VisualAge Professional** icon in that folder.

   After identifying as *Library Supervisor*, VisualAge reconnects the client image to the server library.
9. Save and make a backup of your fresh client workstation image.
10. Load the TCP/IP feature into your image. From the System Transcript window, select **Smalltalk tools**, **Load Features....** From the list of features, select **TCP/IP** and click on **OK**. This step can take quite some time (up to five minutes on slower machines). You may want to save the image after installing the TCP/IP feature.
11. Load the Distributed feature into your image. From the System Transcript window, select **Smalltalk tools**, **Load Features....** From the list of features, select **IBM Smalltalk Distributed** and click on **OK**. A number of new applications will be loaded. This step takes quite some time (20-35 minutes on slower machines).

    After installing this feature, you are invited to save the image. Answer **Yes** to this question.
12. Load the other features that you will use in your application into your image and save the final image.

13. If you are setting up the VisualAge for Smalltalk, Professional environment for the first time, you can add new users to your library now. To accomplish this and other administrative tasks, refer to the *IBM Smalltalk User's Guide*.
14. To ensure that all VisualAge client users identify themselves before using the customized image, execute the following Smalltalk expression from the System Transcript window:

    ```
    EmUser resetImageOwner
    ```

15. Reset the System Transcript window (**File**, **Revert**) and exit from the client image. Be sure to save the image during exit.
16. Make a backup copy of your fresh image configured with the Distributed feature. Copy the `IMAGE` file from the client directory to a shared directory on your LAN. The backup copy can save you time later if you want to install multiple images and load them with various parts of your application. You can use the backup copy to restore your image to its initial state in case of unexpected errors.

You have just completed installing the first VisualAge for Smalltalk, Professional (Client) system. The next step is to install the VisualAge for Smalltalk, Professional (Client) on one or more additional machines that will serve as development workstations that use the Distributed feature.

Additional Clients

Installing an additional VisualAge client is straightforward, particularly if you copied the `IMAGE` file to a shared LAN directory after the first client installation (see Step 13 in the previous section, titled "VisualAge for Smalltalk, Professional Client").

1.-6. Repeat Steps 1 through 6 in "VisualAge for Smalltalk, Professional Client" for the additional client machine.

7. If you made a backup copy of the first client's image file to a shared LAN directory, copy that file as `IMAGE` to the new client's VisualAge directory.

   If you do not use the customized image of the first client, you must reload the required features into the new image by following Steps 8 through 12 in the section titled "VisualAge for Smalltalk, Professional Client" .

Server Activator File

The Distributed feature requires every machine that is running one or more *server object spaces* (see Object Spaces on page 15) to have an *activator*, which is used to automatically start object spaces on a machine when they are referenced. The activator also facilitates object space connections. An activator is not required for a *client object space*.

To set up your activator, edit its configuration file ABTACT.CNF. This file and the executable program ABTACT2.EXE were created in the DISTRIB subdirectory of the directory that holds your VisualAge client installation (for example, D:\VISUALAG). Actually, you can put these files in any directory. We found it convenient to put the files in a shared directory on the LAN and to use the same configuration file for the activators on any machine. A common activator configuration file makes it easier to maintain the object space keys for all developers.

We also found it convenient to make all our object spaces *server object spaces*, to allow any object space to connect to any other object space.

Here are the steps to set up your activator files:

1. Move the ABTACT2.EXE and ABTACT.CNF files to a shared directory on the LAN. After you have modified the ABTACT.CNF file as described in Step , each machine can start the ABTACT2.EXE program from that shared directory. With this approach, the configurations are easy to change.
2. Edit the ABTACT.CNF file to define all related object spaces. The activator uses the ABTACT.CNF file to obtain the key, location, and characteristics of the server object spaces you use. For VisualAge, the configuration file might contain the lines shown in Figure 25 on page 51 to define a server object space with the key *Eddy*.

```
    # Activator Configuration File
#****************************************
_protocol     = tcp
_port         = 1586
_startTimeout = 180
#****************************************
Eddy d:\visualag abt image * * old noautostart ui
```

Figure 25. *Activator Configuration File*

The parameter descriptions, taken from the *VisualAge Distributed User's Guide* are:

#	Starts a comment line.

_protocol Defines the communications protocol through which the activator will receive connections. This line must precede any object space entries to which it applies. Currently, only TCP/IP is supported, so only `_protocol=tcp` is valid. This is also the default value when you omit the _protocol parameter.

_port Specifies the TCP/IP port number through which the activator will receive connections. If you do not specify a port number, the Distributed feature uses the default, port 1586. If you must have more than one activator for a particular machine, you must use the port command in the activator configuration file to ensure that the two activators do not use the same port.

_startTimeout Determines how many seconds the activator waits for an object space to register after being started. This timeout applies to any object space that is not already running when the activator receives a connection bound for that object space. The default is 180.

Eddy ... Following the three optional lines is an object space entry. This example defines an object space called *Eddy* (that is, *Eddy* is the unique object space key that identifies this object space). That entry also provides the activator with the following information about the *Eddy* object space:

- `abt`, in the `d:\visualag` directory, is the command to use to start the object space.
- `image` is the image file to load.
- The two asterisks (* *) indicate that we do not want to specify a different user ID or a different group ID for the object space. User ID and group ID are used in the AIX version only. For non-AIX systems, the IDs must be specified with two asterisks.
- `old` indicates that only one instance will be started at a time; that is, if this object space is already running, incoming connections will be routed to the existing (old) instance.
- `noautostart` indicates that this object space will not be started automatically when the activator starts. Thus, the object space will not start until it receives an incoming connection (or is started manually by a user).
- `ui` indicates that this object space has user-interface capability.

Adjust the drive and path to match your own configurations.

Object space keys are case-sensitive! Here, *Eddy* is the object space key for our sample server object space. Normally there is only one activator for each TCP/IP host name (that is, on each server machine). The activator knows about one or more object spaces on that machine as defined in its activator configuration file.

3. When the Distributed feature was installed, a new Activator folder containing an **Activator** icon for the program invocation was added to your desktop. Change the settings of this icon so that the path names match the LAN directory into which you moved the activator files. First, select the **Activator** icon in the Activator folder, press the right mouse button, and select **Open**, **Settings**. A settings window appears. Change the path for `ABTACT2.EXE` and enter the complete file name of the activator configuration file in the Parameters field.

   You can create a shadow to the program object in your OS/2 Startup folder so that the activator automatically starts when your server workstation is started.

4. Configure the VisualAge image startup icon to include the `-Dk` parameter. The `-Dk` parameter stands for *distribution key* and is used by a server object space to register with the activator on its machine.

   When the VisualAge for Smalltalk, Professional (Client) software was installed, a new folder containing a **VisualAge Professional** icon for the program invocation was added to your desktop. In OS/2 you can change the settings of this icon to add the `-Dk` parameter. Select the **VisualAge Professional** icon, press the right mouse button, and select **Open**, **Settings**. In the settings window, change the Parameters field to include the `-Dk` option with the name of the object space that is started. For example, on *Eddy* server machine, you would enter `-DkEddy`.

   The name specified on the `-Dk` parameter must match a name that is specified in the `ABTACT.CNF` file for the machine where the object space runs. There must not be a space between the `-Dk` and the name. Be aware that the name is case-sensitive.

   If the `-Dk` parameter is not specified, the object space will initialize as a client.

This completes the installation of the Distributed feature environment. Of course, you can add more client systems at a later time by following the guidelines in Additional Clients on page 50 and by adjusting the activator configuration file as described in this section.

Verification

Now we are ready to verify that the installation works and that the client and server object spaces can communicate with each other.

TCP/IP Configuration

Figure 26 shows our sample installation configuration with the TCP/IP parameters.

Figure 26. *VisualAge Distributed Feature Sample Configuration with TCP/IP*

To verify that the TCP/IP connection works between these two machines, follow these steps:

1. Start TCP/IP. On an OS/2 machine there are two ways to ensure that TCP/IP is started on every system startup:
   a. A **TCP/IP Startup** program object icon can be found in the TCP/IP folder. Create a shadow to that program object in your Startup folder, which is in the OS/2 System folder by default.
   b. Include a call to `TCPSTART.CMD` in your `STARTUP.CMD`.

   You can also start TCP/IP from an OS/2 command line by entering `TCPSTART`.

2. Now, test the actual connection by sending a *PING* message to the other machine.[*] Key in.

   ```
   ping eddyhost.sanjose.ibm.com
   ```

   from a command line, where *eddyhost* is the host name of the target machine and *sanjose.ibm.com* is the fully-qualified TCP/IP domain name in the network. (If *eddyhost* is in your TCP/IP name server, you do not need to specify *sanjose.ibm.com*.)

[*] The *PING* program included with the TCP/IP product enables you to send messages to another TCP/IP address and get responses.

If communication is successful, your results will look like this:

```
[C:\]ping eddyhost.sanjose.ibm.com
PING eddyhost.sanjose.ibm.com: 56 data bytes
64 bytes from 9.87.65.123: icmp_seq=0. time=0. ms
64 bytes from 9.87.65.123: icmp_seq=1. time=0. ms
64 bytes from 9.87.65.123: icmp_seq=2. time=0. ms
```

You can stop the ping program at any time by pressing **Ctrl+Break**.

Note: If you successfully "ping" by providing the IP address of the target machine, you are not guaranteed that the VisualAge Distributed feature can connect to the *Eddy* object space. You must verify that TCP/IP can resolve by host name the addresses to which you expect your object spaces to connect. TCP/IP resolves the host name by either explicitly mapping the host name to the IP address in your *host's* file or by using your TCP/IP name server. The TCP/IP name server is not to be confused with the VisualAge Distributed feature's name server.

Distributed Feature Configuration

Next verify the communication between the two object spaces using the Distributed feature.

1. Start the activator on the machine that acts as a server (in our example, *Eddy*) by clicking on the **Activator** icon in the Activator folder. If your activator configuration file resides in a different directory, be sure that you have specified the complete file name as a parameter in the icon settings.
2. Start the client machine's object space (in our example, *Sven*).

   To start the client machine's object space, simply start VisualAge on the client system. The client object space should show the System Transcript and the VisualAge Organizer window. If you reset the image owner after installation, you must provide the user name for that image. After a short delay, Transcript messages similar to these appear:

   ```
   Smalltalk Distributed initializing...
   Object space activated as a client;  with key ''  at
           host'svenhost.sanjose.ibm.com' (no key specified).
   Smalltalk Distributed initialization complete.
   ```

   As you can see from the Transcript messages, this machine is a client because we did not include the `-Dk` entry on the starting parameters of the client image. You can also see that this client machine has the TCP/IP host name `svenhost`.

   Tip: You may prefer to include keys on client object spaces to help identify the client object space in the Transcript messages and distribution tools.

3. Create an object reference that points to the object space of our server, *Eddy*. This object reference will be used to send a message from the client machine to the server object space defined by the -`DkEddy` key.

   From the System Transcript window, select **Distribution tools**, **Open Object Exchange**. From the Object Exchange, select **Reference**, **Add**, **Add New...**. From the object kind list, select **Reference to an Object Space Location**.

   Fill in the object reference fields:

Identifier:	Eddy
Object Space Key:	Eddy
Host Name:	eddyhost.sanjose.ibm.com
Protocol:	TCP/IP

   Note: You must change `eddyhost.sanjose.ibm.com` to match your server's host name.

   You have now created an object reference to *Eddy*'s object space in *Sven*'s name server.

4. To send a message to *Eddy*'s Transcript from your machine, open a *remote workspace* (see The IBM Smalltalk Distribution Toolkit on page 20) on *Eddy*'s machine. Select the object reference you just created, press the right mouse button to bring up the context menu, and select **Referenced Object Space**, **Open Workspace**. These actions open a workspace in the context of *Eddy*'s object space.

5. On the remote workspace, execute the following statement:

```
Transcript cr
 show: 'A message from Sven to Eddy!'
```

If everything was configured properly, a message is sent to the *Eddy* object space. The activator on *Eddy*'s machine will start the *Eddy* object space (if it has not been started already), and the message appears on *Eddy*'s Transcript window. Look at *Eddy*'s machine to verify that communication occurred.

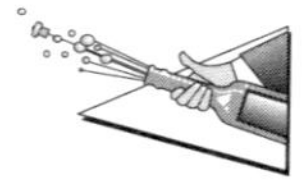

Congratulations! You have properly installed and set up the VisualAge Distributed feature environment and you have successfully sent a message between two object spaces. For a more sophisticated communication example, investigate the card game demo application that comes with the Distributed feature. See the *VisualAge Distributed User's Guide* for instructions on how to run that application.

5

A Quick Tour Through Distributed Object Land

This chapter outlines the development of a simple distributed application to illustrate the main concepts of the VisualAge Distributed feature. We show how to extend an application from stand-alone to a distributed environment.

We encourage you to recreate the application using the steps in the following sections. On the basis of this quick tour, it should be much easier to understand the development process of a real-life application as it is described in Part 2, "Developing Distributed Object Applications" .

This chapter consists of these sections:

- "The Celsius/Fahrenheit Converter" explains the purpose and general outline of our simple sample application.
- "Building the Stand-alone Application" contains the steps to take using VisualAge, to build the stand-alone version of the application.
- "Moving the Model Object to a Remote Object Space" shows how to move a model class of the application to an object space residing on a different machine.
- "Accessing the Same Model Object from Two Clients" shows how to access the same server model instance from two different client machines.
- "Dividing the Application" shows how to add an additional application to separate the view and model class.
- "Using the Distribution Matrix" explains how to use the distribution matrix to control loading the necessary applications into the appropriate object spaces.
- "Experiences" summarizes the experiences made during the quick tour and lists some concerns to be aware of during actual development.

Note

In the sections that follow, we assume that the VisualAge Distributed feature environment has been set up properly with at least two client machines as described in Set Up the Development Environment on page 43.

In our project configuration, we had three clients, with the object space keys `Eddy`, `Matti`, and `Sven`, respectively. The corresponding object spaces were defined in the common activator configuration file (see Server Activator File on page 51).

The Celsius/Fahrenheit Converter

We want to create the small application *EmsThermometerApp*[*] to convert temperature values from degrees Celsius to degrees Fahrenheit and vice-versa.

Our application consists of two classes:

1. *EmsThermometer*

[*] The prefix Ems for our VisualAge application and class names is arbitrary.

The business domain class. An *EmsThermometer* is able to hold and return its actual temperature value in both Celsius and Fahrenheit.

2. *EmsThermometerView*

   The user interface class. An *EmsThermometerView* shows the actual temperature value of its underlying thermometer object in both units. It allows the user to change either of the values and immediately updates the other one. Figure 27 on page 59 shows how the user interface looks.

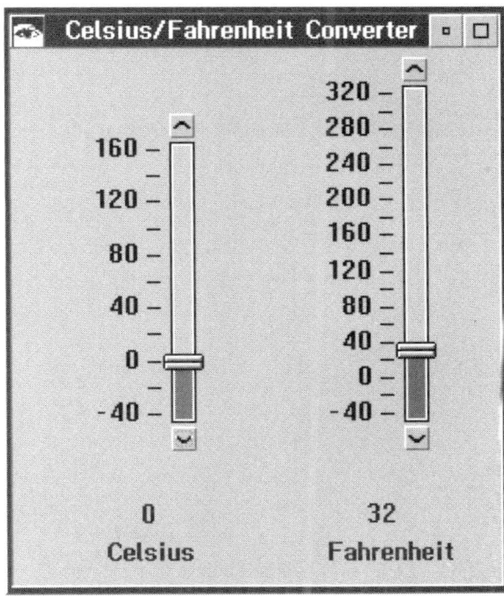

Figure 27. *A Simple Thermometer View*

Building the Stand-alone Application

1. From the VisualAge Organizer, create a new application called *EmsThermometerApp*.
2. Within this new application, create a new nonvisual part called *EmsThermometer*. Since you do not need the VisualAge Composition Editor for any visual construction features, change the superclass of your part from *AbtAppBldrPart* (default) to *AbtPart*.

3. In the Public Interface Editor for your thermometer model, define two instance variables as shown in Table 2.

Table 2. Public Interface of the Thermometer Model

Attribute name	**Get selector**	**Set selector**	**Change event symbol**	**Instance variable class**
celsius	celsius	celsius:	celsius	Integer
fahrenheit	fahrenheit	fahrenheit:	fahrenheit	Integer

Note: Even though we do not store the Fahrenheit value, we want to allow the user to change it. Actually, you will modify the script and in fact change the stored Celsius value.

4. Generate the default scripts for your "real" instance variable *celsius* and for all selectors.

5. In the Script Editor, change the generated code as shown below:

```
celsius
  "Return the value of celsius."
  celsius isNil ifTrue: [ self celsius: 0 ].
  ^celsius
celsius: anInteger
  "Save the value of celsius."
  celsius := anInteger.
  self signalEvent: #celsius with: anInteger.
  self signalEvent: #fahrenheit.
fahrenheit
  "Return the value of fahrenheit."
  ^(self celsius * 1.8 + 32) asInteger
fahrenheit: anInteger
  "Save the value of fahrenheit."
  self celsius: ((anInteger - 32) / 1.8) asInteger.
```

Note that the signaling of the *fahrenheit* event was removed from the *fahrenheit:* method. This event is signaled indirectly by using the *celsius:* method.

6. Now you are ready to test your model. It is good style to implement a specific test class which contains test methods for the actual class. For simplicity of this quick tour, implement the *test* method as a private class method within *EmsThermometer* itself:

```
test
  "Test code for the class."
  | m |
  m := self new.
  Transcript cr; show: m printString.
  m fahrenheit: 100.
  Transcript cr; show: m printString.
```

To see the actual values, implement also the public instance method *printString* as follows:

```
printString
  "Create a string describing the instance."
  ^'an EmsThermometer: ',
      self celsius printString,
      ' degrees Celsius, ',
      self fahrenheit printString,
      ' degrees Fahrenheit.'
```

To run the test method, execute the following code from the Transcript window:

```
EmsThermometer test
```

The Transcript window should display the following lines:

```
an EmsThermometer: 0 degrees Celsius, 32 degrees Fahrenheit.
an EmsThermometer: 38 degrees Celsius, 100 degrees Fahrenheit.
```

7. The next step is to create the visual part *EmsThermometerView*. Use the VisualAge Composition Editor to define the layout as shown in Figure 27 on page 59 and add a part of the *EmsThermometer* class to the free-form surface.

8. Now, define the necessary attribute-to-attribute connections:

   - Unidirectional connections from the actual slider values (*topOrLeftValue* attribute) to their corresponding label parts
   - Bidirectional connections between the actual slider values and the corresponding attributes (*celsius* and *fahrenheit*) of the thermometer part.

   Figure 28 on page 62 shows the Composition Editor after all connections have been defined.

9. Now, let us test the application. You can use both sliders to change the temperature and you should see the corresponding value on the other slider.

10. When everything works fine, assign a version to the two classes, release them, and create version 1 of the application.

Moving the Model Object to a Remote Object Space

To introduce object distribution, we will make the thermometer model reside on a different machine. This is quite simple:

1. Start VisualAge on a second workstation. For our example, this machine's object space has the key `Matti` (see the description of the `-Dk` parameter in Server Activator File on page 51).

2. Load the current version of your *EmsThermometerApp* into that object space and save the image.

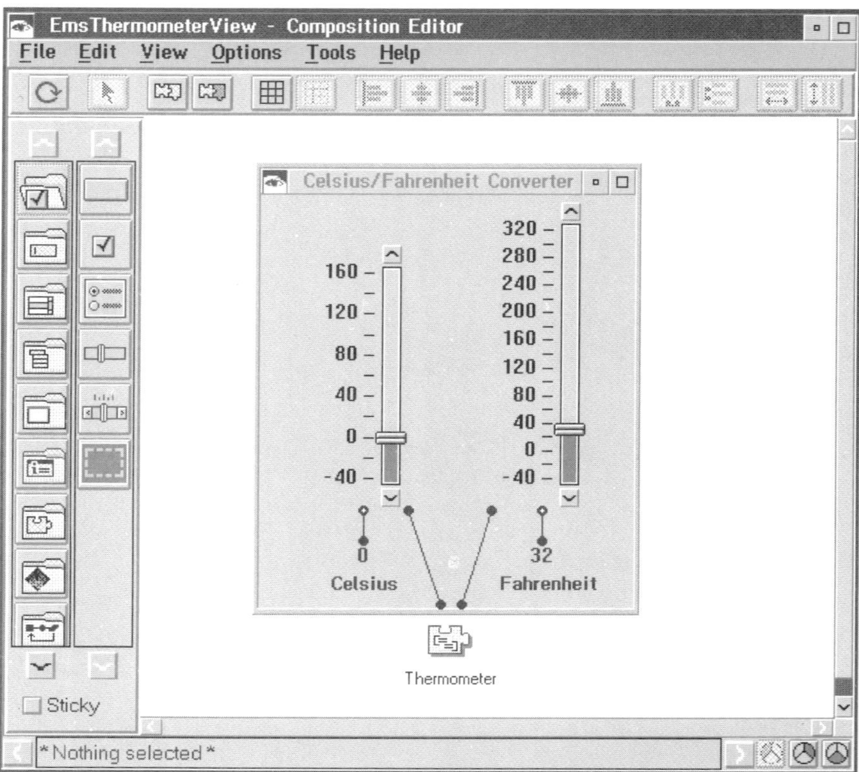

Figure 28. *Thermometer View, Composition Editor*

3. Now, you must change the view class on your development workstation. Create new editions of your application and of the *EmsThermometerView* class.

4. In the thermometer view, you must replace the thermometer part. Instead of creating the thermometer instance in the local object space, we want to instantiate it on the remote machine. To achieve this, you can use the *distributed part* (see Name Server Distributed Part on page 25) and a global object reference to the remote model class, or the model class in the remote object space.

   The reference will be used to create a shadow of the remote class. This shadow, in turn, will create the thermometer instance (see New Terms for Distribution on page 15). Using this approach, the class does not have to be defined in the local object space. On the other hand, you must have explicit references to all those classes you want to use from other object spaces.

5. To define the object reference, activate the Transcript window and select **Distribution tools**, **Open Object Exchange**, **Reference**, **Add**, **Add New...**. From the object kind list, pick **Reference to a**

Global Object to define a reference to a remote class. Use your class name *EmsThermometer* both as *Identifier* and *Global Name*. Provide the key of the remote object space and the corresponding host name.

Figure 29 on page 63 shows the definition screen for the global reference.

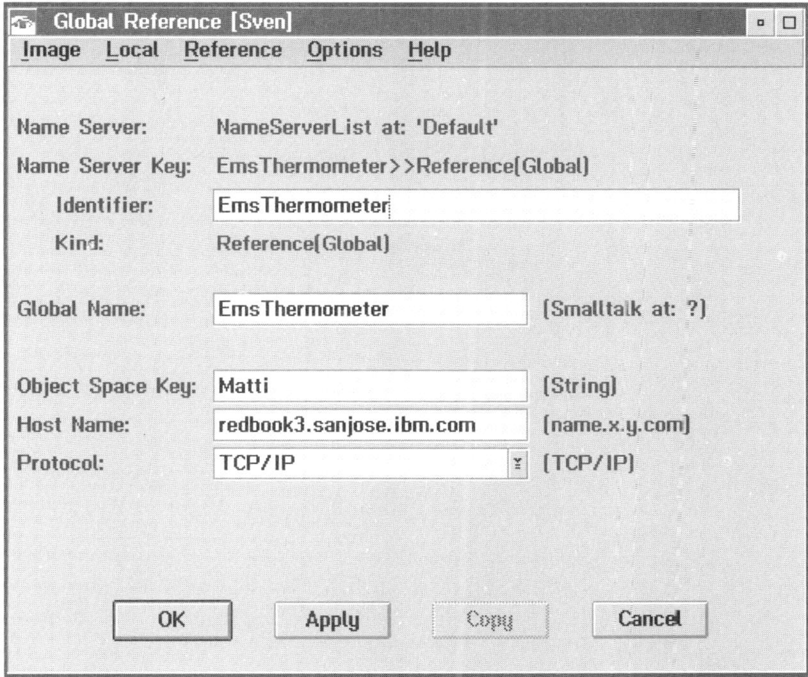

Figure 29. *Global Reference for the Thermometer Model Class*

6. Switch back to the Composition Editor for your view class and add a *Name Server Distributed Part* from the TCP/IP parts category to the free-form surface.* Change the name of that part from *Object1* (default) to *aThermometer*.
7. Change the settings of that part so that the *Id* is *EmsThermometer* (the object reference identifier) and the *Type* is *Reference(Global)*.
8. From the pop-up menu of that part, select **Change type...** to specify *EmsThermometer* as the type (class name).

* That new distributed part is added to the parts palette when the Distributed feature is loaded into a VisualAge image.

9. Drag the two attribute-to-attribute connections from the old thermometer part to the new distributed part. Now, delete the old thermometer part.

10. Because a distributed part is just a reference, you must first get a shadow object for the remote class from the reference. You can then use the shadow object to create the actual remote thermometer instance.

    Creating the shadow is an easy task; you simply define an event-to-action connection between the *aboutToOpenWidget* event of your window and the *getShadow* action of the distributed part.

11. Now that you have a shadow of the remote class, you can use it to create a thermometer instance in the remote object space. Add the following instance method to your view class:

```
createRemoteThermometer
  "Use the shadow currently contained in our thermometer subpart
   to create a new remote thermometer.
   Assign that new instance to the distributed part."
  (self subpartNamed: 'aThermometer') value:
    (self subpartNamed: 'aThermometer') value new
```

    At first glance, the code in this method may appear strange. The subpart value initially holds a shadow object for the remote *EmsThermometer* class, so you can use the *new* class method to create a new instance. Since you do not need the shadow object any further, you can then use the subpart to also store the new instance.

12. The last step is to run the above method after the shadow object has been created. Define an event-to-script connection between the *aboutToOpenWidget* event of your window and the *createRemoteThermometer* method.

    Make sure that the order of the connections is correct. When the window is about to open, the shadow object must be created, and then your new instance method must be executed.

    Figure 30 on page 65 shows the Composition Editor after all these connections have been defined.

13. When you test the changes, the only differences you might notice are short delays during startup time (when the system has to connect to the remote object space) and between the change of one slider and the adjustment of the other one.

14. When everything works well, assign a version to your view class, release it, and create version 2 of the application.

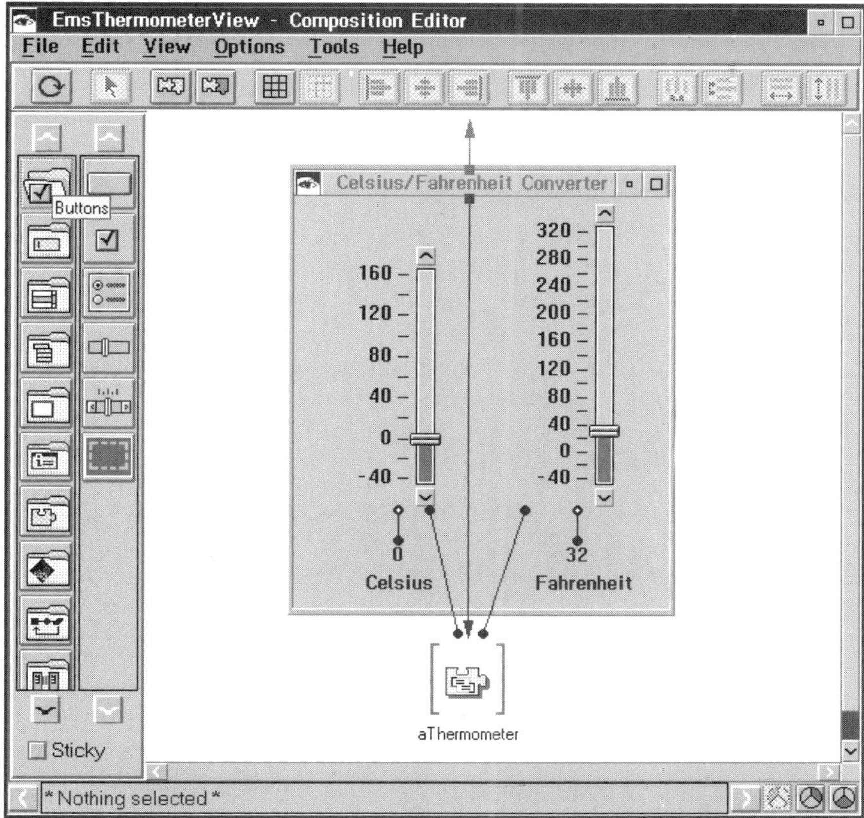

Figure 30. *Thermometer View with Distributed Part, Composition Editor*

Notes:

❑ Instead of following Steps 6 through 12 above, you also could use a standard VisualAge *variable part* of type *EmsThermometer.* In this case, you would have to explicitly use the global object reference and create the shadow object in the *createRemoteThermometer* method as follows:

```
createRemoteThermometer
  "Use the object reference to create a new remote thermometer.
   Assign that new instance to the variable part."
  | oRef |
  oRef := NameServerList default
            referenceAtFirstIdentifier: 'EmsThermometer'.
  (self subpartNamed: 'aThermometer') value:
    oRef shadow new
```

❑ Another way to create the remote instance is to define an object space location reference (see Object References on page 17) and tell your *EmsThermometer* class to create a new instance in that object space.

Using this approach, you must define references only for the remote object spaces you want to use. On the other hand, the class must exist in your local object space too. This does not seem to be a major restriction since you need the class information in the VisualAge Composition Editor anyway to be able to define the connections visually.

These are the steps to follow when using a remote object space location reference:

1. As described in the note , do not follow Steps 6 through 12. Add a standard VisualAge *variable* part of type *EmsThermometer* to the free-form surface of your view class.

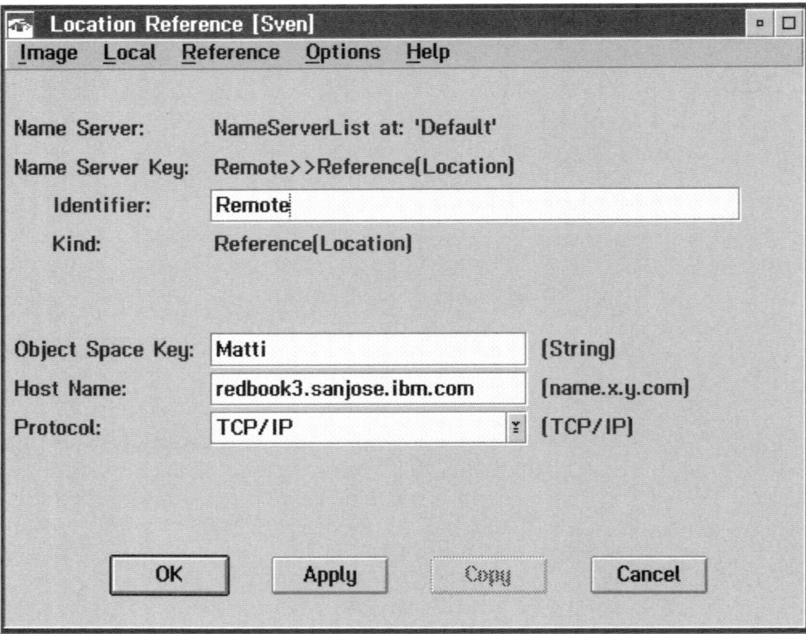

Figure 31. *Location Reference for a Remote Object Space*

2. From the Transcript window, select **Distribution tools**, **Open Object Exchange**, **Reference**, **Add**, **Add New...**. From the object kind list, pick **Reference to an Object Space Location** to define a reference to a remote object space. Use the Identifier *Remote* and provide both the key of the remote object space and the corresponding host name.

Figure 31 on page 66 shows the definition screen for the location reference.

3. Add a new instance method to the view class:

```
createRemoteThermometerByObjSpace
  "Use the class in the remote object space to create a new
   thermometer. Assign it to the variable part."
  | os |
  os := (NameServerList default
          referenceAtFirstIdentifier: 'Remote')
        objectSpace.
  (self subpartNamed: 'aThermometer') value:
    (EmsThermometer dsInSpace: os) new
```

4. In the Composition Editor, you need only one event-to-script connection from the *aboutToOpenWidget* event to the *createRemoteThermometerByObjSpace* methods.

- You could also use a distributed part of type *Reference(Location)* to access the remote object space.

Accessing the Same Model Object from Two Clients

To prove that the thermometer object is used remotely, let us try to access the same object from another object space using the thermometer view.

The thermometer class must be changed so that it creates a new instance only once and returns that instance on subsequent creation requests.

1. Create new editions of your application and of the *EmsThermometer* class.
2. In the Script Editor for your *EmsThermometer* class, add a *Thermometer* class variable by changing the class definition:

```
AbtPart subclass: #EmsThermometer
  instanceVariableNames: 'celsius '
  classVariableNames: 'Thermometer '
  poolDictionaries: ''
```

3. Override the *new* class method as follows:

```
new
  "Create a new instance on first invocation and
   return that instance on subsequent calls."
  Thermometer isNil ifTrue: [ Thermometer := super new ].
  ^Thermometer
```

Be sure to define the *new* method as a *class* method and not as an *instance* method.

4. During the class initialization, make sure that *Thermometer* does not contain an instance from a previous usage. Add the following *initialize* class method:

```
initialize
  "Initialize the class variable."
  Thermometer notNil ifTrue: [ Thermometer become: nil ].
  super initialize.
```

5. Assign a version to the thermometer class and release it. Also, create a new version of the application.
6. On the machine belonging to object space `Matti`, load this new application version into the image.
7. Start VisualAge on a third workstation.
8. On the third system, define the same references as defined in Moving the Model Object to a Remote Object Space on page 61.
9. Load the latest version of your *EmsThermometerApp* into the object space and save the image.
10. To test the changes, open the thermometer view on both clients. You should see that changing a value on one client reflects in the view on the other client. Actually, this proves that both clients are using the same object residing in the server's object space (*Matti*).

Attention

Sometimes the application gets out of synchronization if the values on both clients are changed simultaneously. An out-of-synch situation occurs because of racing conditions between the notification and update messages. (Be aware that IBM Smalltalk supports multiple threads.)

Therefore, in a production application where multiple clients are allowed to change a value of the same object, you would have to provide mechanisms to handle these requests one after the other. We discuss these issues in more detail in Concurrency on page 193 .

An out-of-synch situation can also lock the machines under some circumstances. Pressing and holding the **Alt+SysRq** keys helps you resolve most deadlock situations.

Dividing the Application

A well-designed OO application always separates model and view. We will now take advantage of this model separation to distribute the user interface to the clients and the model, which calculates the temperature conversion, to the server.

In the current state, both the server and client sides have loaded the complete thermometer application. Actually, there is no need for the server object space to contain the user interface class. To divide the classes between different object spaces, you must create an additional application as described in the following steps:

1. Create a new edition of your application.
2. From the VisualAge Organizer, create a new *EmsThermometerModelApp* application.
3. Move the *EmsThermometer* class from *EmsThermometerApp* to the new application, *EmsThermometerModelApp*.

   Note: Be sure that **Full Menus** is selected in the **Options** pull-down menu of the VisualAge Organizer, otherwise, you will not find the **Move...** action in the context menu of a part.
4. Assign a version to the thermometer class in the *EmsThermometerModelApp* application and release it.
5. Switch back to the *EmsThermometerApp* application. Since you are using a variable of the thermometer class to define the connections in the Composition Editor, add *EmsThermometerModelApp* to the list of prerequisite applications.

   To see the list of prerequisites for an application, select the application in the VisualAge Organizer and then select **Applications**, **Prerequisites**.
6. Assign a version to both applications.
7. On the client machines, load the most recent versions of both applications.
8. On the server machine, unload *EmsThermometerApp* and load *EmsThermometerModelApp* instead.
9. You should be able to work with the view on the client machines as before. The difference is that you now have only the necessary classes loaded into each object space.

Notes: It might not be obvious why you need the *EmsThermometer* model class in the client object spaces. There are actually two reasons:

- *EmsThermometer* was defined as a type (class name) of the distributed part in your thermometer view.

  When you open the Composition Editor for the view, VisualAge asks the distributed part's class for its public interface. For that reason, the class must be loaded into the local image.

  For run-time packages (or if you do not use the Composition Editor to run the application) that argument no longer holds. In real projects, you usually place classes and methods that are used only at development time (in the Composition Editor) in a special edit application. When creating the run-time package, you would then exclude this edit application.

Following this approach, only the necessary classes and methods will be contained in every system's object space.

For a detailed description of these aspects, see the discussion of organizing your code in the *VisualAge Programmer's Guide to Building Parts for Fun and Profit*.

- If you use the *createRemoteThermometerByObjSpace* method in your thermometer view as described in the note , that method references the *EmsThermometer* class. However, that argument is no longer valid if you use the distributed part as recommended.

Using the Distribution Matrix

To automate the loading and unloading of the right applications into the different object spaces, create a configuration map and use the distribution matrix feature.

1. Before defining the distribution information, add a reference to your local object space. From the Transcript window, use **Distribution tools**, **Open Object Exchange**, **Reference**, **Add**, **Add New...**. From the object kind list, pick **Reference to an Object Space Location** to define a reference to your local object space. Use the Identifier *Local* and provide the key (in our example, this is `Sven`) of the local (client) object space and of the corresponding host name.
2. The distribution information is part of a configuration map, which defines a set of applications that work together. To define the distribution information, you must create a new configuration map that will contain your two applications.
3. Open a TrailBlazer browser by selecting **Browse Configuration Maps** from the **Smalltalk tools** menu in the Transcript window.
4. Select **Create...** from the pop-up menu in the Configuration Maps list. Provide *EmsThermometerMap* as the name for the new configuration map.
5. Select the new edition created by VisualAge for the new configuration map.
6. With the **Applications** property showing in the bottom window of the TrailBlazer browser, select the **Available Applications** button. Select *EmsThermometerApp* and release the last version into your configuration map. Repeat this step for the *EmsThermometerModelApp* application.

The TrailBlazer window now looks like the window in Figure 32 on page 71.

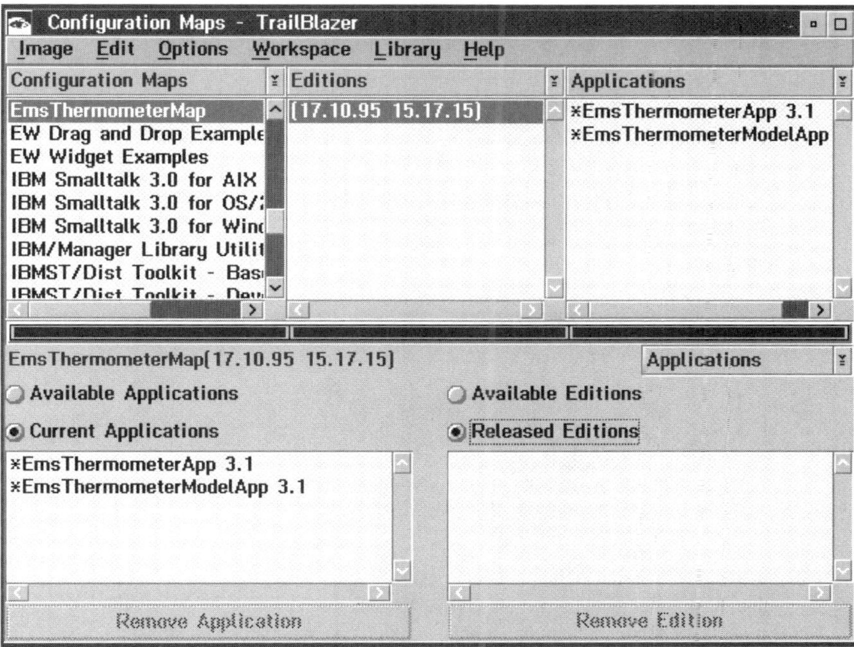

Figure 32. *Configuration Map for the Thermometer Application*

7. Edit the distribution-specific attributes of the configuration map. From the **Editions** list in the TrailBlazer, use the pop-up menu to show the locations by selecting **Show**, **Locations**.
8. Using **Add Location...** from the pop-up menu in the **Locations** list, add *Local* and *Remote*. These are references to object space locations that were previously defined.
9. In the bottom pane of the TrailBlazer, change to the **Distribution Matrix** property. Edit the distribution matrix by using the pop-up menus of the icons that represent how each application is loaded into each object space. Make the selections listed in Table 3, " Distribution Matrix for the Thermometer Configuration Map," on page 71.

Table 3. (Part 1 of 2) Distribution Matrix for the Thermometer Configuration Map

	Local	**Remote**
EmsThermometerApp	Full Load	Do Not Load

Table 3. (Part 2 of 2) Distribution Matrix for the Thermometer Configuration Map

	Local	**Remote**
EmsThermometerModelApp	Full Load	Full Load

Note: For now, do not specify *Shadow Load* for the *EmsThermometerModelApp*; we will explain the difference in Real Distribution: Using a Distribution Matrix for the Run-time Scenario on page 73.

The TrailBlazer window should look like the window in Figure 33 on page 72.

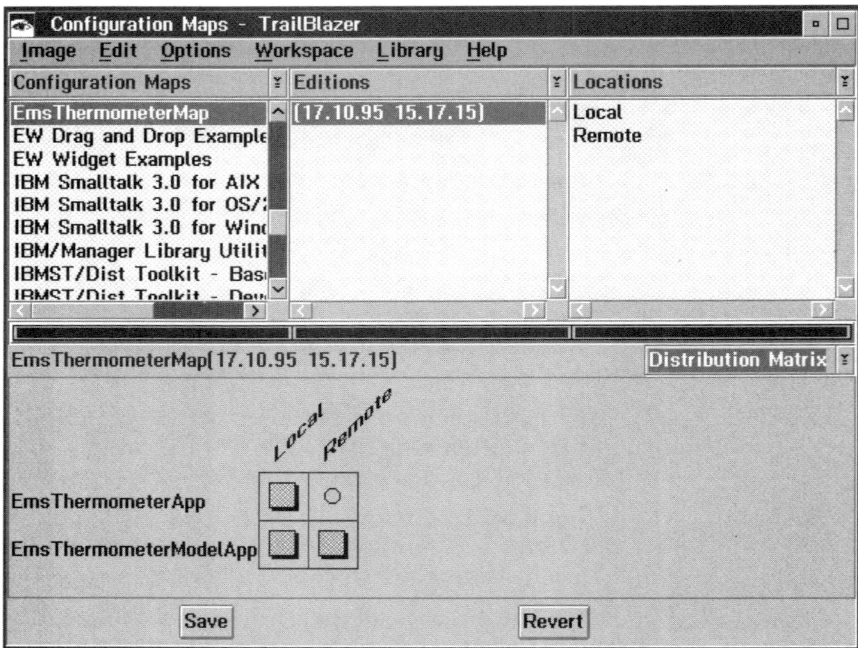

Figure 33. *Distribution Matrix for the Thermometer Application (1)*

10. Select **Save** to save the distribution matrix.
11. Now that the configuration map that includes the distribution matrix is defined, you can initiate loading of the thermometer application into the object spaces specified by the distribution matrix.
12. To use the distribution matrix, select **Distributed Load** from the pop-up menu in the **Editions** list.

As specified by the distribution matrix, the Distributed feature now processes the request as follows:

- Fully loads *EmsThermometerApp* and *EmsThermometerModelApp* into the *Local* object space
- Fully loads *EmsThermometerModelApp* into the *Remote* object space (after starting the object space, if necessary).

13. Since you have automated only Steps 7 and 8 from the section titled Dividing the Application on page 68 , there should be no difference when working with the application.

Real Distribution: Using a Distribution Matrix for the Run-time Scenario

To simulate the run-time scenario for your application, you must change the distribution matrix by specifying **Shadow Load** instead of **Full Load** for the *EmsThermometerModelApp* on the *Local* object space.

For this approach, you cannot use the distributed part and its *getShadow* action any longer to get a shadow object for the thermometer class. Since the shadow load automatically creates shadows of all classes contained in the corresponding application within the local object space, you do not have to create remote objects through special methods. Instead, you can create and use an instance of the *EmsThermometer* class as if it existed locally.

1. Before making any changes, assign a version to the old configuration map.
2. Create a new edition of the *EmsThermometerApp* application.
3. In that edition, load the original (stand-alone) version 1 of your *EmsThermometerView* class.
4. Release the *EmsThermometerView* class and create a new version 4 of the *EmsThermometerApp* application.
5. Create a new edition of your configuration map, *EmsThermometerMap*.
6. Release the last version 4 of *EmsThermometerApp* into the configuration map.
7. Change the distribution matrix of your configuration map so that *EmsThermometerModelApp* is now shadow-loaded into the *Local* object space.

   Figure 34 on page 74 shows the TrailBlazer window after the changes.

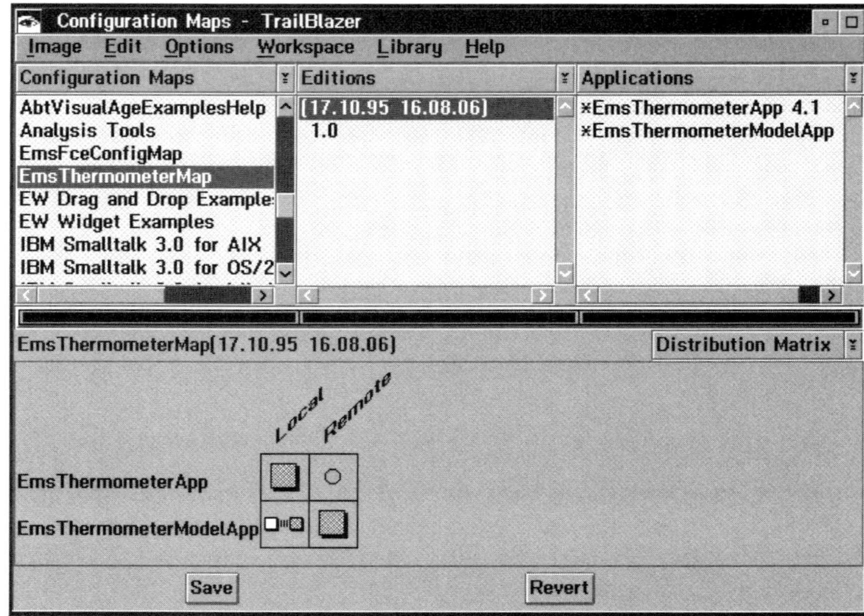

Figure 34. *Distribution Matrix for the Thermometer Application (2)*

When loading the new configuration map, the Distributed feature processes the request as follows:

- Fully loads *EmsThermometerApp* into the *Local* object space
- Fully loads *EmsThermometerModelApp* into the *Remote* object space (after starting the object space, if necessary)
- Loads shadows for the classes of *EmsThermometerModelApp* into the *Local* object space.

Be aware that after you execute the distributed load of the configuration map, you cannot open the Composition Editor for the thermometer view anymore. Opening the Composition Editor for the view will bring up the debugger since VisualAge cannot obtain the necessary information about the *EmsThermometer* part from the shadow class. But, if you either use the **Test** button in the VisualAge Organizer or execute

```
EmsThermometerView newPart openWidget
```

from a Workspace window to open the thermometer view, everything will work fine.

If you want to make changes using the Composition Editor, you must select **Load** instead of **Distributed Load** from the pop-up menu of your configuration map edition. The difference between distributed and local load is that the latter fully loads the shadow applications also. Then, since all necessary classes are locally available again, you can use the Composition Editor. From now on, however, everything will run in the local object space only.

Switching between local and distributed load enables you to use the same configuration map for local development and testing, as well as for run-time testing.

Experiences

Since we wanted to provide Chapter 18, "Lessons Learned, Hints, and Tips," as the focal point for all hints and tips, our experiences during the quick tour are described there. As a convenience for the reader, the following list is a summary of the results:

- Operations can usually be interrupted by pressing **Alt+SysRq**.
- Local load can be used to load all classes into the local object space for development iterations. Use the distributed load again to test distributed processing.
- Use *“allInstances become nil”* to remove instances from your object space before trying to unload the corresponding class.
- The event/notification mechanism provided by VisualAge for connections defined in the Composition Editor results in numerous messages and impacts performance when remote objects are used.

For a detailed description of the items above, see “Experiences During the Quick Tour” .

Part 2

Developing Distributed Object Applications

6 The Foreign Currency Exchange Application

This chapter provides an overview of the Foreign Currency Exchange (FCE) application and the distributed extensions we made to it.

We selected the FCE application because we wanted to:

- Explain how to use distribution within a business application's problem domain
- Explore how to extend an existing application with distribution
- Have a common application across different IBM International Technical Support Organization (ITSO) projects. The FCE application has been used previously in various ITSO publications, such as:

- *Client/Server Computing: The Design and Coding of a Business Application*. This document describes a traditional analysis and design approach.
- *Object-Oriented Application Development with VisualAge in a Client/Server Environment*. This publication introduces the *Visual Modeling Technique* (VMT) methodology.
- *Developing Distributed Object Applications with VisualAge Smalltalk and SOMobjects*. This book exploits the DSOM support of VisualAge while using VMT as the underlying methodology.

This chapter is divided into the following sections:

- "The Original (Nondistributed) FCE Application" summarizes the original (nondistributed) implementation of the FCE application which was the basis for our residency project.
- "Scenarios for a Distributed FCE Application" describes how the different application types suitable for the Distributed feature can be applied to the FCE application.
- "The Residency Project" explains the scope of the residency project.

The Original (Nondistributed) FCE Application

The FCE application provides foreign currency exchange services. The services include the trading of foreign currencies in cash and travelers checks to customers. Trading is based on current exchange rates.

Each bank has a number of branches worldwide. These branches perform foreign currency exchange services. Customers who have an account in a bank branch are considered bank customers. Customers who do not have an account in any bank branch are considered non-bank customers. Both bank customers and non-bank customers can use the exchange services.

The FCE application provides the branch cashiers with country information, for example, country name, currency name, denominations of both cash and travelers checks, and foreign country currency restrictions.

The cashiers get customer information, create an order, and receive an immediate response regarding the requested stock availability in their drawers and in the local branch. Customer orders can be pending, in process, or completed. Orders become pending only if sufficient stock is not available in the cashier's drawer or in the local branch.

The system manages foreign currencies, orders and payments, and stock availability.

Requirements Specifications Summary

This section summarizes the specifications of the FCE application that are related to our scenarios. For the complete requirements specifications, see Requirements Specifications on page 201. It is important to understand the functional requirements for the branch and the central bank and see how they differ from each other.

Branch Functions

The most common function performed at the branch regarding foreign currency is *customer order management*. The most usual operations are:

- Customer purchases from the branch cashier

  This is the most frequently performed function of this subapplication. Some of the usual activities of this function are:

  - Determine currency and or check denominations.
  - Obtain exchange rate.

- Customer sales to the branch cashier

  Tourists and travelers returning with foreign currency or travelers checks sell or cash them in to the bank. Some of the usual activities of this function are:

  - Obtain exchange rates.
  - Handle multiple currencies and checks.

Central Bank Functions

The central bank is responsible for supplying foreign currency and travelers checks to the branches and for selling off excess foreign currency received from the branches. The most common function performed at the central bank regarding foreign currencies is *bank management*. The most common operations are:

- Branch order

  Orders from branches are normally for several currencies and checks. Some of the usual activities of this function are:

  - Check currency and check denominations.
  - Obtain exchange rate.

- Central stock reconciliation

  At the end of each day, or more frequently, the central bank verifies that the travelers checks and foreign currency in its stocks are equal to the totals held in the system. Some of the usual activities of this function are:

  - Obtain the exchange rate for each currency or check.
  - Display each currency or check totals and local currency equivalents.
  - Send excess, if maximum stock quantity is exceeded, to other banks (U.S.A. and abroad) through foreign note dealers.

The Object Model

Figure 35 on page 83 shows the object model of the current FCE application.

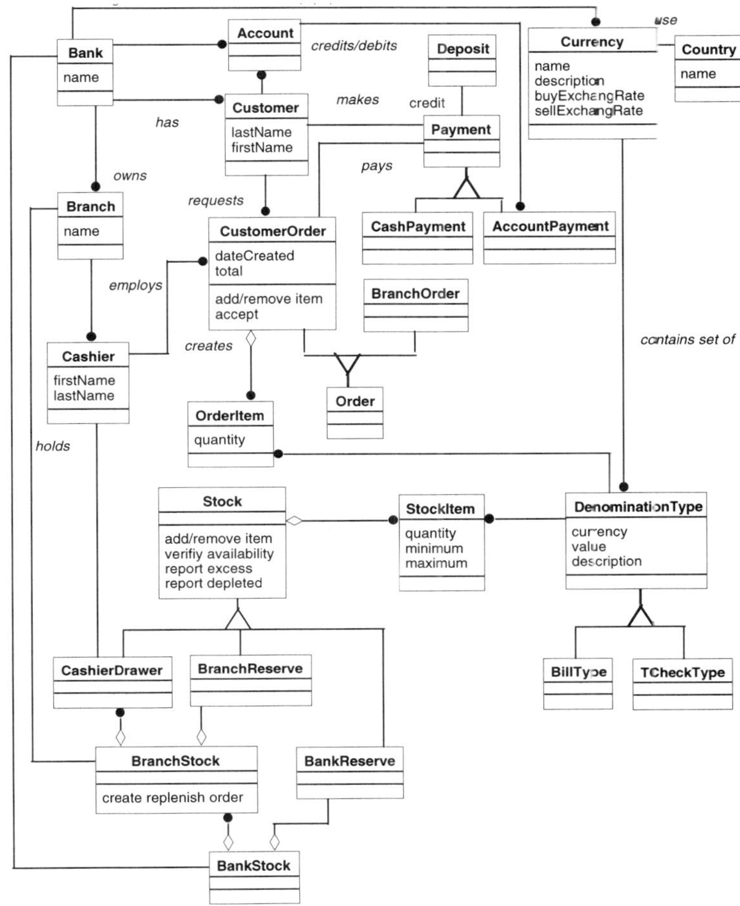

Figure 35. *Object Model of the Original FCE Application*

The following lines can help to read and understand the notation used in the object model:

- 1:n relationship: A bank owns *many* branches.
- 1:1 relationship: A bank has *one* bank stock.
- Inheritance: A cash payment *is a* type of payment.
- Aggregation: Many cashier drawers *are part of* a branch stock.

The Nondistributed Implementation

Figure 36 on page 84 shows the main view of the original FCE application. One push button with the VisualAge logo, enables you to log onto the system. Four other push buttons enable you to work with currencies, cashier stocks, orders, and customers. The application does not include any central bank functions. It covers only branch functions, most of which correspond to cashier operations and a few to branch management operations.

Figure 36. *Main View of the Original FCE Application*

The original FCE application was revised during another residency project. The main view was changed to look like Figure 37 on page 85.

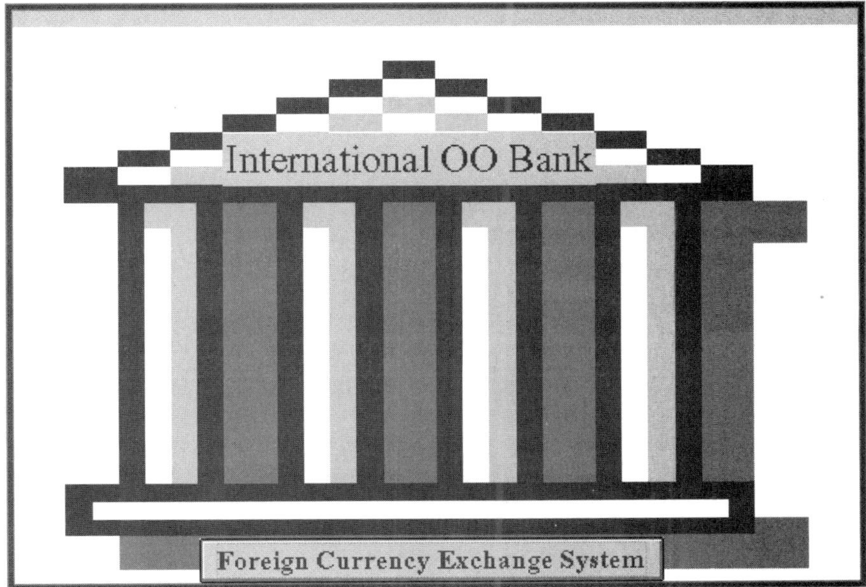

Figure 37. *Main View of the Original FCE Application (Revised)*

Clicking on the large push button labeled **Foreign Currency Exchange System** opens the toolbar shown in Figure 38 on page 85. The toolbar contains the well-known push buttons for currency, stock, order, and customer management. It also has a pop-up menu that lets the user log onto the system.

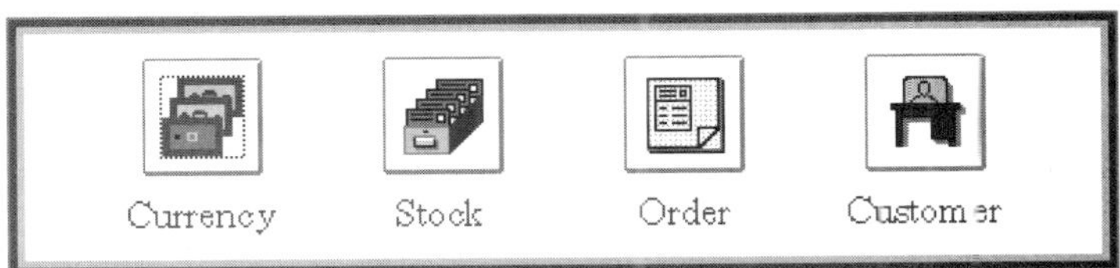

Figure 38. *Toolbar of the Original FCE Application (Revised)*

Scenarios for a Distributed FCE Application

In Chapter 3, "Applications Suitable for the Distributed Feature" we introduced the concepts of *object server*, *active server*, and *peer-to-peer*. In this section we explain how these application types can exist within the FCE application scenarios.

Object Server: Currency Management

In many cases, we develop an application that runs in a client machine and executes queries against a database that resides in another machine. With the existing Distributed Relational Database Architecture (DRDA) databases we can have a centralized database and access its data from clients as if it were local.

For example, if we have a list of all currencies, we have each currency object instantiated as many times as clients have that list at the same time. Also, if the client application does not keep the list in memory, it must execute a query against the remote database as many times as it requires the list.

Is this what we want? Is this the way it should be? When we talk about object-oriented we must not forget about encapsulation. And what is encapsulation all about? *Encapsulation* means that only an object has access to its data. If any other object needs access to that data, it must request the data from the owner object because it cannot read or change the data directly.

But, if we read the same data from different client machines using direct database access, we do not have real encapsulation. Do you think it is more desirable to have just one list of real currency objects, and let this list provide information to the client machines? We do. The advantages are as follows:

- ❑ Database access is required only on the server machine. Client machines do not need to execute queries to remote databases.
- ❑ Only one object, the currency list that resides in the server object space, has direct access to the data.
- ❑ Installing the database client software in each machine is not required.

The disadvantage is that the initialization of the list on the client can take more time compared to direct access. Also, topics such as concurrency and locking must be addressed. Chapter 17, "Optimization and Performance Tuning" contains information on how to overcome these problems.

If the client application keeps the list in memory and allows changes to the list (adds, updates, or deletes) to be made online, it is required to include the notification mechanisms covered in the previous section, Active Server: Exchange Rate Management on page 87.

Active Server: Exchange Rate Management

As mentioned in Appendix A, "Requirements Specifications" the cashiers in each branch obtain the exchange rate for each currency. This information is maintained by the central bank.

The original FCE application assumes that the exchange rates for all currencies are updated overnight and remain fixed during the day. The branch cashiers obtain the exchange rate for each currency to perform foreign exchange transactions. The implementation creates and maintains all objects in a client machine. No consideration was given to distributing objects across the network.

To allow the cashiers to use a fluctuating exchange rate for currency trading, a list of all currencies with their corresponding exchange rates can be located on a server (a computer in the central site). All clients (the personal computers in the branches) must have access to the information provided by that central list.

The list of currencies is an active server in the sense that it informs all the interested clients when a change occurs. The clients can reflect that change on their corresponding views of the user interface.

See The Residency Project on page 88 for more information regarding our implementation and its relationship with the active server.

The event/dependency notification mechanism between clients and server can be implemented in one of two ways:

- ❑ Automatically, through internal messaging between an object and its shadows
- ❑ Manually, by adding dependent objects for a specific event of a changing object.

These are design issues, so we do not discuss them any further in this section.

Peer-to-Peer: Trading Currencies Between Banks

By the term *peer-to-peer application*, we mean direct connections between two client machines.* Within the FCE application, a good example of a peer-to-peer scenario would be the currency trading between two different banks.

---

* See Peer-to-Peer Applications on page 41

As described in Appendix A, “Requirements Specifications”, the central bank must maintain the central stock and trade with many banks around the world.

We can assume there is an external system that offers the foreign currency trading facilities across a large number of banks. Each bank would be required to pay a fee to use this system. The main requirements for this system are:

- ❑ Maintain a list of all or most of the existing currencies and the rates each bank assigns to them. This helps each bank to increase or decrease their own internal exchange rate.
- ❑ Maintain a list of all trading requests that the member banks send to the system. A trading request specifies the available currency, the requested amount, the requested currency, the requested exchange rate, and the bank that originated the request.
- ❑ A bank can start a direct negotiation with another bank. Without intervention of the central system, a connection can be established between a bank and the bank that originally sent a trading request. In this way, the bank can negotiate the rate, bulk transportation, date, time, and additional considerations.

The Residency Project

Due to time constraints, we decided in our residency to concentrate our effort on a single application type. We selected the *active server* scenario since it also has the capabilities of the *object server*. This was accomplished through the implementation of exchange rate management.

Obviously our application is not ready for use in a bank. Our application just consists of a list of currencies that is maintained on the server side and is accessible by all clients through object distribution. Each currency contains a country object. The currency has an ID, description, exchange rate, and can return the corresponding country name by asking its country component.

We used two database tables (`COUNTRY` and `CURRENCY`) with the same definitions as used in the original FCE application. The data definitions can be found in Appendix B, “Database Definition”.

We have done three iterations, trying different approaches, that we hope you find helpful when dealing with the Distributed feature.

7 Planning a Distributed OO Development Project

In general, a distributed OO development project should follow the same guidelines that have been proven efficient for standard (nondistributed) OO development projects. However, adding object distribution to the scope of the application architecture results in some additional tasks that must be included. Minor refinements to already known tasks are also necessary.

In this chapter we focus on the additions and refinements for a development project involving distributed objects:

- "Considerations for Distribution Using the Visual Modeling Technique" summarizes the Visual Modeling Technique (VMT) methodology and focuses on the steps related to object distribution.

- "Project Team Structure: Roles and Responsibilities" summarizes the different roles, including responsibilities for object distribution, within a project team.
- "Iterative Development" shows where to add a *distribution phase* in the well-known iterative development life cycle of an OO project and also explains the *"Develop and test locally, then split and perform distributed testing"* strategy for using the Distributed feature.
- "Incremental Development" gives some ideas on how to extend (or migrate) existing nondistributed VisualAge applications to the Distributed feature environment.

A detailed description of how to plan an OO development project is beyond the scope of this book. For fundamental project planning considerations and a complete elaboration of IBM's Visual Modeling Technique, we strongly recommend reading *Object-Oriented Application Development with VisualAge in a Client/Server Environment.*

Considerations for Distribution Using the Visual Modeling Technique

The Visual Modeling Technique (VMT) [Tkach96] is a methodology designed for OO visual programming environments. The methodology combines several techniques derived from existing modeling methodologies, and it is geared toward the use of a visual programming tool, such as VisualAge.

The backbone of the VMT methodology is the *Object Modeling Technique* (OMT), developed by J. Rumbaugh et al. [Rumba91]. To capture user interactions, main aspects from the use cases requirement modeling technique (*Object-Oriented Software Engineering*, OOSE) developed by I. Jacobsen [Jacob92] were added. Finally, to establish the responsibilities and distribution of responsibilities among the classes, Rebecca Wirfs-Brock's *Responsibility-Driven Design* (RDD) approach using Class-Responsibility-Collaboration (CRC) cards was applied [Wirfs90].

Table 4 summarizes the analysis and design steps defined by VMT. The notes refer to additional design considerations for object distribution.

Table 4. (Part 1 of 2) Visual Modeling Technique, Summary

VMT Steps	Notes
I. Object-Oriented Analysis	1
1. Specify requirements.	2

Table 4. (Part 2 of 2) Visual Modeling Technique, Summary

VMT Steps	Notes
2. Develop use cases.	3
3. Develop user interface sketches and an analysis prototype with VisualAge.	4
4. Develop the object model (first version): - Find objects (candidates). - Identify associations. - Prepare class dictionary.	
5. Conduct CRC exercise.	
6. Develop the dynamic model.	
7. Validate the model and iterate.	
II. Object-Oriented Design	
1. Design the system: - Define subsystems. - Choose client/server platform.	5
2. Design the objects and prototype using VisualAge: - Map object classes to VisualAge classes. - Design nonvisual classes. - Design visual classes. - Iterate the design prototype.	6
3. Design the persistent objects: - Define the units of work. - Map the objects to a database system.	7
4. Design the object distribution.	8
5. Iterate...	9

Notes:

1. In theory, Object-Oriented Analysis (OOA) that focuses on the problem domain should be conducted independently of the distributed object technology applied in system design. However, it is not unusual when some requirement specification or problem statement provides useful information about the target distributed environment during the OOA phase. Although we should defer any design decisions on object distribution to the design phase, having object distribution in mind provides useful insight during the early phase of software development.

2. This step usually contains both business specifications and system design specifications. Often, customers have system-specific requirements at a very early phase.

   System design specifications can contain requirements for distributing objects. Constraints such as line speed, message volume, and data flow may affect application design.

A detailed description of both the functional and physical (geographical) hierarchies at the customer site must be provided. For deciding how to distribute objects in the design phase, knowledge of where their object spaces will be located is required.

3. Since we are dealing with distribution, it is important to specify on which workstations the use cases will run (for example, the use cases for a bank cashier will never be run on the branch manager's machine).

   This should be specified now even if it does not seem important for pure problem analysis. It will be used during the design phase when dealing with distribution.

4. Usually, the prototype GUI should not be influenced by distribution matters, at least during initial iterations. However, if for some reason distribution aspects must be included, the scope of the application GUI must be limited to the use cases that will run in a specific location.*

5. System design should include the decision of whether to use the Distributed feature. Is the analyzed application suitable for distribution? (See Chapter 3, "Applications Suitable for the Distributed Feature," on page 37.)

   When the answer is yes, decide whether to use the Distributed feature or a different solution (for example, DSOM; see SOM and DSOM and the Distributed Feature on page 30). The following assumes that the Distributed feature was chosen.

   During system design using VMT, we begin with decomposing the analysis object model into subsystems and define VisualAge applications according to the resulting subsystems. This is an initial design strategy for application architecture structure and development work assignment. During the design process, including the design for the distribution of objects, further refinement and changes to the initial subsystem definition and mapping will be necessary.

   The distribution of objects is usually designed at a later stage (see 8). We recommend making the initial mapping based on a first guess, keeping in mind that it will be refined later.

6. Use variables within the Composition Editor instead of parts for classes that might be remote. Provide scripts or connections to fill the variables with the actual instance during run-time.

   If possible, choose *location-independent data types* for attributes that will be accessed over the network. The same holds for return values.

   Introduce additional (technical) *light objects* when appropriate.

* By the term *location*, we mean a certain type of workstation, such as all bank cashier machines.

A more detailed explanation of these and other items dealing with optimization is contained in Chapter 17, "Optimization and Performance Tuning".

7. Compared with traditional design for nondistributed solutions, the design trade-offs of the following two cases must be considered when you design a distributed solution:

   a. Objects in server object spaces with local access to the database:

      The corresponding persistence manager class should reside in the same object space.

   b. Objects in server object spaces without local access to the database:

      You can choose from three different approaches:

      1). Place the corresponding persistence manager class into the object space that has local access to the database. Use a shadow of the persistence manager to access its services. Using this approach, object and data access are combined within the same object space, but the complete object is transferred between the object spaces over the network.

      Since the persistence manager uses instance methods to populate the object's data, the object class must reside in that object space too.

      2). Place the corresponding persistence manager class into the same server object space and use remote database access. Using this approach, the object class and its persistence manager class will reside within the same object space, but the SQL query and results will be transferred over the network.

      3). Move the object class and persistence manager into the object space that has local access to the database to minimize SQL traffic. Use a shadow to access the object. Using this approach, the object class and its persistence manager class will reside within the same object space with local SQL traffic, but every message to the object instances (and its return value) will be transferred over the network.

8. During the design of object distribution, several sources help to decide how to divide the classes between different object spaces; for example:

   Requirements specification. The customer might have specified requirements that are related to object distribution. (See note on page 21.)

   Use cases. Which use cases will run in which workstation types? (See note on page 87.)

Object model. Clusters of objects, that is, closely related objects with a high degree of interaction, should remain in the same object space to minimize the message traffic between object spaces. Are there typical *server* objects, that is, common objects that are used by many different client workstations at the same time?

Dynamic model. Are there interactions between similar kinds of objects within different machines (peer-to-peer requirements)?

System design. Are there subsystems to be mapped only into certain object spaces? On which platform does the server system run? Are there LANs that run their own server? Objects can be distributed to platforms currently supported by VisualAge.

Persistent objects design. See note on page 92.

Having designed the distribution of objects, we must refine the mapping of analysis subsystems to VisualAge applications. This refinement process is described in detail in System Design Considerations on page 100.

9. Multitasking features are already included in the standard IBM Smalltalk and VisualAge products. Consider adding the enhanced multitasking facilities provided by the Distributed feature. For example, you are now able to use not only multiple threads but multiple processors as well (see Third Rule: Do Not Wait Unless You Have To on page 181).

   Concepts to handle concurrency must be provided. If you allow multiple clients to update the same server object by means of a local shadow, deadlock situations can occur. An example of such a situation is discussed in Chapter 5, "A Quick Tour Through Distributed Object Land" . To avoid these deadlocks, use IBM Smalltalk mechanisms like *semaphores* or *critical blocks*.

Project Team Structure: Roles and Responsibilities

The project team structure required to develop a distributed application is not much different from the one required to develop a nondistributed application. Each application should be developed by one or two developers. There must be a library supervisor to manage the assignment of versions configuration of the applications. The library supervisor has new roles such as manipulating the distribution matrix and maintaining the configuration map.

The tester must coordinate with the library supervisor for the distribution of the application. A tester must keep the distribution of objects in mind when preparing test cases. For more information on testing, refer to Testing Distributed Applications on page 167.

In addition, there is a new role: the name server administrator. This administrator is responsible for the maintenance of the servers list (refer to Name Servers on page 19 for more information on name servers) and the installation and provision of technical support for TCP/IP (see TCP/IP Configuration on page 46).

Iterative Development

Most existing systems were not analyzed, designed, and implemented correctly in a single development cycle. The currently accepted OO development strategy is both iterative and incremental. Under an iterative development process, a system is usually developed through changes incorporated in new versions. Every version of the system is the result of a complete development cycle and usually includes a considerable number of changes. VisualAge, Professional, is probably the best tool on the market to manage changes between the different versions in a Smalltalk development environment.

Within the production stage of every iteration, there is a testing process, in addition to the analysis, design, and coding activities. The strategy for application development with the Distributed feature is *"Develop and test locally, then split and perform distributed testing"*. Therefore, the testing process must be divided into local testing and distributed testing. Figure 39 on page 96 shows how the testing process may be split into two phases separated by the activity of distributing (or splitting) the application. However, you may want to skip distributed testing in the first few iterations when you initially concentrate on the development of the system as a local application.

For more on testing, refer to Chapter 15, "Testing Distributed Applications".

Incremental Development

It is common to build applications incrementally, satisfying some requirements in a later stage. There are many reasons to do incremental development, including:

- Initial requirements can change during the development process
- Some subsystems can require the existence of others which are not yet implemented
- Resources can be insufficient to accomplish all requirements at once.

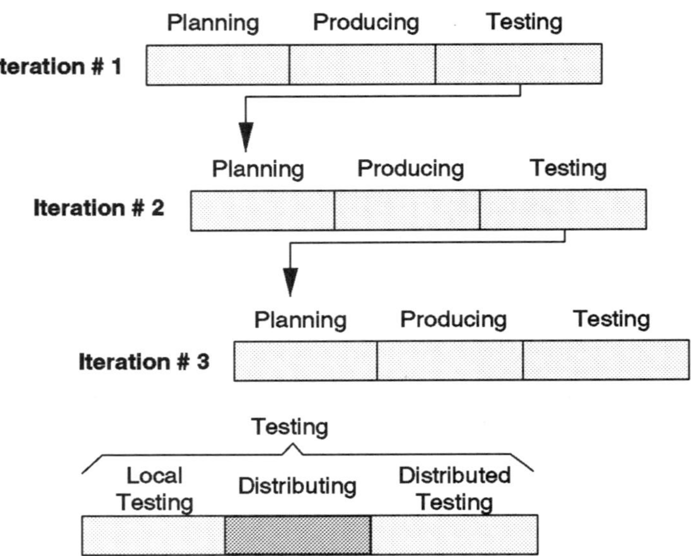

Figure 39. *Iterative Development with Distribution*

What happens now if we have an existing nondistributed application and want to add new functions to it that use distributed features? If previous classes are affected by the changes (for example, some of them are moved to a different object space), we can expect a major redesign of the original application. On the other hand, if the new functions involve only new classes to be distributed, the necessary changes to the old application should be very moderate. Figures 40 and 41 illustrate this idea.

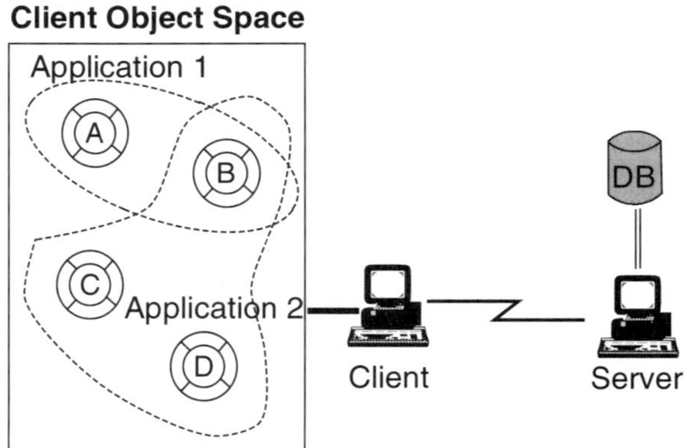

Figure 40. *Incremental Development (Nondistributed)*

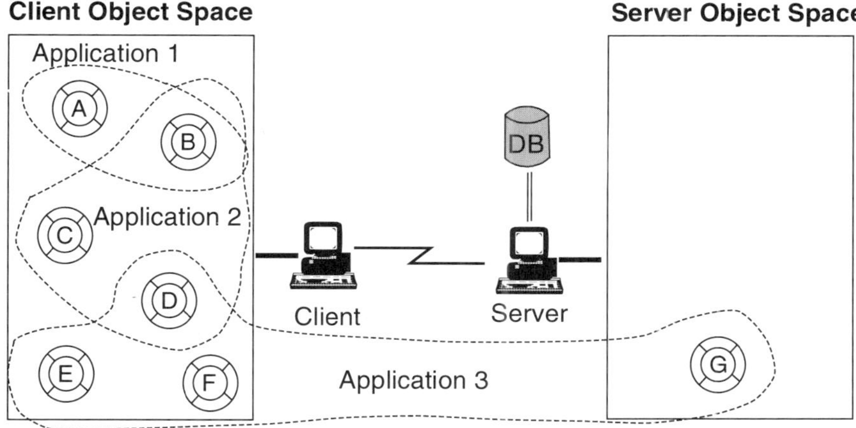

Figure 41. *Incremental Development (Distributed)*

8

Designing Distributed Object Applications

This chapter describes some design issues of distributed object applications that use the VisualAge Distributed feature.

This chapter consists of the following sections:

- "System Design Considerations" discusses some system design-related issues of distributed VisualAge applications.
- "Object Design Considerations" contains object design-related considerations when distributing applications using the Distributed feature.
- "Distribution Techniques" describes the alternative distribution techniques to use.

If you are developing a new application, you start by identifying the business needs that your application must satisfy, and then you design the application to best meet those needs. During the design and development phase, you can concentrate on your business requirements without being concerned about distribution design.* In fact, you can build the complete, working application on a single computer and within a single Smalltalk image.

After the application is completed, tested, and functional, you can use the event profiler to identify the best places to divide the application between object spaces. Using the Distributed feature toolkit, you can then distribute the application modules among computers on the network and start testing and tuning the distributed version.

The design activities of an OO application can be categorized into two tasks groups: *system design* and *object design*.

System Design Considerations

The outcome of the system design task group is a high-level *system architecture* and *application architecture* for the proposed solution. The system and application architectures include a definition of the major building blocks of the system, called subsystems, the allocation of these subsystems to processes and platforms, and their high-level connectivity.

During system design we must make initial decisions about the placement of objects and the distribution of processes. Several sources help us to decide how to divide classes between different object spaces (see Considerations for Distribution Using the Visual Modeling Technique on page 90, and note on page 100). We must look closer at the system environment in which the application will be running. Consider the following examples:

- Network-related topics:
  - What kind of network is or will be used?
  - What is the estimated traffic rate between the clients and servers?
  - Will the bandwidth of the network be able to handle this traffic load?
- Geographical locations and their roles:
  - How many different kinds of locations will there be for servers and clients?
  - Will there be several layers of servers (department, company, enterprise)?

---

* Nevertheless, thinking about distribution concerns from the very beginning of your application design makes it easier to change things during later iteration steps.

- ❑ Security, reliability, and usability topics:
  - ➢ What are the security and reliability requirements for servers and clients?
  - ➢ Who has the right to use an object and how is the verification accomplished?
  - ➢ Which servers are responsible for maintaining persistent data?
  - ➢ How is recovery done after a system crash?

Here we must also decide which client/server enabling technology to use and for what purpose. For example, we can use the Distributed feature to distribute only some objects. Other objects will be local to the client object space or might use some other distribution technique like DSOM.

During system design using VMT, we begin with decomposing the analysis object model into subsystems, and map the resulting subsystems to separate VisualAge applications. This is a design strategy for the initial application architecture structure and for development work assignment among the developers. For example, if a requirements analysis shows three subsystems, the result of the mapping process is a simple structure as shown in Figure 42 on page 101. This division of the business application into a number of VisualAge applications will allow a team of developers to proceed with development work concurrently. Each can take on one or more VisualAge applications.

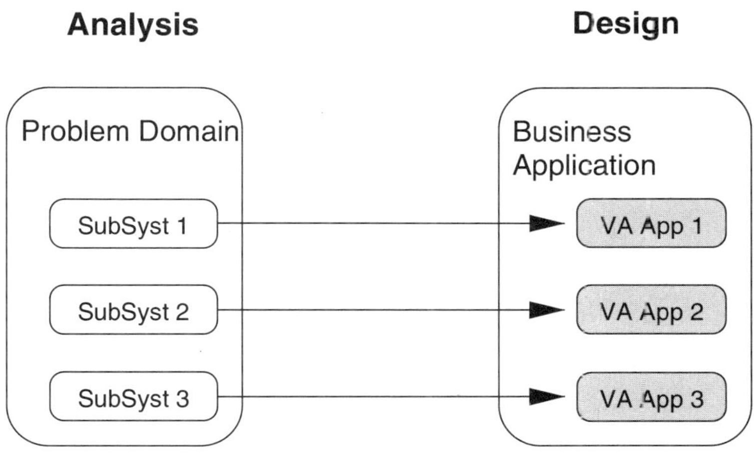

Figure 42. *Defining VisualAge Applications (Nondistributed)*

In partitioning the object model into subsystems, we will initially find some candidates for object space boundaries. But, we must keep in mind that we should minimize object references that are made across object space boundaries. We should only divide those subsystems into different object spaces that are loosely coupled and will not interact with each other very often.

Unfortunately, design becomes more complicated with object distribution. If we use the distribution matrix to handle the creation of shadows, applications are the smallest unit within the Distributed feature to separate classes between object spaces. Therefore, distribution design affects the necessary VisualAge applications.

Tip: It is better to err on the side of too many applications than too few. This will allow you to redistribute your classes more freely between object spaces.

Physical and logical object spaces add one dimension to the matrix that shows the project's classes and the containing applications. The Distributed feature distribution matrix defines which application is to be loaded into which object space. This means that every subsystem is actually further divided into multiple applications, each destined to be loaded into a dedicated object space. Figure 43 on page 102 shows the resulting applications for the same problem domain as shown in Figure 42 on page 101, but with three different configurations of object spaces.

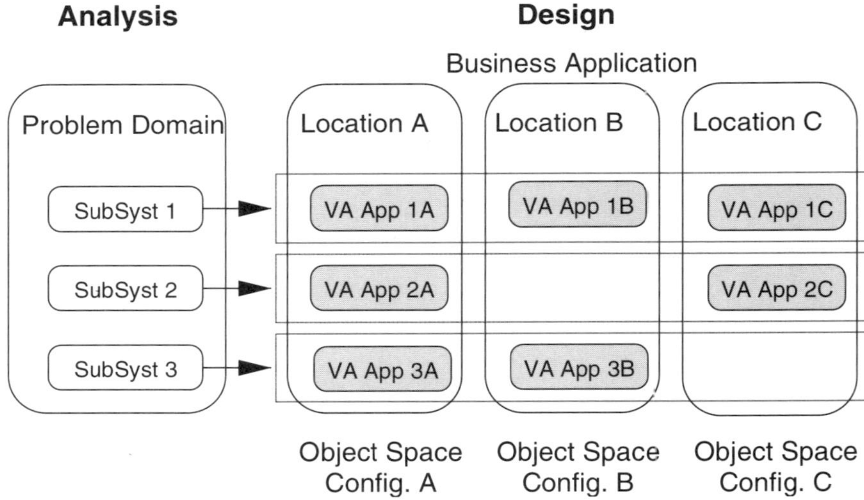

Figure 43. *Defining VisualAge Applications (Distributed)*

Object Design Considerations

In the initial iteration, we might not concentrate on distribution design concerns. But during later iterations we must pay closer attention to the optimizing rules for distributed VisualAge applications.

The final application usually consists of a larger set of classes than just those classes found during the analysis phase. The extra classes are needed in the solution to provide the concrete functionality of the application. These classes can be divided into two categories: service classes and interface classes.

Service classes are used to provide database access and system services. For distributed applications, additional service classes can be used as optimized interfaces to remote objects. We may have an optimized client object space service class for each remote server object space class. If we do not want to use service classes, we must improve performance of the application by providing optimized public interfaces for those classes that will be distributed. This means that, whenever possible, we must combine multiple messages into one message to reduce the number of messages that will go through the network. Interface classes are used to bind the user interface to the business model and the business model to the service classes. The same considerations hold for these classes when designing for distribution. If instances of server object space classes are used simultaneously from multiple clients, we must provide a mechanism that can handle concurrent invocations of setter methods of these instances. We must make sure that a single update process of some attribute is not interrupted by another update process. In the IBM Smalltalk environment, you can use semaphores to accomplish this task (see Concurrency on page 193).

There are some issues that we must consider when we are designing the user interface classes for a distributed application using the Distributed feature. It is a good idea to use variables instead of parts in the user interface classes (views) for those classes that will be in a remote object space. If we use parts, we actually create instances of a class in our working image. Consequently, if there are instances of a class in the image, we cannot simply unload that class to move it to a different object space.

Distribution Techniques

You must consider which method of distribution you will use during your design. Your choice may include one or both of the two techniques to make references to remote objects:

- **Manual**, which is reference-based distribution
- **Automated**, which is matrix-based distribution.

The choice of distribution technique affects the actual implementation of classes. Each approach has its advantages. To use reference-based distribution, you must write some Smalltalk code to (1) get the object reference from the *NameServerList* global dictionary, and (2) send the *shadow* message to the object reference to get a shadow of the remote class.

To use matrix-based distribution, you must get a shadow of an instance transparently whenever you need a new instance of the remote class. Using distribution matrix, you must put server object space classes in a different application than client object space classes.

Generally speaking, reference-based distribution is simpler and more straightforward than matrix-based distribution. The chief advantage of matrix-based distribution, however, is that it does not require explicit distribution awareness in your Smalltalk code. Here are some items for consider when choosing a distribution technique:

Use reference-based distribution:

- When you are building a completely new application and have a fairly good idea of what your distribution design will be
- When you want to explicitly control the creation and manipulation of object references and shadows
- When you have instances of the same classes both on the server object space and the client object space.

Use matrix-based distribution

- When you have clear separation between server object space classes and client object space classes
- When you do not know in advance in which object space your classes will reside
- When you are not interested in controlling the creation of object references and shadows
- If you have an existing application and you want to distribute it without making any changes.

Part 3

The Distributed Foreign Currency Exchange Application

9

An Approach to VisualAge Application Architecture

This chapter describes the underlying VisualAge application architecture we developed during our residency project. The purpose of that architecture was to get a solid base on which we were able to implement our distributed application.

- "Introduction" contains our motives for implementing a base architecture first.
- "Implementation of Layering Within the Residency Project" explains in short terms how we categorized and layered the objects of our application.

- ❑ "Implementation of Instance Uniqueness Within the Residency Project" describes how to overcome the problem of having multiple versions of the same instance.
- ❑ "Questions to Be Addressed" lists some of the key points not yet addressed.

Introduction

When we started to develop any production application with VisualAge, sooner or later we noticed two major tasks:

1. VisualAge is based on the *Construction from Parts* paradigm, meaning that software is developed by assembling and connecting reusable components, called *parts*. Reusability is one of the strengths of OO application development. Reusability can best be achieved by using *layering*, which separates presentation, business logic, and data-access related components.

   Unfortunately, we do not get these advantages for free. Layering has to be planned and implemented.
2. Using multitasking operating systems like OS/2 offers you the ability to develop applications with multiple views on the same object opened at the same time. Changes to the object's data from one view can immediately be reflected within other views. We can achieve this by using the same object instance in every view that presents data of that object. This requires a conceptual approach that we call *uniqueness of instances* (UNI). The built-in VisualAge dependency/notification mechanism takes care of synchronizing the values.

   But again, we do not get this for free; it must be planned and implemented.

Layering and UNI are already important for conventional VisualAge applications, and they are an absolute must for distributed VisualAge applications. Let us look at an example to understand the reason.

In our Foreign Currency Exchange (FCE) application, we want to move the currency's exchange rate to a server object space so that we can use the current value in all client views at any time (see Active Server on page 40). When two clients want to connect to the object that holds the exchange rate for a given currency, our underlying application architecture must ensure that they are really accessing the *same* (that is the identical) object.

Applying both the layering and UNI concepts, we designed and implemented a solution suitable for the primary objective of our project, which was to investigate the Distributed feature.

Our solution is far from being a complete framework for the development of production applications. But, we believe it provides a good basis, so we included the main ideas here as a kind of added value.

Implementation of Layering Within the Residency Project

We categorize objects based on their particular responsibilities. Objects that present data to users and receive data from users we can call *user interface* objects (like views or forms). Objects that represent business entities we call *business domain* objects. Objects that operate behind the scenes, for example to access databases, we call *infrastructure* objects.

We built our application by layering components from these three categories. For example, when we look at currency management in the FCE application, we find these three major objects:

1. The *EmsCurrencyListView*, a user interface object, which presents a list of all currencies, including their exchange rate to the user.
2. The *EmsCurrencyList*, a business domain object, which contains and manages information for a list of currencies.
3. The *EmsPersistenceManager*, an infrastructure object, which supports the business function of *EmsCurrencyList* by retrieving currency information from the database.

Let us have a closer look at the different classes.*

A User Interface Class: EmsCurrencyListView

The *EmsCurrencyListView* presents data from the business domain object *EmsCurrencyList* described below. The interlayer interface protocol between the user interface and business domain layer was constructed visually. We used an event-to-script connection to instantiate the *EmsCurrencyList* variable each time the view was opened. We connected the *currencies* attribute of that variable to the *items* attribute of the table.

Figure 44 on page 110 shows the VisualAge Composition Editor for the *EmsCurrencyListView*.

* A detailed description of the public interface for the FCE classes and their methods can be found in Appendix C, "Sample Code".

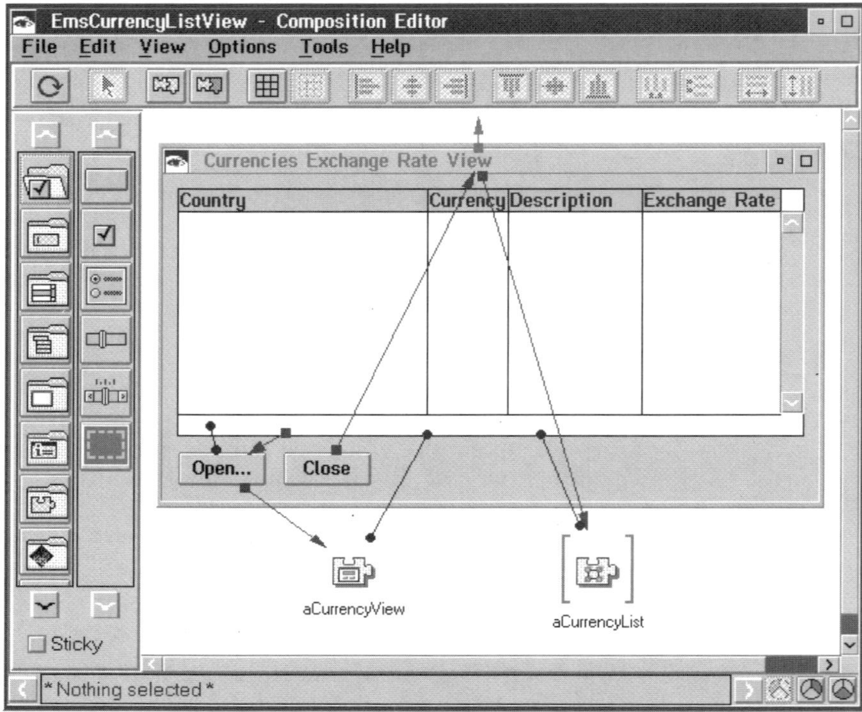

Figure 44. *EmsCurrencyListView, Composition Editor*

A Business Domain Class: EmsCurrencyList

EmsCurrencyList is a collection class containing references to a list of currencies. In the getter method for that list, an instance of the *EmsCurrencyList* class calls a method of its class to retrieve the value if that value is not yet defined.

The class is responsible for routing the request to the corresponding persistence manager, which provides services like *retrieve* and *save*.

Using this approach, the business domain class defines the interlayer interface protocol between the business domain and infrastructure objects. This approach hides the internal implementation of the persistency from user interface objects using a specific business domain part.

An Infrastructure Class: EmsPersistenceManager

The *EmsPersistenceManager* holds the database query part that we used to construct the necessary SQL queries visually. For each different query, we added a private method to perform the query and update the corresponding instance depending on the query's result. Each of these methods expected a business domain object instance as a parameter. For example, we defined *allCurrencies:* to retrieve a list of all currencies from the database.

For each basic request (*retrieve*, *create*, *save*, and *delete* an instance of a supported business domain class), we added an action with the same name to the *EmsPersistenceManager*'s public interface. Each action was associated with an instance method that expected an instance of a supported class as a parameter. In the corresponding Smalltalk script, we called the appropriate method based on the instance's class.

For example, the *retrieve:* method associated with the *retrieve* action was implemented as follows:

```
retrieve: anInstance
  "Retrieve the persistent data for anInstance.
   At the moment, only EmsCurrencyList instances are supported."

  (anInstance isKindOf: EmsCurrencyList) ifTrue: [
    ^self allCurrencies: anInstance
  ].
  CwMessagePrompter
   error: 'Retrieving instances of class ', anInstance class name,
          ' not supported yet'.
  ^false
```

Figure 45 on page 112 shows the VisualAge Composition Editor for the *EmsPersistenceManager*.

Implementation of Instance Uniqueness Within the Residency Project

As we pointed out at the beginning of this chapter, we do not want to allow the existence of two different instances representing the same business object at the same time within the same object space. Why do we want to avoid this?

Let us consider the situation when a cashier opens the currency list view to see the actual exchange rate of the German Mark (DM). The view creates an instance for the DM exchange rate within the server object space.

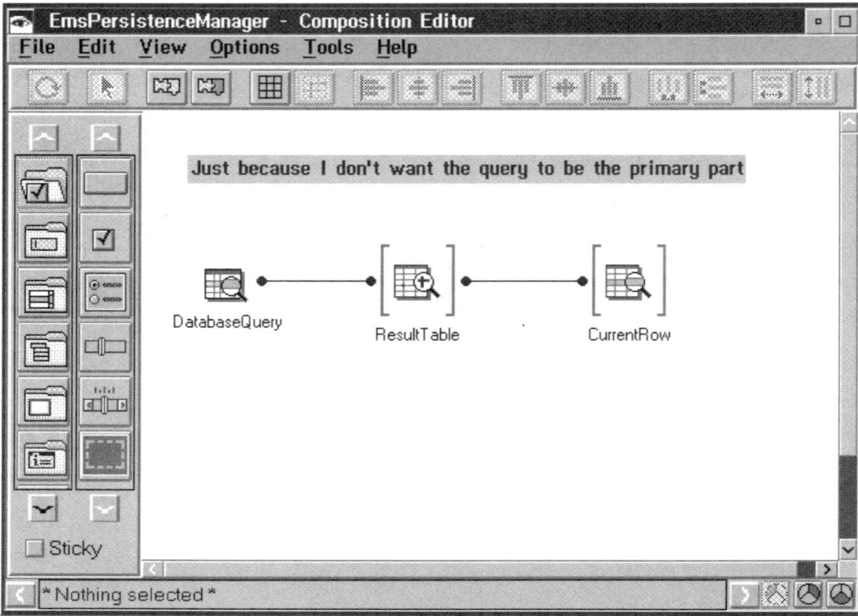

Figure 45. *EmsPersistenceManager, Composition Editor*

Now, a broker in the bank opens the currency list edit view for the same currency. That view also creates an instance in the server's object space for the DM exchange rate. Using the persistence manager, each of these instances retrieves its data from the relational database.

Nothing bad has happened so far (except for one unnecessary database access).

But, if the broker now modifies the exchange rate for DM and saves that update, only the broker's view shows the new value. Figures 46, 47 , and 48 illustrate the different stages of the involved objects.

A New Superclass: EmsUniquePart

The challenge is for all views to show the most current value automatically. A new class named *EmsUniquePart* can be used as a superclass for all of our business domain objects. It inherits from AbtPart and serves to implement our UNI architecture. Every time a new instance is created through an appropriate class method, the class registers that instance. All following requests of the same data held by that instance do not result in the creation of new instances. Instead, the class returns the existing object.

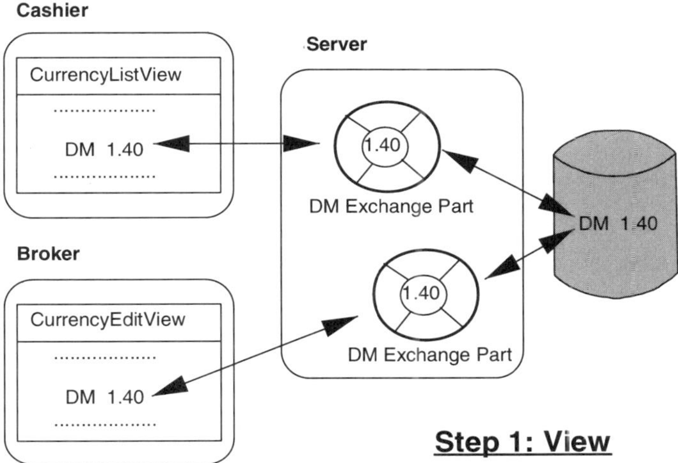

Figure 46. *Instances Without Uniqueness, Step 1 of 3*

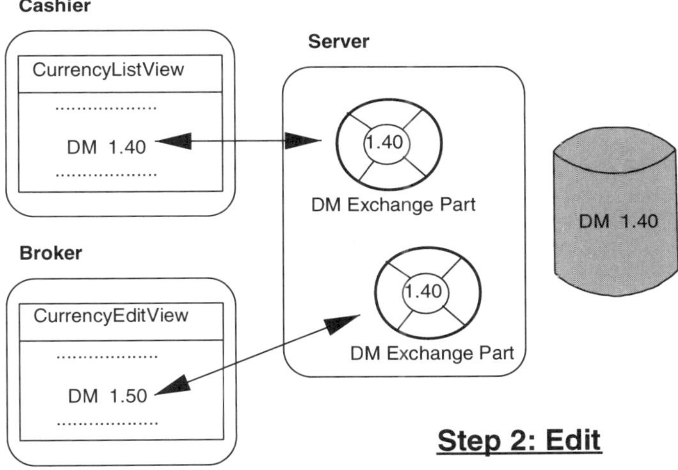

Figure 47. *Instances Without Uniqueness, Step 2 of 3*

But how can we know that two requests refer to the same instance? We have to provide an identifier (ID) for every business domain object. Each requester has to use a new class method `newFor: anId` to get an instance of that class.

The class uses the ID to decide whether to create a particular object or to simply return an existing instance. To maintain all its instances, the class uses a class instance variable of type Dictionary. That dictionary holds an entry for every existing instance with the ID as key and a pointer to the instance as value.

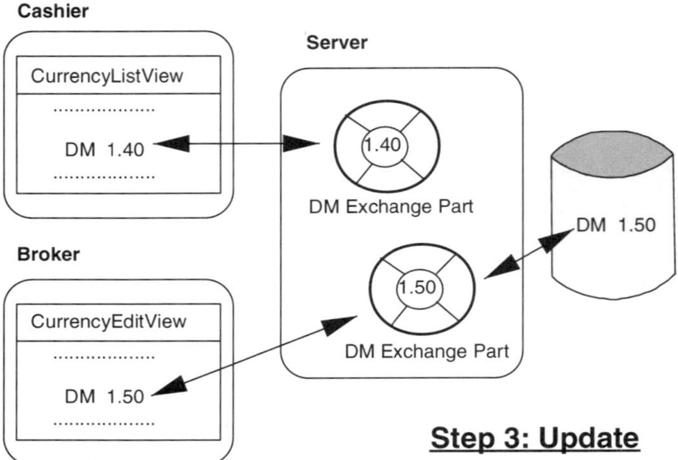

Figure 48. *Instances Without Uniqueness, Step 3 of 3*

In our example above, the first view requesting an instance with the identifier DM creates a new exchange rate object. To answer the request of the second view, also providing DM as ID, the class just returns the same (identical) object. So, both views use the identical source, and updates to one side immediately reflect on the other side. Figures 49, 50 , and 51 show the new data flow.

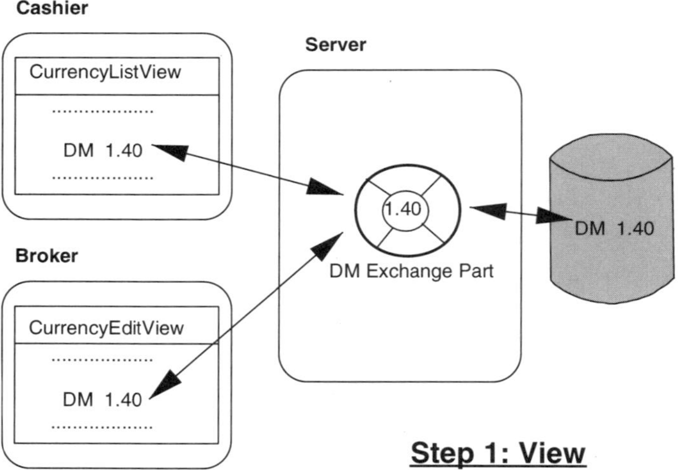

Figure 49. *Uniqueness of Instances (UNI), Step 1 of 3*

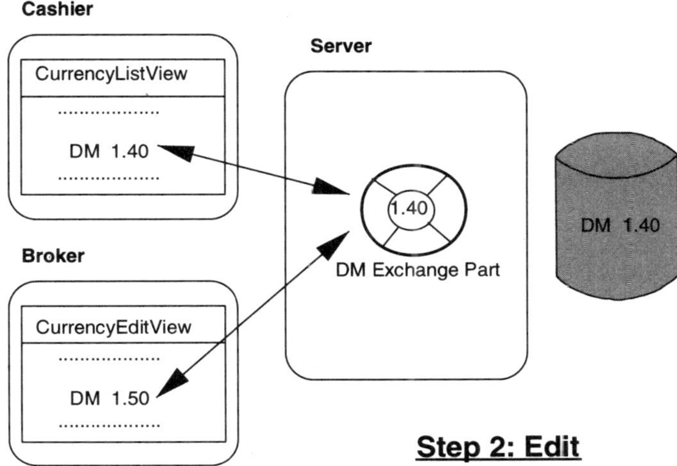

Figure 50. *Uniqueness of Instances (UNI), Step 2 of 3*

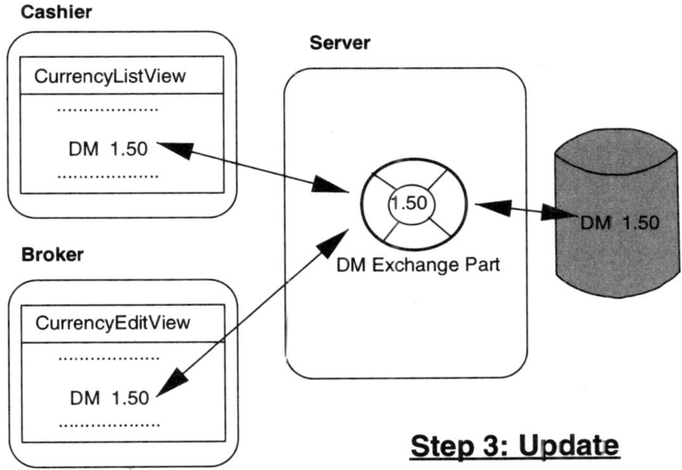

Figure 51. *Uniqueness of Instances (UNI), Step 3 of 3*

Maintaining references to instances within a class keeps Smalltalk from removing these instances from memory through garbage collection. We implemented a release mechanism in the superclass *EmsUniquePart*. This mechanism is used by every requester of a specific instance to release the instance explicitly when it is no longer needed.

This enables the instance to inform its class when there are no requesters left, and the class can also release its pointer to that instance. The memory occupied by that instance will be freed during the next Smalltalk garbage collection. This is very important, especially for the server object space.

Unfortunately, the Composition Editor bypasses this mechanism when we use a business domain part. If any business domain parts are added in the Composition Editor, VisualAge creates an instance for these parts each time the Composition Editor is opened. Closing the Composition Editor of course does not call our `releaseRequester` method. To get rid of these instances, we added an `initialize` class method to EmsUniquePart as follows:

```
initialize
  "Remove all existing instances and initialize class variable."
  Transcript cr;
    show: 'Initializing ', self name.
  self instances do: [ :each |
    Transcript show: '.'.
    each become: nil
  ].
  instances := nil.
  ^super initialize.
```

Then, we defined the following `startUp` method* for our application:

```
startUp
  "Initialize all included model classes."
  Transcript cr;
    show: 'Initializing all visible subclasses of EmsUniquePart'.
  EmsUniquePart allVisibleSubclassesDo: [ :aModelClass |
    aModelClass initialize.
  ].
  Transcript cr; show: 'Done!!'; cr.
  ^super startUp.
```

Sample Code on page 209 contains a detailed description of the interface and methods of the EmsUniquePart class.

Singleton Classes

Using EmsUniquePart as the superclass, it is easy to implement *singleton classes* that have only a single instance at a time. All we must do is override the class `new` method as follows:

```
new
  "Use a fixed identifier to ensure there will be only one instance."

   ^self newFor: #AnyIdentifierIsFine
```

Using the above code and the inherited `newFor:` method, a new instance with the specified ID is created. Each following request that uses the `new` method will get that same instance.

* The `startUp` method of an application class is run every time after an image is loaded.

We used this approach for our *EmsCurrencyList* business domain object since it always holds *all* currencies. Multiple instances of the *EmsCurrencyList* would lead to update synchronization problems.

Questions to Be Addressed

As we mentioned before, our approach to implement layering and UNI is not yet complete. In fact, we expect it to result in a complete project on its own to extend that basis to a framework for a real application. The following list contains some of the points that must be addressed:

- Should we use only one *EmsPersistenceManager* instance for all persistent objects of the same class? Using one *EmsPersistenceManager* instance within each persistent object means a lot of overhead. On the other hand, sharing one *EmsPersistenceManager* instance among several objects could lead to concurrency problems.
- How can we use the Object Factory part provided by VisualAge to create instances dynamically? The prefabricated part uses the `new` method of the referenced class, but we want to force requesters to use the `newFor:` method.
- How can we get rid of instances created by the Composition Editor? It should release the instance at the same time we close the Composition Editor view.
- How do we handle insertions of new objects? How do we handle deletions?

10 Introduction to the Distributed FCE Case Study

Notice

In this part of the document, we discuss the design and implementation steps we took during our case study project. We assume that you are familiar with the basic terms and tools of the Distributed feature and know how to apply them (see Chapter 2, "The VisualAge Distributed Feature", and Chapter 5, "A Quick Tour Through Distributed Object Land").

Our FCE application accesses data from a DB2/2 database. Appendix B, "Database Definition", provides a definition of the required database tables. Appendix C, "Sample Code", contains a complete listing of all classes and methods used throughout the three project iterations. As a convenience to the reader, we repeat parts of the code in the description of the implementation steps to illustrate the main ideas.

The objectives of our residency project were to redesign and implement the distributed FCE application as we extended it with both object server and active server capabilities to manage exchange rates.*

Our redesign was based on the architecture described in An Approach to VisualAge Application Architecture on page 107. To simplify the demonstration of both the object and active server implementation, we implemented only the currency and country classes from the original FCE application.

We used the distribution matrix (see The IBM Smalltalk Distribution Toolkit on page 20) to partition the FCE application into a client part and a server part. Two separate IBM Smalltalk applications were created: one for the classes required only on the client machines, and another for the classes required only on the server. These applications can have subapplications, but remember that applications are the smallest unit of distribution. Figure 43 on page 102 shows an example of such a configuration.

We chose the descriptive names *EmsAFceServerApp* for the server application and *EmsAFceClientApp* for the client application. *EmsAFceClientApp* has *EmsAFceServerApp* as a prerequisite application.

The redesign during our second iteration produced classes that we needed on both the client and server sides. For these classes, we created a third application, *EmsAFceClientServerApp*, and defined it as a prerequisite application for both *EmsAFceClientApp* and *EmsAFceServerApp*.

* The sections titled Object Server: Currency Management on page 86 and Active Server: Exchange Rate Management on page 87 explain this scenario in more detail.

11

The First Iteration

In this chapter we provide an overview of the distributed FCE application and describe the first iteration of the application. We implemented the first iteration using the following approach:

Develop and test locally, then split and perform distributed testing.

This chapter consists of the following sections:

- "Overview" summarizes the categories and classes contained in our VisualAge applications.
- "Business Domain and Infrastructure Layers" introduces the business domain and infrastructure classes of our applications.
- "The User Interface Layer" describes the visual parts that make up the user interface.
- "Performance Analysis" describes how we used the object visualizer and event profiler to analyze the first iteration.
- "Conclusions" summarizes the results of the first iteration.

Overview

According to our layering architecture for VisualAge applications, we categorized our objects into user interface, business domain, and infrastructure objects. The *EmsAFceServerApp* application contains the business domain and infrastructure classes that reside on the server side. The *EmsAFceClientApp* application contains all user interface classes that reside on the client side.

Figure 52 on page 122 shows the applications and their classes.

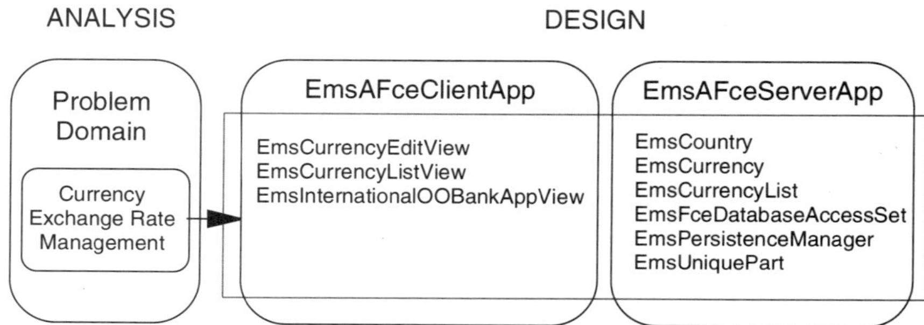

Figure 52. *Applications and Classes of the First Iteration*

Business Domain and Infrastructure Layers

We implemented the following business domain classes:

- *EmsUniquePart*
- *EmsCountry*
- *EmsCurrency*
- *EmsCurrencyList*.

EmsUniquePart is the superclass for all business domain objects according to the UNI concept discussed in Implementation of Instance Uniqueness Within the Residency Project on page 111 . For implementation details, refer to EmsUniquePart on page 220.

EmsCountry and *EmsCurrency* are the business domain classes for single country and currency objects. The public interface and methods of these classes can be obtained from EmsCountry on page 213 and EmsCurrency on page 214 , respectively.

Countries and currencies are instantiated by a currency list, which is an instance of the *EmsCurrencyList* class (see A Business Domain Class: EmsCurrencyList on page 110). A currency list has a collection of all currencies that are stored in our database. It is instantiated in the server object space during the first request of a currency list from a client object space. Subsequent requests to the server from any client return the already instantiated currency list. We implemented *EmsCurrencyList* as a *singleton class* to allow the use of the same instance from multiple clients (see Singleton Classes on page 116).

Because the currency list is unique within an object space, all clients actually use the same instances. So, if the exchange rate attribute of a currency instance is changed within the server object space, all clients automatically see that change.

The infrastructure layer of our application contains two classes:

- ❑ *EmsFceDatabaseAccessSet*
- ❑ *EmsPersistenceManager.*

The persistent data of countries and currencies is kept in the server's database. We created *EmsFceDatabaseAccessSet* as the database access set class for our *EmsAFceServerApp* application. *EmsPersistenceManager* is the infrastructure class as discussed in An Infrastructure Class: EmsPersistenceManager on page 111. It contains a multi-row query part that we used to visually define our currency query.

For our distributed FCE project we needed only one SQL query to retrieve a list of all currencies from the database. Because the *EmsPersistenceManager* class used some of the VisualAge database support classes, we added *AbtDbmIbmBaseApp* and *AbtRunDatabaseQueryPartApp* to the prerequisite applications of *EmsAFceServerApp*. Otherwise, warning messages such as:

```
#abtBuildInternals should not reference AbtMultiRowQuery
```

would appear in the System Transcript window when we would save our persistence manager part.

The User Interface Layer

The user interface layer contains all program components that interact with the user. When the application is started, the main view appears as in the previous FCE implementation. Figure 53 on page 124 shows the Composition Editor for the main view.

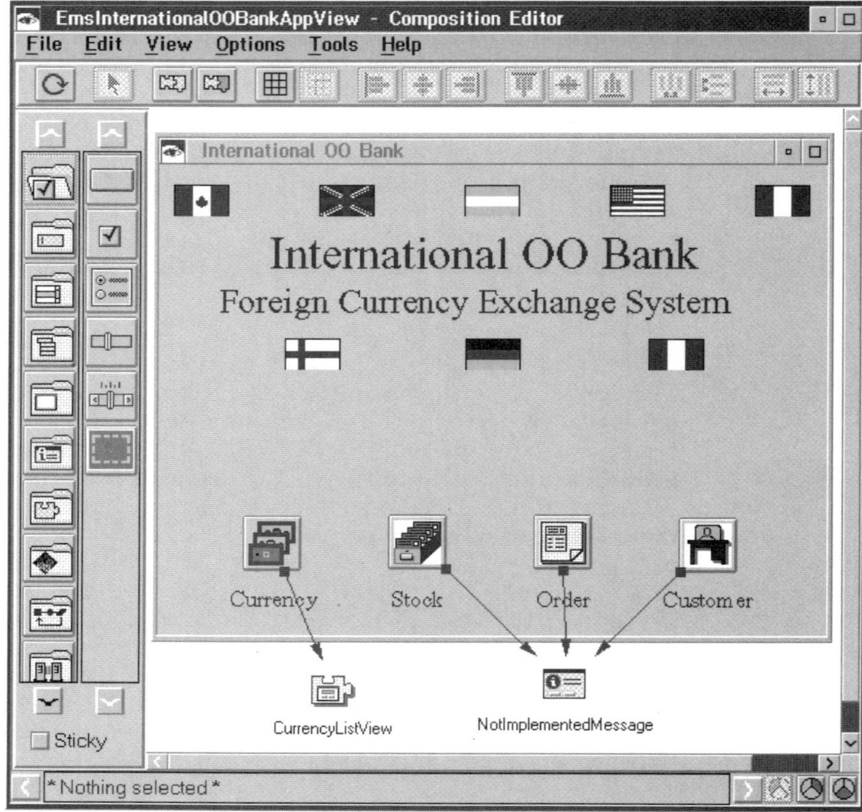

Figure 53. *Main View*

As mentioned before, we implemented only the management of currency exchange rates; therefore, we connected the *clicked* event of the **Stock**, **Order**, and **Customer** push buttons with the *openWidget* action of a message prompter part that provides the user with such information as "Not available yet."

By clicking on the **Currency** push button, we can get to the currency list view. Figure 54 on page 125 shows the Composition Editor for this view.

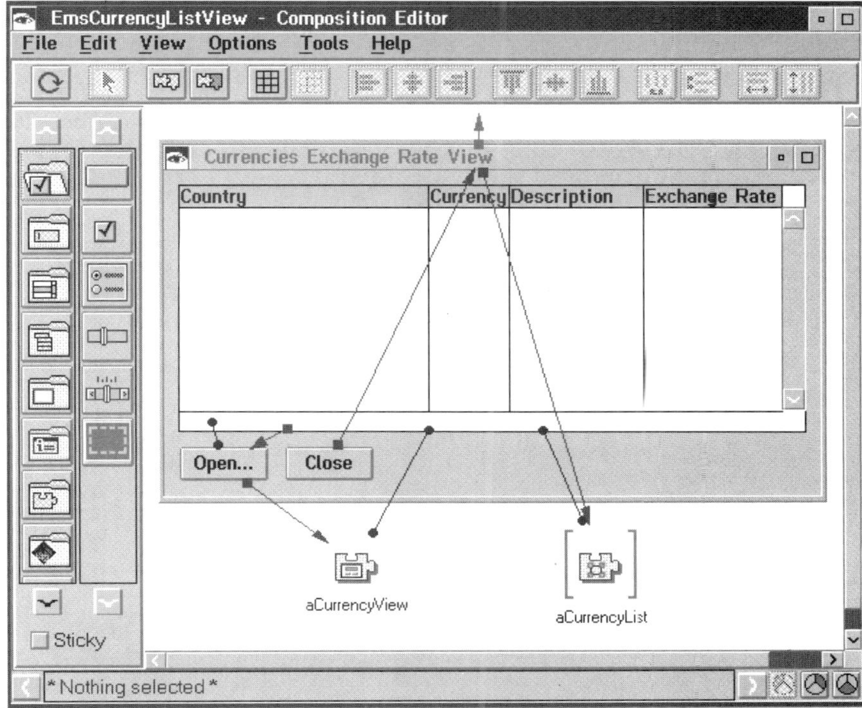

Figure 54. *Currency List View*

The currency list view has a read-only table that shows all currencies with their current exchange rates. We set the exchange rate column to display right-justified floats with four decimal places. We used an *aCurrencyList* variable of the *EmsCurrencyList* class to get the currency list for the table. We made an attribute-to-attribute connection between the variable's *currencies* and the table's *rows*.

Because we used a variable and not a part, we had to write some code to fill the *aCurrencyList* variable with an actual instance. We used a *getCurrencyList* script and an event-to-script connection from the *openedWidget* event of the window to run the script when the view was opened. The *getCurrencyList* script is as follows:

```
getCurrencyList
 "Get an instance of the currency list and assign it to the variable."
  (self subpartNamed: 'aCurrencyList') value: EmsCurrencyList new.
```

The *EmsCurrencyList* class is defined in the server application and therefore resides only within the server object space after the distributed load. However, we shadow-load the server application to the client object space, so we can still use the class as if it were local. Thus, by using this script, we actually get a shadow of a remote *EmsCurrencyList* instance.

There is also an event-to-script connection from the *aboutToCloseWidget* event of the window to the *release* action in the *aCurrencyList* variable. The purpose of this connection is to inform the currency list instance that this view no longer needs that instance (see A New Superclass: EmsUniquePart on page 112).

By clicking on the **Open...** push button, we can open the currency edit view for a selected currency object to change its exchange rate. (Using another attribute-to-attribute connection, we enable the **Open...** push button only when a table row is selected.)

Note: Our application does not take advantage of the Distributed feature's security services. In a real application there would probably be an authorization check, so that only authorized users would be allowed to edit exchange rates.

Figure 55 on page 126 shows the Composition Editor for the currency edit view.

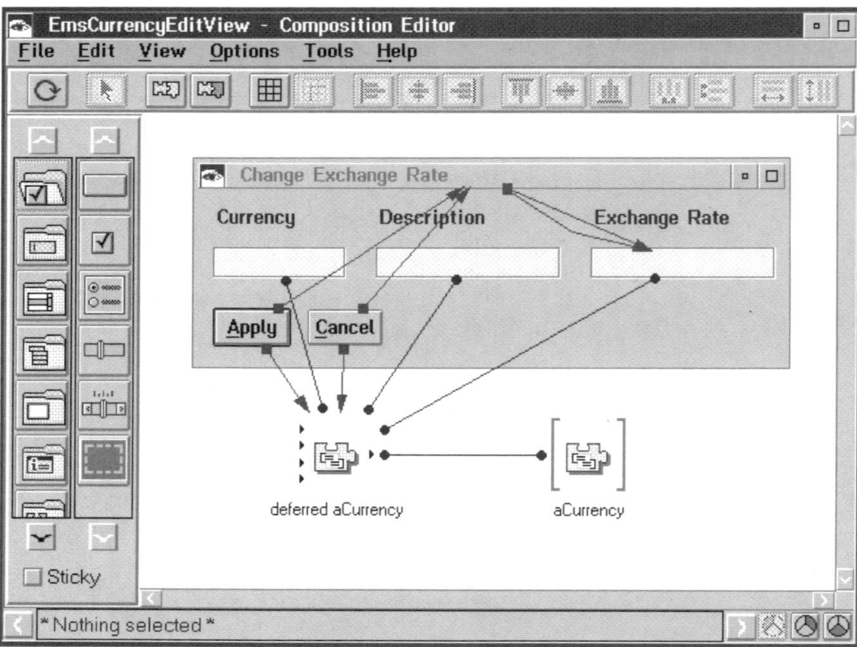

Figure 55. *Currency Edit View*

The currency edit view uses a variable of the *EmsCurrency* class. We added a deferred update part so that we could abort the intended exchange rate update; its *apply* and *cancel* actions were connected with the corresponding **Apply** and **Cancel** push buttons. Clicking either of the push buttons also closes the view.

Two connections were defined to position the cursor in the *Exchange Rate* entry field and to select the current value when the currency edit view is opened. We set the data type of the entry field to display a float with four decimal places.

We promoted the *aCurrency* variable to the public interface of the edit view part. This enabled us to make an attribute-to-attribute connection in the *EmsCurrencyListView* between that currency variable and the *selectedRowObject* attribute of the currency list table.

Testing and Distributing the Application

First, we tested the application locally and verified that it worked correctly. During the local test, the application used the local DB2/2 database access and instantiated all objects locally. The performance of the local application was pretty good.

After the successful local test, we assigned a version and released all classes, and we also assigned versions to our two applications. In preparation for the distribution process, we set the local instances to become *nil* for those classes that we were about to move to the server object space.

Attention

If there are instances of a class in an object space, we cannot unload the class. To enable unload, we must set all existing instances of the class to *nil*. For example, to remove all instances of the class *EmsCurrency*, execute the following script:

```
EmsCurrency allInstances do: [ :each | each become: nil ]
```

After "cleaning" the client object space by setting all instances of our *Ems* classes to nil, we defined two object references , *Local* and *Remote*, in our common name server. *Local* and *Remote* are references to the object space locations of the client machine and server machine, respectively.

Next, we created a configuration map, *EmsFceConfigMap*. Within that configuration map, we defined the distribution matrix for our FCE application as shown in Figure 56 on page 128.

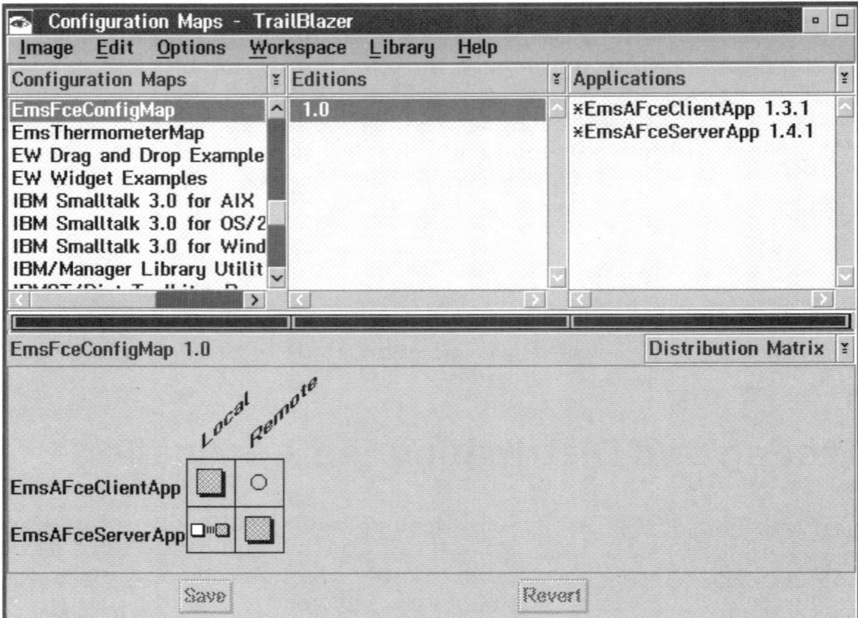

Figure 56. *FCE Distribution Matrix for the First Iteration*

We loaded the applications into the different object spaces by selecting **Distributed Load** from the pop-up menu in the **Editions** list. As defined within the distribution matrix, *EmsAFceClientApp* is fully loaded and *EmsAFceServerApp* is shadow loaded to the client object space called *Local*. *EmsAFceServerApp* is fully loaded to the server object space called *Remote*.

On the server machine, we issued a local logon and started the database manager. Note that, because there are no longer persistent objects within the client object space, the client machines need not be connected to the database, nor do they need the database client software for this application.

Then we started testing and waiting...

Note: If you now open the currency list view we suggest that you have a cup of coffee or do something else. Do not touch the mouse or keyboard while the table is being refreshed. (This might take the application out of synchronization.)

You can verify that the first iteration of our distributed application works correctly (if you have enough patience and time). After you issue a distributed load of the *EmsFceConfigMap* on another client machine, open the *EmsCurrencyListView* on the other client with the

VisualAge *Test* Button. You will see that a change of an exchange rate on one machine is propagated to the other client workstations, and that their tables are refreshed automatically.

Attention

When we verified the first iteration of our application with the general available version of the Distributed feature, updates to the exchange rate were not reflected in the server. This problem prevented the currency table from being refreshed.

We removed the deferred update part in the *EmsCurrencyEditView* to work around the bug. Because the problem did not manifest itself in our later iterations, the workaround was no longer required.

The performance of the first iteration is not acceptable, however. It takes far too long to populate and refresh the currency list table. The reason for this bad performance is that we actually send many messages to the server object space, and these messages create many shadow objects in the client object space.

Figure 57 on page 129 shows the object spaces and contained objects of the first iteration.

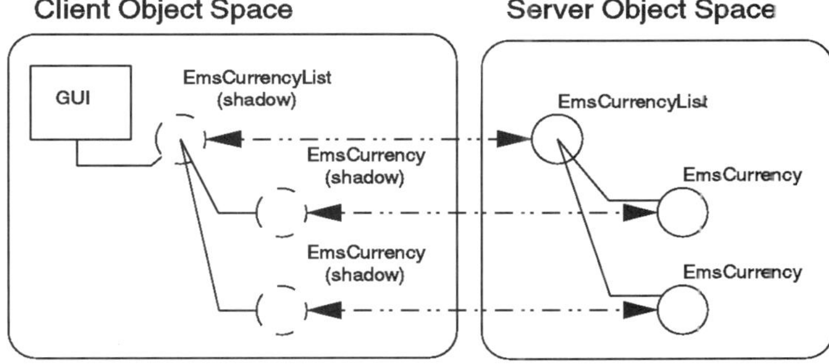

Figure 57. *Object Spaces of the First Iteration*

Performance Analysis

To analyze the poor performance of our first iteration, we used the event profiler and object visualizer tools provided by the Distributed feature toolkit. (See The IBM Smalltalk Distribution Toolkit on page 20.)

Visualizing the Application Before Distribution

The object visualizer highlighted the objects we would focus on to achieve the goals outlined in Optimization and Performance Tuning on page 175. The event profiler enabled us to take a closer look at the message traffic and processor time spent for remote messages.

After developing and testing the first iteration locally, we opened an object visualizer to observe program execution before distribution. We selected all but the *App* and *Package* classes to visualize. It was important to set up the object visualizer *before* our application ran so that we could watch the animation of object creation from the beginning. After startup of the FCE application, the object visualizer produced the views shown in Figure 58 on page 131 and Figure 59 on page 132 .

The object visualizer highlighted the "hottest" objects in red, message frequency color at the left side of the box, processor time at the right. The hottest objects were those that sent the highest number of messages or consumed the most processor time. It was obvious that *EmsCurrency* and *EmsCurrencyList* were the most active business model objects. Of all the view classes, *EmsCurrencyListView* was the most active.

The class cluster view (Figure 59) animated attraction and repulsion forces according to the total instance message traffic of each class visualized. It confirmed the wisdom of model-view separation. Our model classes, *EmsCurrency* and *EmsCountry*, were repelled farthest from the view classes and attracted to each other. Because the *EmsUniquePart* is an abstract class, there were no instances of it and therefore no message traffic. It was repelled farthest from all other classes.

The class cluster view grouped the business model objects. From this view, we concluded that a division between the business model objects and views was a good starting point.

Because the object visualizer highlighted the *EmsCurrency* instances as the "hottest," we decided to take a closer look at them. The behavior browser provided insight as to which methods were being sent most often and how much time was spent processing them. We simply selected one of the *EmsCurrency* instances from the object visualizer and selected **Browse Behavior** from the pop-up menu. Figure 60 on page 133 shows the resulting window.

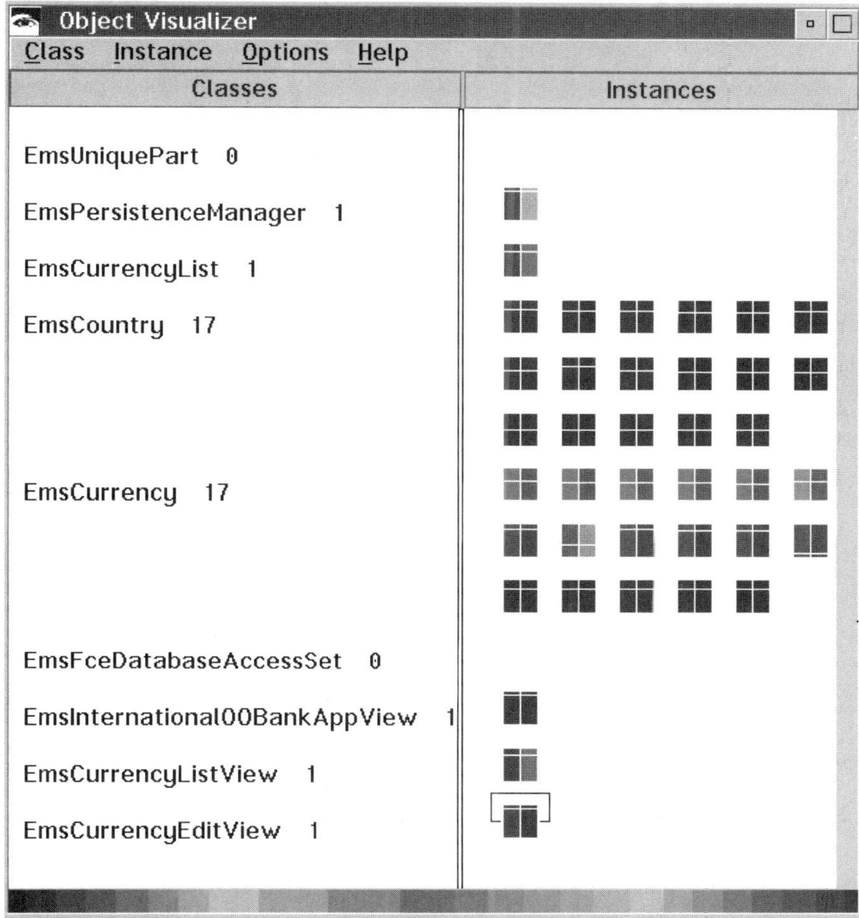

Figure 58. *First Iteration, Object Visualizer Before Distribution*

We noticed that some methods had been added to our class by either VisualAge or the object visualizer. Those added by VisualAge appeared to be the "hottest" (red):

- *valueOfAttributeNamed:ifAbsent:*
- *abtFeatureNamed:ifAbsent:*
- *abtPrivateInterfaceSpecFeatureNamed:ifAbsent:*.

This exercise enabled us to select focus areas for the performance analysis we carried out after distribution.

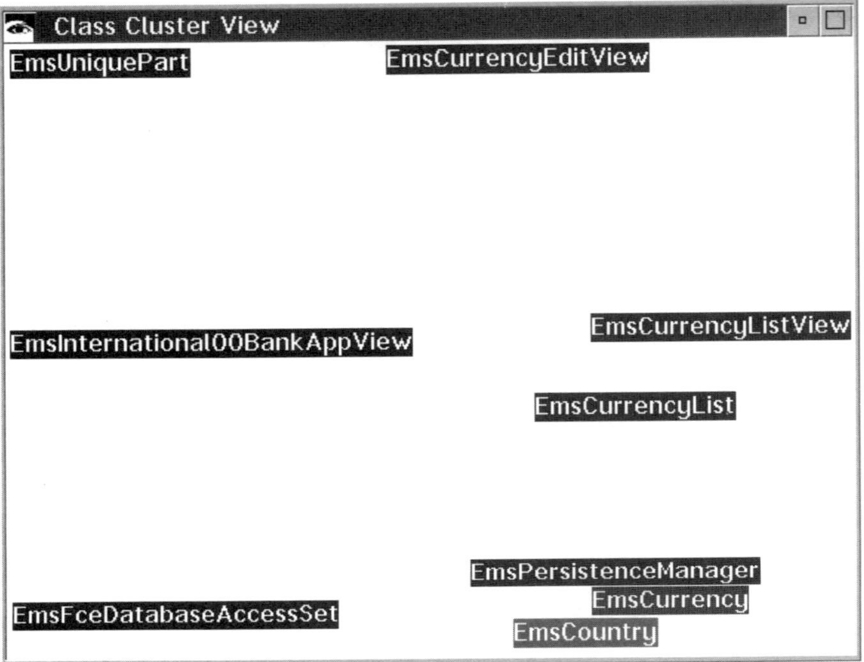

Figure 59. *First Iteration, Class Cluster View Before Distribution*

Profiling the Application After Distribution

After distribution, the event profiler recorded and summarized message traffic between object spaces. In this iteration, both the client and server object spaces were profiled to provide the clues necessary for pinpointing the performance problems we observed in Testing and Distributing the Application on page 127.

Before starting our distributed application, we set up our profiles to record all message traffic during startup. As shown in Figure 61 on page 134, we created five profiles on the *LocalClient* object space. The most interesting profile for this analysis was *allDsRemoteObjectInstances.1*. It recorded all messages sent to remote objects.

From the profiles browser, we picked the *allDsRemoteObjectInstances.1* profile and selected **Browse Event Tree** from the pop-up menu to open the event tree browser shown in Figure 62 on page 134.

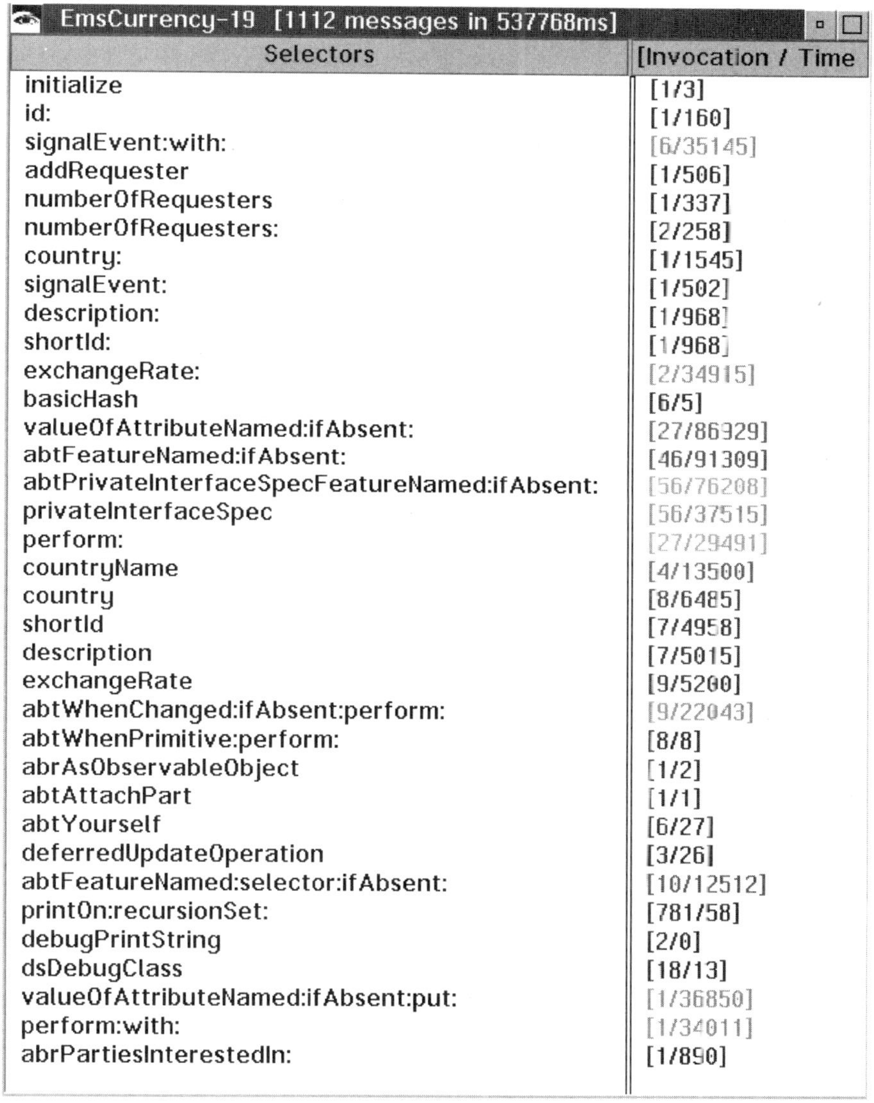

EmsCurrency-19 [1112 messages in 537768ms]

Selectors	[Invocation / Time
initialize	[1/3]
id:	[1/160]
signalEvent:with:	[6/35145]
addRequester	[1/506]
numberOfRequesters	[1/337]
numberOfRequesters:	[2/258]
country:	[1/1545]
signalEvent:	[1/502]
description:	[1/968]
shortId:	[1/968]
exchangeRate:	[2/34915]
basicHash	[6/5]
valueOfAttributeNamed:ifAbsent:	[27/86929]
abtFeatureNamed:ifAbsent:	[46/91309]
abtPrivateInterfaceSpecFeatureNamed:ifAbsent:	[56/76208]
privateInterfaceSpec	[56/37515]
perform:	[27/29491]
countryName	[4/13500]
country	[8/6485]
shortId	[7/4958]
description	[7/5015]
exchangeRate	[9/5200]
abtWhenChanged:ifAbsent:perform:	[9/22043]
abtWhenPrimitive:perform:	[8/8]
abrAsObservableObject	[1/2]
abtAttachPart	[1/1]
abtYourself	[6/27]
deferredUpdateOperation	[3/26]
abtFeatureNamed:selector:ifAbsent:	[10/12512]
printOn:recursionSet:	[781/58]
debugPrintString	[2/0]
dsDebugClass	[18/13]
valueOfAttributeNamed:ifAbsent:put:	[1/36850]
perform:with:	[1/34011]
abrPartiesInterestedIn:	[1/890]

Figure 60. *First Iteration, Behavior Browser for EmsCurrency Before Distribution*

The event tree browser revealed that our application was spending most of its time processing user interface messages remotely! (Remember, all messages prefixed with *abt* or *abr* are either part of or generated by VisualAge.) Just to give you an idea of how much time, this is the first line from the event tree:

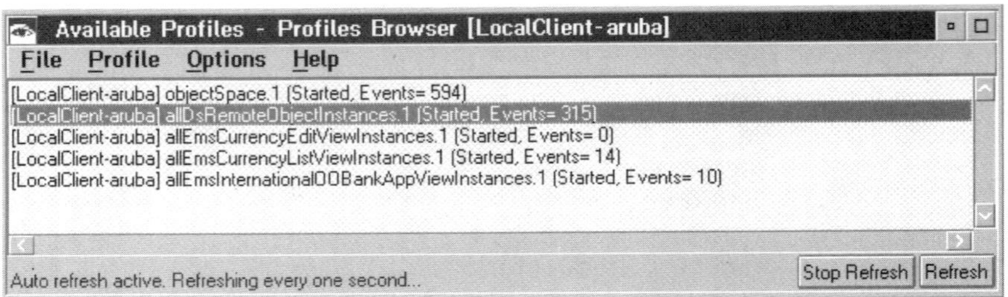

Figure 61. *First Iteration, Profiles Browser on LocalClient*

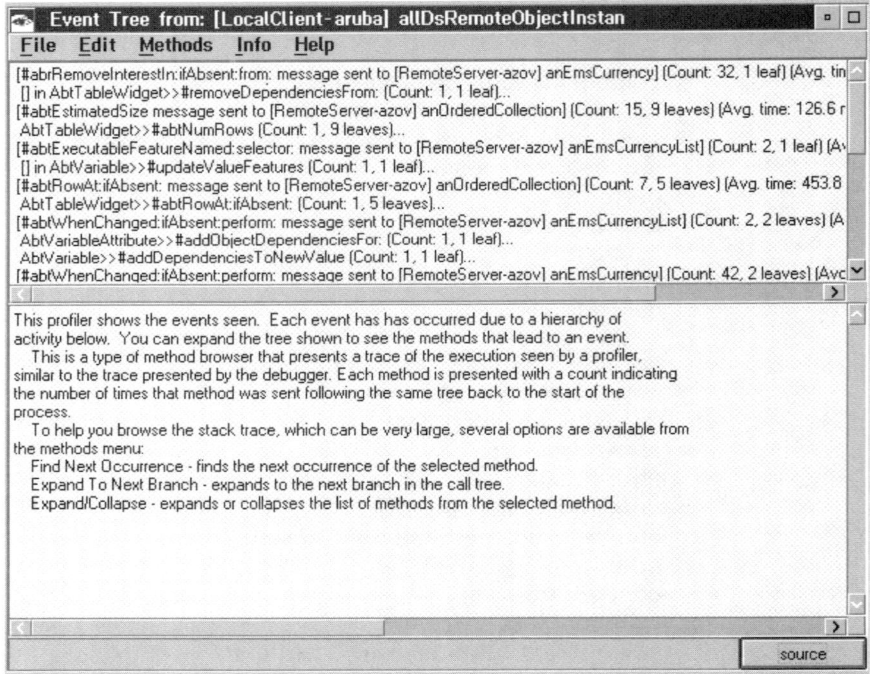

Figure 62. *First Iteration, Event Tree Browser on LocalClient*

```
[(#abrRemoveInterestIn:ifAbsent:from: message sent to
        [RemoteServer-azov] anEmsCurrency] (Count: 32, 1 leaf)
        (Avg. time: 573.2 ms, 18343 ms total)...
```

As you can see, the total time for this method was more than 18 seconds!

The profiles browser had another browser we could open on the *allDsRemoteObjectInstances.1* profile. From the profiles browser, we picked the *allDsRemoteObjectInstances.1* profile and selected **Browse Event List** from the pop-up menu to open the event list browser shown in Figure 63 on page 135. This list revealed that the *AbtPart>>#callHandlers:* selector is sent the most, 112 times to be precise. You will see in later iterations that we greatly reduced this number by applying our golden rules.

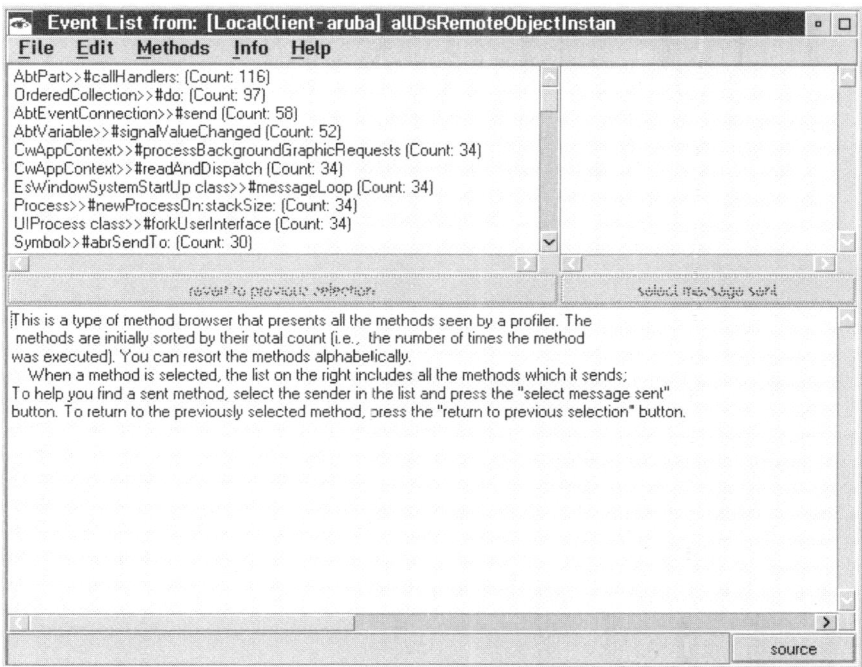

Figure 63. *First Iteration, Event List Browser on Local Client*

The server object space deserved attention as well. We profiled our application classes on the *RemoteServer* before we started our application on *LocalClient*. This recorded the message traffic occurring on the *RemoteServer*. Our model and database access code all resided on the *RemoteServer* object space. Figure 64 on page 136 lists the profiles we started.

We selected the *allEmsCurrencyInstances.1* profile on the basis of our analysis from Visualizing the Application Before Distribution on page 130. You may recall, that we previously observed that the instances of *EmsCurrency* seemed to be the "hottest." Opening an event tree browser on this profile revealed that the *abrRemoveInterestIn:ifAbsent:from:* method noted in the example discussed in Figure 62 on page 134 was on the top of the event tree browser list . We noted, once again, that all of the methods taking most of the processor time were user interface-related.

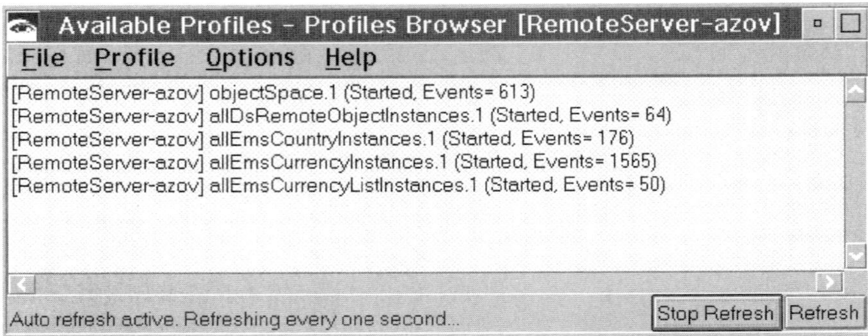

Figure 64. *First Iteration, Profiles Browser on RemoteServer*

Conclusions

One remarkable result of the first iteration was that, because of the Distributed feature architecture, we did not have to change any code from our single object space implementation! Nevertheless, performance was poor. Our observations in Profiling the Application After Distribution on page 132 led us to the conclusion that, although model and view were separated, additional layering was required.

Table 5 shows the "Golden Rules" for optimization and what went wrong in our first iteration. For more information about optimization and a detailed discussion of the golden rules, see Optimization and Performance Tuning on page 175.

Table 5. Optimization Rules

Rule	What Went Wrong
Maximize local references.	We maximized **remote** references. (Almost every object is in the remote object space.)
Minimize remote messages.	We **maximized** remote messages. The table part asks for the value of the corresponding attribute from the remote object, column by column, row by row. This behavior also leads to creating more shadow objects in the client object space.
Do not wait unless you have to.	We waited because we did not implement any parallelism on the server side.

From the first iteration, we are forced to conclude that we really must start planning for distribution from the very beginning of our application design. Early planning should make it easier to change the design during later iteration steps. Nevertheless, we are convinced that we should still start the application development in one object space and test the application locally first. When we are sure that the application works well enough, we can then distribute it, test it remotely, and tune it.

12 The Second Iteration

In this chapter we describe the changes and improvements we made to our application during the second iteration. The chapter consists of the following sections:

- "Overview" introduces the modified partitioning of our VisualAge applications.
- "Applying the Golden Rules" describes how we enhanced the distributed FCE application to conform to the rules of optimization (see Table 5).
- "Performance Analysis" describes how we used the object visualizer and event profiler to analyze the second iteration.
- "Conclusions" summarizes the results of the second iteration.

Overview

For the second iteration, we decided to follow the optimizing rules. To achieve better performance, we re-examined our design to identify an approach that would minimize remote messages.

We created a third application, *EmsAFceClientServerApp* and defined it as a prerequisite application for both *EmsAFceClientApp* and *EmsAFceServerApp*. Its purpose is to hold all classes that are required in both the client and server object spaces.

Figure 65 on page 140 shows the modified distribution matrix.

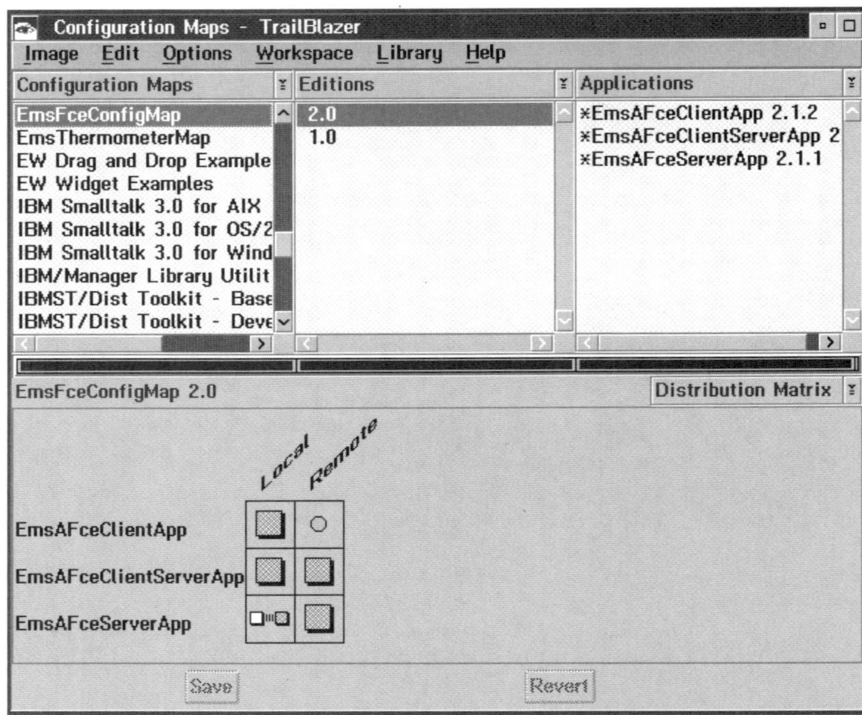

Figure 65. *FCE Distribution Matrix for the Second Iteration*

Applying the Golden Rules

To follow the golden optimization rules in the second iteration, we changed the application to:

- ❑ Maximize local references
- ❑ Minimize remote messages
- ❑ Add parallel processing.

Maximizing Local References

We made the assumption that only exchange rates could be modified and that all other attributes of currency were not subject to change. Therefore, to maximize local references, we decided to make the exchange rate a separate class and put it in the server object space. We moved every other class back to the client object space so that we had nearly the same situation as in the nondistributed version of our application.

Figure 66 on page 141 shows the implementation of object spaces and their objects during the second iteration of our distributed application.

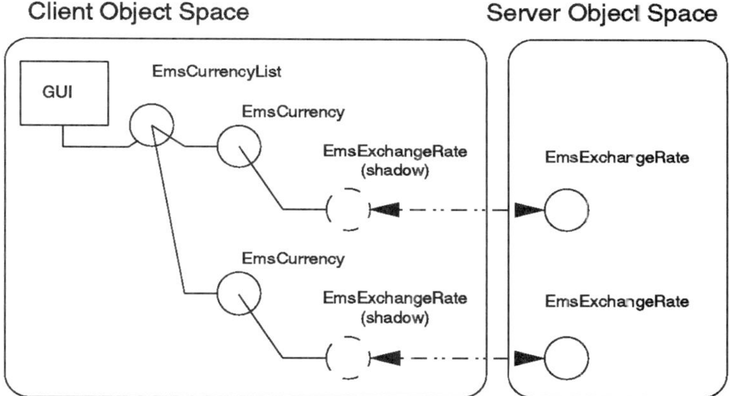

Figure 66. *Object Spaces of the Second Iteration*

In the VisualAge Organizer we moved *EmsUniquePart* from *EmsAFceServerApp* to *EmsAFceClientServerApp*, because that class is required as the superclass for both client objects and server objects. We moved all other classes of *EmsAFceServerApp* to *EmsAFceClientApp*. The only class in our server application is the new business domain class, *EmsExchangeRate*, for exchange rate objects. The public interface and methods can be obtained from EmsExchangeRate on page 228.

Figure 67 on page 142 shows the modified object model. Compare it to the original object model in Figure 35 on page 83.

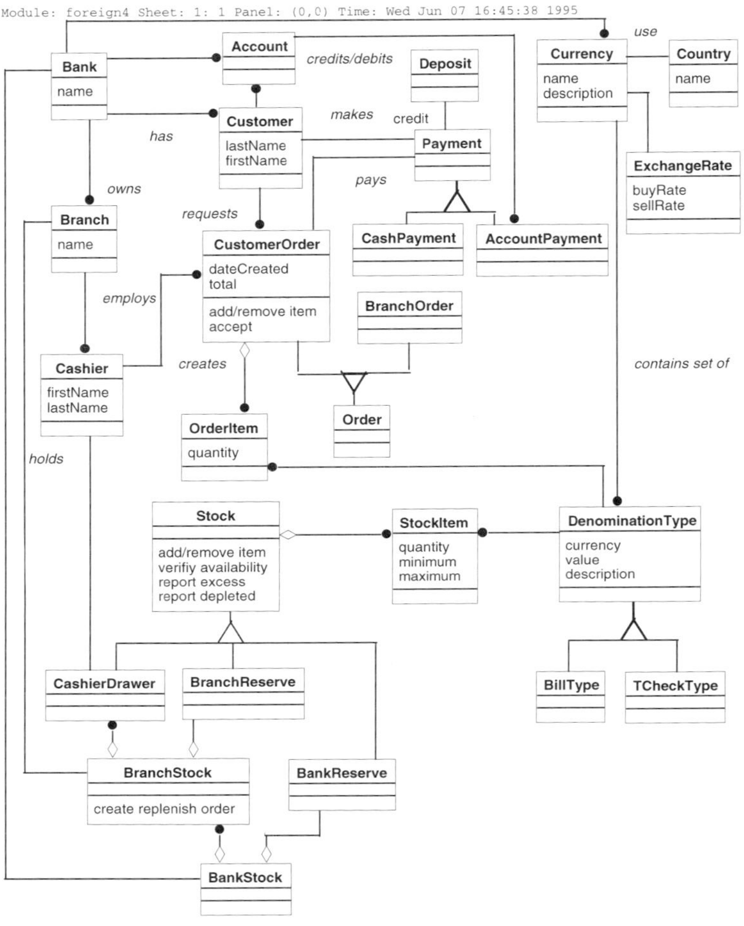

Figure 67. *Modified Object Model of the FCE Application*

Minimizing Remote Messages

In our application, maximizing local references results in minimizing messages that go across object space boundaries. In addition, we combined some methods to further minimize the number of messages sent between object spaces. The following example shows the *EmsExchangeRate* class method to create and initialize a new exchange rate instance:

```
newFor: anId requester: anObject currencyId: aString exchangeRate:
 aFloat
    "Create a new instance for anId and provide its instance
variable values."
    ^(self newFor: anId)
      currencyId: aString;
      exchangeRate: aFloat;
      addDependent: anObject;
      yourself.
```

In this particular method, we combined four messages into one to reduce network traffic between the client and server machine.

Adding the Dependency Mechanism and Parallel Processing

During the second iteration, we also implemented a dependency mechanism to propagate the modification of exchange rate values to all clients interested in the notification; that is, to all clients that have a shadow object for the affected *EmsExchangeRate* instance.

In the first iteration, the exchange rate was a direct attribute of a currency instance. When the exchange rate was modified, the change was automatically propagated to the user interface by means of the standard VisualAge notification mechanism. Because we implemented the exchange rate as a separate object in the second iteration, we had to inform the currency instance that the exchange rate had changed.

The *Object* class has methods that enable the Smalltalk programmer to build such a dependency and notification mechanism. First, we must make an object dependent on another object by using the *addDependent:* method. Then, whenever a specific instance is changed, it can inform all of its dependents by sending the *changed:* message to itself. This in turn causes the *update:* message to be sent to all the dependents. The dependent objects must react on that notification by implementing an *update:* instance method.

In the FCE application we had to add each *currency* instance of a client object space as a dependent on the corresponding *exchange rate* instance of the server object space. We also modified the *addDependent:* method so that it guaranteed that one object did not add itself as a dependent more than once. We overwrote the method in our *EmsUniquePart* class as follows:

```
addDependent: anObject
  "Overwritten to make sure that there are no duplicates."
  (self dependents includes: anObject) ifFalse: [
  ^super addDependent: anObject ].
```

Every time an exchange rate instance value was changed on the server object space by using the corresponding setter method, the exchange rate informed all of its dependents about this event. The new *exchangeRate:* setter method looked like the following:

```
exchangeRate: aFloat
  "Save the value of exchangeRate. Check if the value has changed
 at all. If it has changed, signal an event and inform all dependen
ts using the asynchronous broadcast mechanism."

  exchangeRate ~= aFloat ifTrue: [
    ...
    ...
    self changed: aFloat.
    ...
  ].
```

On the client side, we had to implement the *update:* method in the *EmsCurrency* class to react to the notification message as follows:

```
update: anObject
  "Process the information from the server exchangeRate object
   about the new exchangeRate value.
   Signal the corresponding event and also show a message box."
  self signalEvent: #exchangeRate with: anObject.
  CwMessagePrompter message: 'Attention:', LineDelimiter,
     'Exchange rate for ', self description trimBlanks,
     '(', self shortId, ') has changed to ',
     anObject asFloat printString.
```

That implementation led to a problem in our distributed client/server application. As shown in the example above, we used a *CwMessagePrompter* part to inform the user about the modified exchange rate. The resulting window was a system modal dialog by default. The user had to confirm the message before he/she could continue with other work. Thus, if we used the standard dependency mechanism, the server object waited for every confirmation and did not return the control until every client had confirmed the message. That is not what we really wanted. We wanted to inform the clients asynchronously, and we wanted to continue the processing on the server immediately without waiting for the confirmations. (See Modal Dialogs on page 189.) To accomplish this we had to add parallelism to our application.

We were required to change the standard *changed:* and *broadcast:with:* Smalltalk methods to use parallel informing of the dependents. We chose the names *dtChanged:* and *dtBroadcast:with:* for these new methods. In the *exchangeRate:* setter method listed above, we changed the line `self changed: aFloat` to `self dtChanged: aFloat`. Our *dtChanged:* method changed as follows:

```
dtChanged: anObject
 "Inform all dependents that the receiver has changed in an aspect
  represented by the argument anObject.  Answer self."
  self dtBroadcast: #update: with: anObject.
```

Our new *dtBroadcast:with:* method used the *dtForkEachAndContinue* method, which the Distributed feature adds as an API method of the *Collection* class. *dtForkEachAndContinue* is sent to a collection of blocks. It evaluates each block in parallel and then continues without waiting for a response. We implemented the *dtBroadcast:with:* method as follows:

```
dtBroadcast: aSymbol with: anObject
  "Send the argument aSymbol as a keyword message with argument a
nObject to all of the receiver's dependents. Use parallel blocks to
 send the messages. Answer self.
    Fail if aSymbol is not a Symbol.
    Fail if the number of arguments expected by aSymbol is not 1"

  | aCollectionOfBlocks |
  self dependents notEmpty ifTrue: [
    aCollectionOfBlocks := OrderedCollection new.
    self dependents do: [ :dependent |
      aCollectionOfBlocks add:
      [ (dependent respondsTo: aSymbol) ifTrue: [
        dependent perform: aSymbol with: anObject ]
      ]
    ].
    aCollectionOfBlocks dtForkEachAndContinue.
  ].
```

Performance Analysis

In the second iteration, the response time for building the list of currencies was still less than desirable. We decided to focus on improving the response time at the client. At this point, the event profiler was the tool for the job. In the sections that follow, we recap our observations.

Profiling the Local Client

As in the first iteration, we started our profiles before we tested our application. Figure 68 on page 146 lists the profiles.

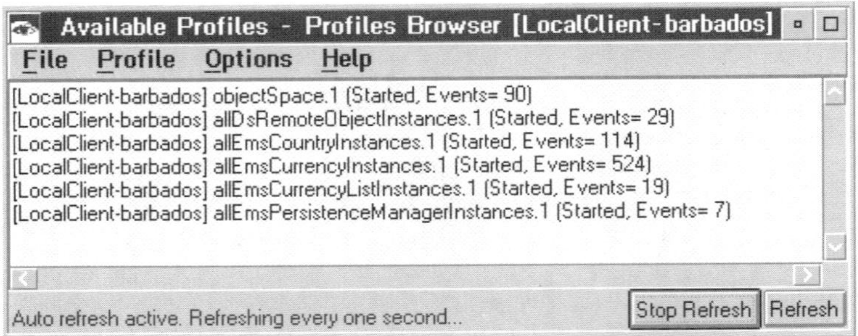

Figure 68. *Second Iteration, Profiles Browser on LocalClient*

Browsing the event tree for the *allDsRemoteObjectInstances.1* profile, we were rewarded with the messages listed in Figure 69 on page 146. This profile proved that our efforts to minimize remote messages paid off in this iteration.

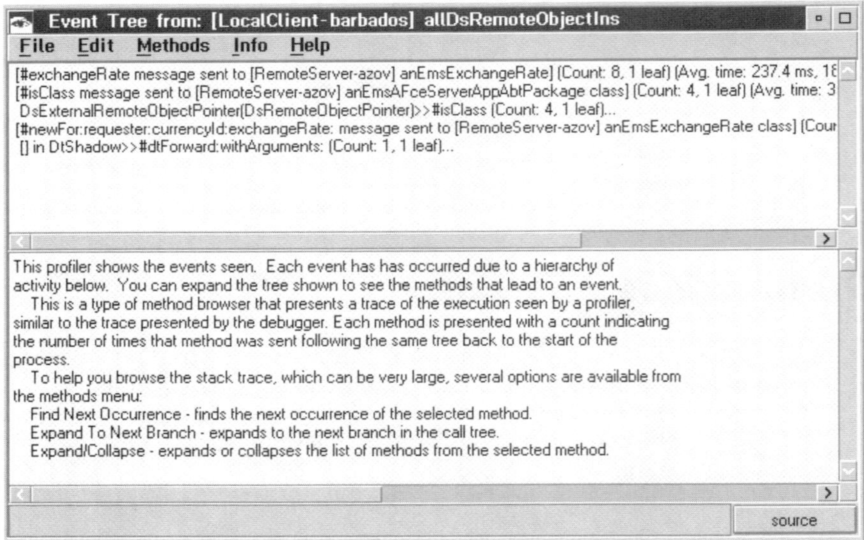

Figure 69. *Second Iteration, Event Tree Browser on LocalClient*

We examined the event list for the *allDsRemoteObjectInstances.1* profile as well. Figure 70 on page 147 shows the event list browser. Note that the count on the *AbtPart>>#callHandlers:* selector has improved by an order of magnitude over the first iteration!

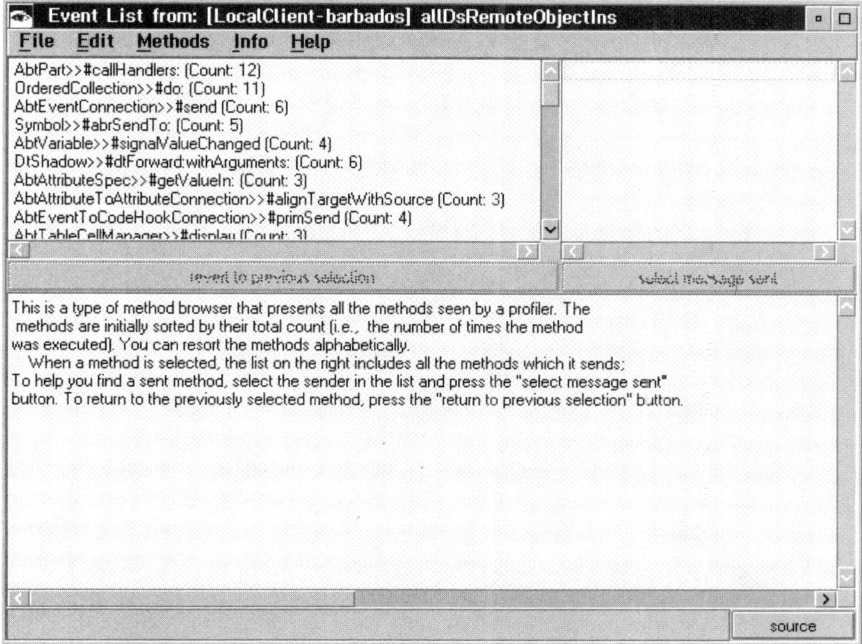

Figure 70. *Second Iteration, Event List Browser on LocalClient*

Not bad! But as you will see in the third iteration, we can do better.

Conclusions

The performance of the application for the second iteration was acceptable. We were able to test and see the advantages of an active object server application. The second iteration also proved that it pays to follow the optimization rules (see The Golden Rules on page 176).

Nevertheless, we decided to further refine the application in a third iteration. We wanted to improve not only the initial creation of the list, but the interaction with it as well. You will see in our third iteration that we can move even more objects to the client to speed things up.

13 The Third Iteration

In this chapter we describe our project's third and final iteration of the performance-tuned FCE application. This chapter consists of the following sections:

- "Overview" presents our approach to optimize the application's performance.
- "Creating Local Copies of Remote Objects" describes how we changed our application to have only local objects connected to the user interface layer.
- "Controlling Message Flow Between Object Spaces" describes how we propagated exchange rate updates among different object copies.
- "Performance Analysis" describes how we used the object visualizer and event profiler to analyze the third iteration.
- "Conclusions" summarizes the results of the third iteration.

Overview

Even after the second iteration, scrolling the currency list table still resulted in some unwanted network traffic. Because VisualAge uses the object connected to the table to retrieve the necessary row data, any scrolling of the table results in messages being sent to the server object space. To make the view work faster and to prevent needless network traffic, we decided to redesign our class locations.

In the third iteration, we returned to the same class structure as we used in the first iteration, but we created local copies of the *EmsCurrencyList*, *EmsCurrency*, and *EmsCountry* objects in the client object space instead of generating shadow objects. The only shadow object that was created was a shadow of the server's currency list instance. This shadow was used in the client object spaces, in addition to the local copy. The local copy was connected to the table; therefore, scrolling the table was as fast as in a nondistributed application. We used the shadow object to transfer the exchange rate update messages between the client and server.

Figure 71 on page 150 shows the distribution matrix we defined for the third iteration.

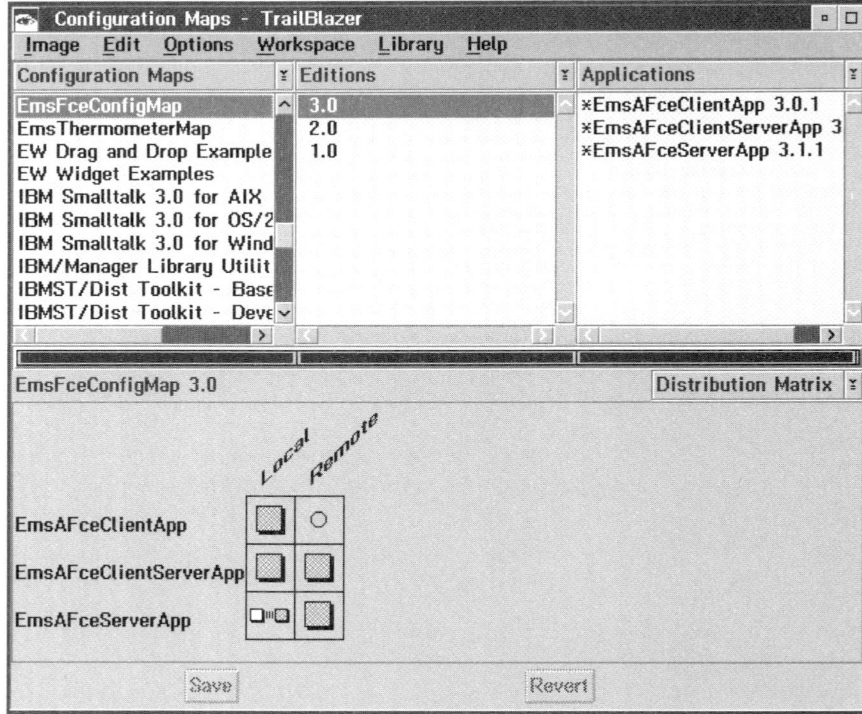

Figure 71. *FCE Distribution Matrix for the Third Iteration*

Creating Local Copies of Remote Objects

Using local copies instead of shadows minimizes the generation of remote messages. Only update messages must be sent through the network to synchronize local copies with their remote objects. With this solution, the view's table asks the local objects for their attributes each time the table must be refreshed, instead of going over the network to the remote objects.

Figure 72 on page 151 shows object spaces and their objects of the third iteration:

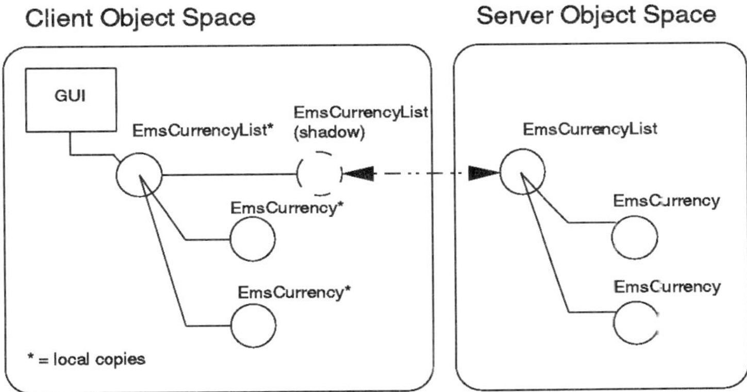

Figure 72. *Object Spaces of the Third Iteration*

Having local copies of the remote objects in the client image requires that the *EmsCurrencyList*, *EmsCurrency*, and *EmsCountry* classes are defined in both the client object space and server object space. Therefore, we could no longer use the distribution matrix to make automatic remote object references. Instead, we had to use explicit object references for remote objects.

We (1) defined a global object reference, *EmsServerCurrencyList*, for the *EmsCurrencyList* class of our server object space, and (2) requested a shadow from that object reference. Figure 73 on page 152 shows the global object reference definition.

In the *EmsCurrencyList* class definition, we added a new instance variable, *serverCurrencyList*. In a client object space, that variable holds the shadow object of the server currency list. In a server object space, that variable has the value *nil*.

To use the object reference to create and store the shadow object, we also overwrote the *newFor:* class method as follows:

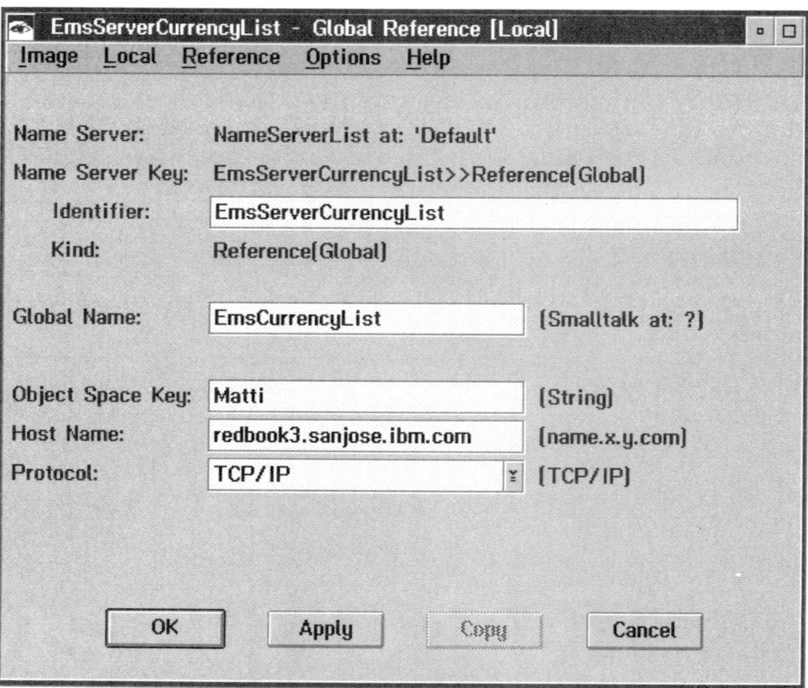

Figure 73. *Global Reference for the Server Currency List Class*

```
  newFor: anId
     "Create a new instance for anId, if it doesn't already exist.
Create also a 'master' currency list within the server object space
. Return the instance."

     | anInstance temp oRef |
     anInstance := self instances at: anId ifAbsentPut: [

      "Use the global reference to get an object reference for the
      CurrencyList class within the server object space. Create a
     remote object by using a shadow, then store a pointer to that
     object in the local currency list."
       oRef := NameServerList default referenceAtFirstIdentifier:
                 'EmsServerCurrencyList'.
   temp := super new.
   temp id: anId;
     serverCurrencyList: (oRef shadow newFor: anId dependent: temp);
          yourself
     ].
     ^anInstance addRequester; yourself.
```

On the first invocation of its *currencies* getter method, an *EmsCurrencyList* object sends itself the *retrieve* message to get its currency list from the database. In our third iteration, only the currency list in the server object space actually retrieves its data from the database. An

EmsCurrencyList instance in a client object space routes the *currencies* message to the corresponding server currency list, using the shadow stored in the *serverCurrencyList* instance variable. We used the *dsPerformWithLocalResult:* method to send the *currencies* message to the server object space.* Using this approach, a local copy of the return value is created in the sender's object space.

To summarize, with the following new *retrieve* method, a client currency list gets a copy of all currency and country objects from the server currency list:

```
retrieve
  "If I have a serverCurrencyList, I route the request to that re
   mote object."
 self serverCurrencyList notNil ifTrue: [
  self currencies:
   (self serverCurrencyList dsPerformWithLocalResult: #currencies)
  ] ifFalse: [
    super retrieve
  ].
```

Controlling Message Flow Between Object Spaces

Because we now have currency list objects in both the client and server object spaces, we must take precautions to control the message flow when an exchange rate value is changed on a client machine.

Figure 74 on page 154 shows the new message flow. The numbered messages in the figure are explained below.

1. In the currency edit view, the user modifies the exchange rate value and clicks on the **Apply** push button. This causes the execution of the corresponding *EmsCurrency* setter instance method:

   ```
   exchangeRate: aFloat
   ```

2. Each currency object has the currency list as its dependent. In the *exchangeRate:* method, the currency informs all its dependents about the modified exchange rate as follows:

   ```
   self dtBroadcast: #localRateUpdate:for:
     withArguments: (Array with: aFloat with: self shortId)
   ```

* For a detailed explanation of the *dsPerformWithLocalResult:* method, see First Rule: Maximize Local References on page 176.

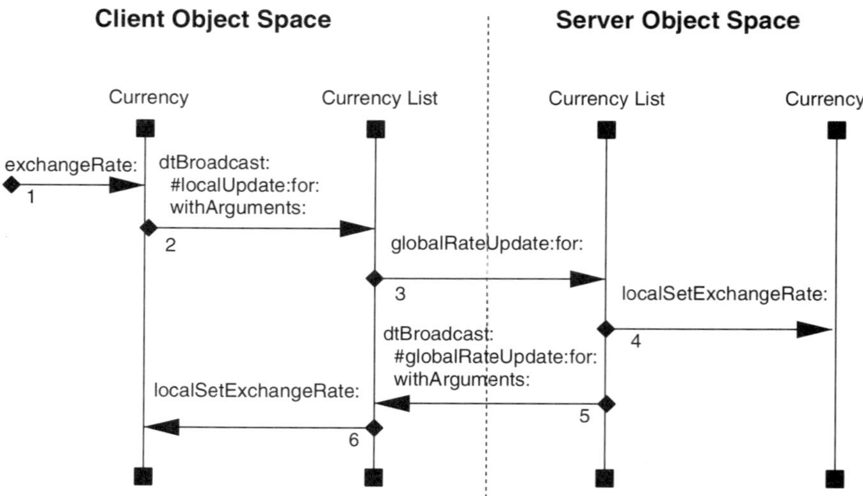

Figure 74. *Event Trace Diagram for an Exchange Rate Update*

3. The currency list in the client object space executes the *localRateUpdate: aFloat for: aCurrencyId* method. The currency list holds a shadow object of the server currency list in an instance variable, *serverCurrencyList*. It routes the modification to that server currency list by executing:

```
serverCurrencyList
  globalRateUpdate: aFloat for: aCurrencyId
```

4. In its *globalRateUpdate* method, the server currency list first finds the currency instance for the given currency id and then sets the exchange rate value of that instance, using the following *EmsCurrency* private instance method:

```
localSetExchangeRate: newRate
```

Note: To avoid an endless notification loop, we added this private setter method. In contrast to the *exchangeRate:* method, there is no further broadcasting.

5. The server currency list has all client currency lists as its dependents. So, the next step is to inform them about the modified exchange rate:

```
self dtBroadcast: #globalRateUpdate:for:
  withArguments: (Array with: aFloat with: aCurrencyId)
```

6. Executing the *dtBroadcast:withArguments:* method leads to the execution of the *globalRateUpdate* method in the client object spaces. As described in Step for the server currency list, the client currency list first finds the currency instance for the given currency ID and then sets the exchange rate value of that instance, again using the *EmsCurrency* private instance method:

```
localSetExchangeRate: newRate
```

Every client currency list object has a shadow to the server currency list. The local currency list knows that it is really a client and does not have to send a broadcast message (in contrast to Step 5 for the server currency list). Instead, the client currency list opens a message box that informs the user about the changed currency with its ID and new value.

In some methods of this application, we must know whether we are executing the code in the client object space or the server object space. This is very important because we want only the server currency list, not the client currency list, to send update broadcast messages to its dependents. The *serverCurrencyList* instance variable indicates whether a currency list resides in a client object space or server object space.

By testing the *serverCurrencyList* variable we can provide the correct behavior of methods in different object spaces although the classes are actually identical in both locations. For example, in the *retrieve* method shown on page page 153 , only a currency list in the server object space calls the *retrieve* method of its superclass. This superclass method, in turn, causes the data to be retrieved from the server's database.

When the client's view asks for currencies from the local currency list for the first time, the local currency list gets a copy of all currencies from the server. The server currency list adds the client currency list as a dependent. The server currency list instance knows about all of its dependents (see Adding the Dependency Mechanism and Parallel Processing on page 143) and can inform them about modified currency exchange rates.

Performance Analysis

We wanted to look one last time at how well we had implemented our golden rules in the third iteration. For a cross-iteration comparison, we followed the same line of reasoning in our final analysis. We profiled the client's object space where response time is most noticeable.

Profiling the Local Client: Last Pass

We used the same approach in this analysis as we used in the first and second iterations. We focused on the profile of remote object instances at the client. The profile browser in Figure 75 on page 156 lists the profiles we started before we tested our application.

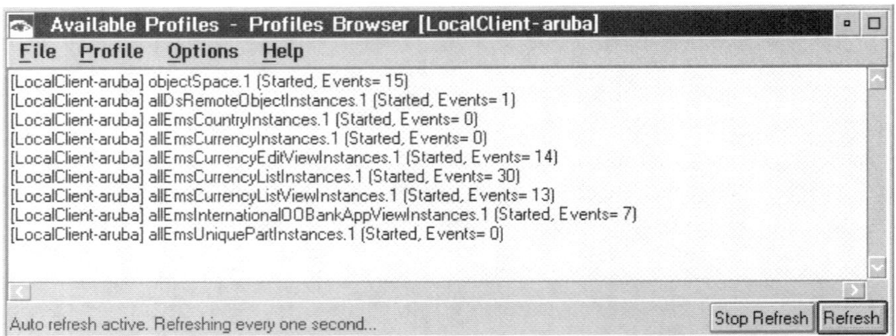

Figure 75. *Third Iteration, Profiles Browser on LocalClient*

Looking at an event tree of the *allDsRemoteObjectInstances.1* profile, we found that we had improved our remote message traffic once again.

In the second iteration, the same profile reported 13 remote messages (see Figure 69 on page 146).We added all of the top-level branches to arrive at this conclusion: 8 + 4 + 1 = 13. Figure 76 on page 156 shows a 12-count improvement.

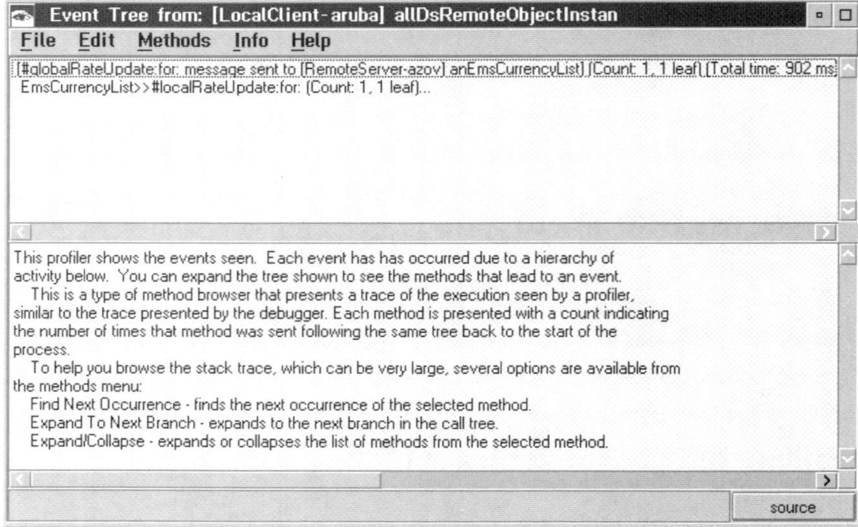

Figure 76. *Third Iteration, Event Tree Browser on LocalClient*

We found the Distributed feature analysis tools quite helpful in observing the behavior of our application. Through using the tools provided by the Distributed feature we verified many of the design choices we made during the three iterations. The object visualizer gave us a bird's-eye view of the system before we distributed its components. Using the complementary tools of the object visualizer, we could watch the utilization of any object's selector or the change in any object's instance variables. Clustering in the class cluster view verified our separation design.

The event profiler enabled us to analyze performance in-depth and provided us with an easy way of collecting the required data to observe the communication between object spaces. Imagine the enormity of the task of instrumenting your application to collect similar information whenever a remote message is sent!

Conclusions

The performance of the application after the third iteration was quite satisfactory. Refreshing the table caused no delays in network traffic. In addition to good performance, with the third iteration, we did not have to extract the exchange rate attribute to a separate object. We were able to use the original object model as before the distributed version of the application.

The third iteration proved to us that, in some cases, we should not connect shadow objects to user interfaces. The use of local copies (or so-called *light objects*) instead relayed only the required messages to remote objects.

14 Applying the Event Services Framework

At the time we implemented our three application iterations, the event services framework of the Distributed feature was not available. Therefore, we developed our own dependency and notification mechanisms, as described in previous sections.

In the third iteration of our application, we registered the currency list as a dependent of its currencies, and all client currency lists as dependents of the server currency list. With these underlying dependencies, we used a somewhat complicated message flow to propagate exchange rate updates to the server and all other clients.

The CORBA-compliant event services framework provides a more general solution for applications that propagate events independently of source or target. In this chapter we discuss two possible enhancements to the third iteration of the distributed FCE application that take advantage of the event services framework. In the first enhancement, we explore the possible use of a single event channel to propagate events to the server. We improve this approach in the second enhancement making use of two event channels to enable the server to guarantee synchronization with the database.

This chapter consists of the following sections:

- "Using a Single Event Channel for Each Server Currency" describes how a single event channel per currency object can propagate exchange rate updates.
- "Using Two Event Channels for Each Server Currency" describes a design to further enhance the single event channel approach.

For a detailed description of the event services framework, refer to the *VisualAge for Smalltalk User's Guide*.

Using a Single Event Channel for Each Server Currency

The simplest way of adapting the event services framework to our distributed FCE application is to create a single event channel for each currency that resides in the server object space. For each currency that resides in the server's object space, the server must provide both a push supplier and a push consumer. The event channel, push supplier, and push consumer can be created in the server object space during initialization of the currency object.

After a client object space has requested its local copies from the server (see Creating Local Copies of Remote Objects on page 151), each currency's push supplier and push consumer must be connected to the corresponding server event channel. Figure 77 on page 161 illustrates these connections for a configuration with two client object spaces.

To clarify the remainder of this enhancement, we define the following notations:

`X`	a given currency of our FCE currency database table.
`Client1`	the first client object space.
`Client2`	the second client object space.
`Server`	the server object space.
`CurrXin[os]`	the currency object for `X` in the object space denoted by `[os]`. For example, `CurrXinClient2` is the currency object in the second client object space.

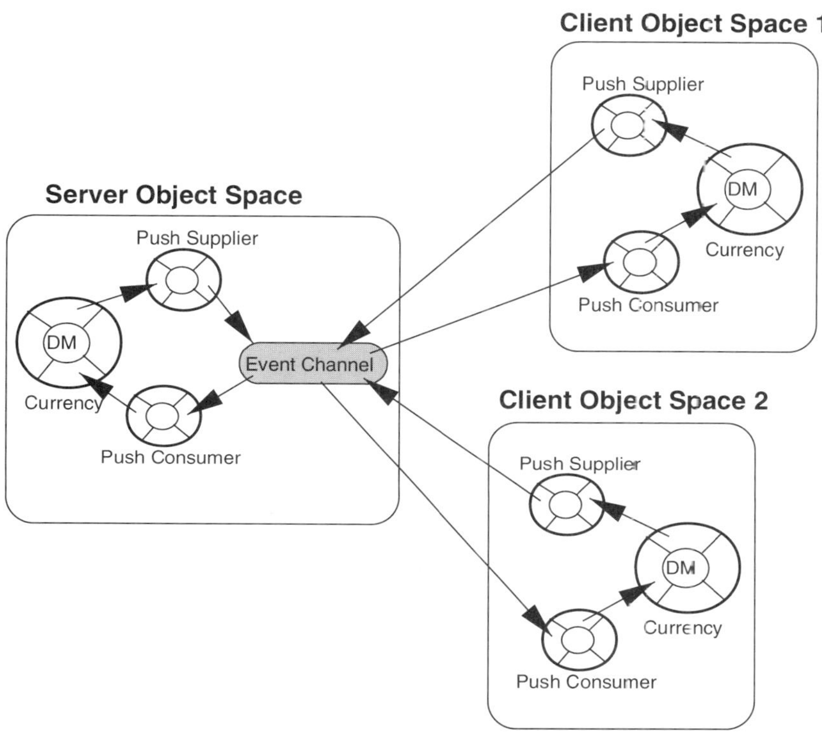

Figure 77. *Using a Single Event Channel for Each Server Currency*

`PushSuppXin[os]`	the push supplier for currency `X` in the [os] object space.
`PushConsXin[os]`	the push consumer for currency `X` in the [os] object space.
`ChannelX`	the event channel for currency `X`. (**Remember:** All event channels reside in `Server`.)

Now we are ready to describe how to use event services to propagate exchange rate updates in the distributed FCE application.

1. Click on the **Apply** button on the currency edit view in `Client1` to update the exchange rate for `X`.
2. The exchange rate setter method of `CurrXinClient1` does not directly update the exchange rate value. The client transmits a currency update event to the server by sending a *push:* to `PushSuppXinClient1`.
3. The push consumers of currency `X` in each of our object spaces are connected to `ChannelX`. Therefore, the notification of the exchange rate update arrives in each object space.

4. PushConsXinClient1, PushConsXinClient2, and PushConsXinServer set the new exchange rate value in their corresponding currencies, namely CurrXinClient1, CurrXinClient2, and CurrXinServer.

   Note: To avoid a loop in this message flow, the exchange rate setter method cannot be used in Step 4 because it would lead to Step 2 again. The value of exchange rate must be set by some other method, such as *localSetExchangeRate:*.

The following changes are required to adapt this approach to the third iteration of our FCE application:

- An *EmsCurrencyEventChannel* class is required in the *EmsAFceServerApp* application. *EmsCurrencyEventChannel* is a subclass of *EmsUniquePart* and has an instance method that returns the corresponding event channel. This event channel must be an instance of class *CosEventChannel*.
- Two new classes are required in the *EmsAFceClientServerApp* application: *EmsCurrencyPushSupplier* (subclass of *DfPushSupplier*) and *EmsCurrencyPushConsumer* (subclass of *DfPushConsumer*). No additional logic is required for the supplier class. In the consumer class, we must define an instance variable to store the corresponding currency object. We also must implement a *push:* instance method, which uses the given argument to set the exchange rate in its currency object:

```
push: newRate
  "Modify the local exchange rate without any
   further notification."
  self currency localSetExchangeRate: newRate
```

- The *EmsCurrency* class needs an additional instance variable to store the instance's push supplier. In the exchange rate setter method, the push supplier object propagates the new exchange rate value:

```
exchangeRate: newRate
  "Propagate the new exchange rate, but do
   not update it yet."
  self pushSupplier proxy push: newRate
```

- The *EmsPersistenceManager* instance must create the event channel, push supplier, and push consumer along with each corresponding currency. The push supplier and push consumer must be connected to the event channel.
- In the *EmsCurrencyList* class, the local push supplier and push consumer must be connected to the corresponding server event channel, after the currency objects are copied from the server object space.

At first glance, following the above steps appears to be a major effort. However, the event service framework provides a standardized interface, exception handling, buffering, and additional features such as pull suppliers, pull consumers, and typed events. We are convinced that using event services is a better solution for our third iteration. The implementation of event services would make the following code obsolete:

- *dtBroadcast:*, *dtBroadcast:with:*, *dtChanged*, and *dtChanged:* methods in the *EmsUniquePart* class
- *globalRateUpdate:for:*, *localRateUpdate:for:*, and *update:* methods in the *EmsCurrency* class
- Dependency management of the instance; registering the currency list as a dependent of its currencies, and all client currency lists as dependents of the server currency list
- The *serverCurrencyList* instance variable and its corresponding getter and setter methods in the *EmsCurrencyList* class.

In summary, we prefer using the event services framework because of its standardized interface and overall simplicity.

Using Two Event Channels for Each Server Currency

There is still room for improvement over the first enhancement. With the single event channel approach, updates to an exchange rate are propagated to all clients connected to the event channel even if the server itself cannot process the update. This could be a problem in a production application. To ensure that currency objects in client object spaces receive the update event notification only after processing on the server is successful, we must provide an additional event channel for each currency.

One event channel sends an exchange rate update request from a client currency to its corresponding instance in the server object space. The second event channel sends the update message from the server currency to all corresponding instances in the client object spaces after the exchange rate modification is processed on the server.

To implement these modifications, the *EmsPersistenceManager* instance must create *two* event channels for each currency object. It must then connect the push supplier to the first event channel and the push consumer to the second event channel. In the *EmsCurrencyList* class, the push supplier and push consumer must be connected as follows:

- The push supplier of a client currency must be connected to the same event channel as the push consumer of the corresponding server currency

- The push consumer of a client currency must be connected to the same event channel as the push supplier of the corresponding server currency.

Figure 78 on page 164 illustrates these connections for a given configuration with two client object spaces.

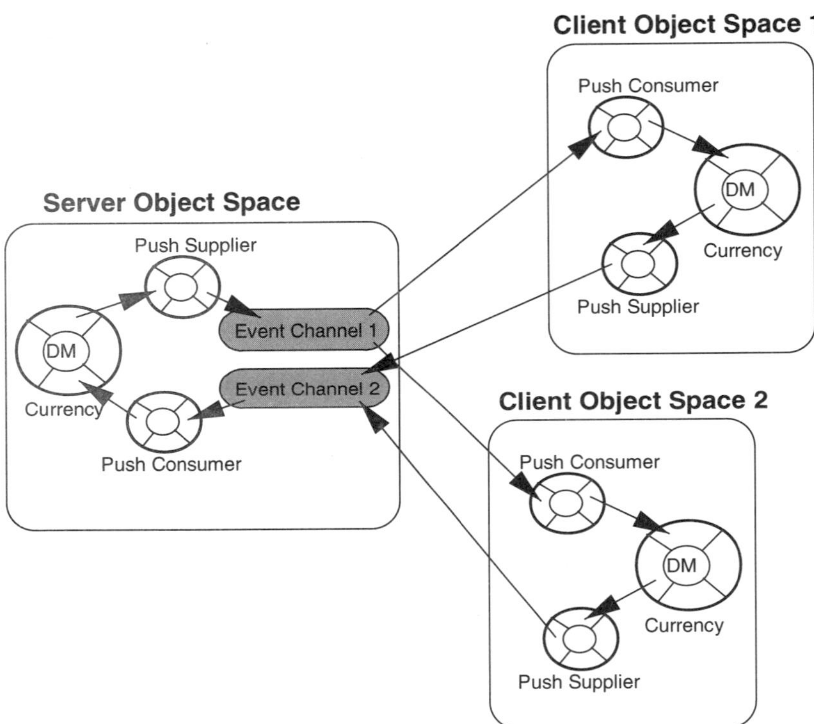

Figure 78. *Using Two Event Channels for Each Server Currency*

With this approach, an exchange rate update request sent from any client currency's push supplier is received only by the corresponding push consumer on the server. The server currency processes this event and then uses its push supplier to propagate the new exchange rate to the clients. This time, only the corresponding push consumers on the clients receive the event.

Using the two event channels approach ensures that clients modify an exchange rate value only after the server has successfully applied the change.

Part 4

Distributed Object Applications: The Rest of the Story

15 Testing Distributed Applications

Object-oriented testing starts early and spans the development life cycle, validating the quality and effectiveness of an application. There is no best testing methodology, because every project has its own requirements. Object-oriented testing varies substantially from traditional testing because of the following characteristics of OO software development:

- Incremental and iterative development
- Inheritance.

In general, the testing concept should establish a sequence of tasks that must be carried out to measure the quality of the different work products being developed. These tasks fall within three main testing categories:

- Model testing

- Class and unit testing
- Integration testing.

Below we briefly discuss these testing categories.

Model Testing

Although each project can have different models, all models must be validated for consistency and completeness.

Class and Unit Testing

Although continuous unit testing is performed during the development process, a formal testing process is required. The formal testing process can include the partial results obtained from the unit tests done during development. In the formal testing process, each class method and each instance method should be categorized as one of the following methods:

- **Simple** So simple that a visual inspection is sufficient
- **Inspect** Not complex and requires only a formal inspection
- **Test** Complex enough to be formally inspected and subject to dynamic testing.

The tester must have a list of all methods from all of the classes of a subsystem. On this list the tester can see and change, if required, the category of each method and the result of each test.

All errors found during class and unit testing must be reported in an appropriate way so that the analysis and design models can be updated if required.

Integration Testing

Besides class and unit testing there must exist a *subsystem testing* during which a number of test cases are performed and results are obtained. If the testing process is executed by using an advanced testing tool, some important information can be gathered, such as how many times each method is called (this also identifies unused methods), the average time that it takes to execute each method, the number of instantiations of each class, and the variables used and not used.

When we deal with distributed applications, there are additional items to consider when testing an application:

- ❑ What happens if the activator is not working?
- ❑ What happens if the remote object space is down?
- ❑ How are TCP/IP problems handled?
- ❑ Are error messages displayed in the right object space? When a remote object is used, errors within that object's method should not be signaled in the remote object space, but in the local object space.

It is also important to know about the tools that the VisualAge Distributed feature provides to help the developer test and debug a distributed application.

At the end of every iteration, the testing process may go through distribution. However, we think it is more worthwhile for most applications to be developed through the first iteration before testing distribution.

16

Run-time Configuration Considerations

Once an application has been implemented and tested through several iterations, the final product must be built and distributed.

This chapter includes the following sections:

- "Building the Final Product" introduces the packaging process.
- "Keeping Application Components in Sync" explores ways to manage a deployed application.

Building the Final Product

The building process of a distributed application is very similar to the one required for a nondistributed application. There are, however a few additional steps and items to consider. The building process utilizes the IBM packager tool.

Preparation

The following activities must be done prior to packaging:

1. Load the desired application versions.
2. Ensure that the correct prerequisites for your distributed application are set. Use the following guidelines to decide which applications from the Distributed feature to include as prerequisites:

   - ❑ If your application uses the basic functions of distributed object spaces, include *DsPackagingApp*. This prerequisite applies to any application that uses the Distributed feature.
   - ❑ If your application uses a name server to manage object references, include *DtNameServerApplication*.
   - ❑ If your application uses object references but does not use the name server, include *DtObjectReferenceApplication*.

   Remember also to include the normal prerequisites for any Smalltalk or VisualAge application.
3. In the Transcript window, select **Options**, **Reset Distributed System...**. This step ensures that there are no connections to your object space. You cannot package your image if you currently have connections to other object spaces.
4. In the Transcript window, select **Options**, **Enable packaging** from the **Distribution tools** menu. This option loads special configurations of the Distributed classes that are required for runtime packaging.
5. When you select **Enable packaging**, you disable communication with other object spaces, delete all object profiles, and disable the object visualizer. To re-enable communication, profiling, and visualizing, you must select **Options**, **Enable communication** from the **Distribution tools** menu.
6. Set the name server to be archived.

   If your application uses a persistent name server, the name server loads its contents from an archive file during image startup. Be sure to include any required name server archive files along with your packaged application.

   Using a persistent name server also makes it possible for you to dynamically modify the contents of the name server without repackaging your image. Because the archive file is separate from the image file, you can change the object references in the name server by changing the contents of the archive file. You can do this by editing the persistent name server from within the name servers browser on a development system. After you have made the necessary changes, do one of the following to save the new information to the archive file:

- ❑ Enter the Smalltalk development environment
- ❑ Select **Archive**, **Save To Archive Now** from the pop-up menu in the name servers list.

After you have saved the archive file, you can copy the updated file to the run-time system. The next time you start the run-time image, the name server will use the object references in the new archive file.

If your packaged application uses a temporary name server rather than a persistent name server, the contents of the name server are saved as part of the image. To change the contents of a temporary name server, therefore, you must repackage the run-time image.

Packaging the Application

You can now proceed with packaging the run-time image just as you would any IBM Smalltalk or VisualAge application. (See the IBM Smalltalk User's Guide for more information about packaging run-time images.)

Keeping Application Components in Sync

The Distributed feature verifies that connections between object spaces are made with the same level of the object space run-time services at either end. The distribution matrix enables you to use configuration maps to store the necessary configuration information for the final layout of your subsystems.

It is the application's responsibility to ensure that the components packaged within the images are compatible with one another. Maintaining systems in the production environment can cause mismatches across components if some users do not update their software. Here are some suggestions to safeguard against these problems:

- ❑ Include verification code within your application which matches application version numbers found in the development library with those packaged for run-time.
- ❑ Use the name server in each object space to store supported version identifiers. These identifiers could be checked upon object space connection to validate compatibility. If these version identifiers are stored in a persistent name server, the name server archive file can be updated at run-time to specify new versions which are compatible. String references are ideal for this purpose.

We hope these suggestions will generate additional ideas suitable for your environment.

17

Optimization and Performance Tuning

This chapter is meant to be the focal point for all optimization and performance issues related to the Distributed feature.*

- "The Golden Rules" introduces the general guidelines for improving the performance of a distributed application.
- "Optimization Through Design" covers additional issues to be considered during application design.
- "Optimization Summary" contains a summary to be used as a quick reference during an actual project.

* You might also want to check Chapter 18, "Lessons Learned, Hints, and Tips" which contains further hints and tips.

Note: Paragraphs that begin with **Distributed FCE** contain comments on the tuning steps we applied in our residency project, described in Introduction to the Distributed FCE Case Study on page 119.

The Golden Rules

Distribution must be designed!

Every consideration of how to optimize and tune a distributed application is based on the following "Golden Rules":

The Golden Rules

1. Maximize local references!
2. Minimize remote messages!
3. Do not wait unless you have to!

First Rule: Maximize Local References

Our first golden rule tells us to *Maximize local references!*. The reasons are obvious:

- Local messages are faster than remote messages
- Local debugging is faster than distributed debugging.

To adhere to the first rule, consider the following recommendations:

- Make temporary copies.

  Several methods (all starting with *dsPerformWithLocalResult:*) are available within the distribution toolkit to perform remote methods and get a local copy of the result value. In addition, *asDsByValueObject* can be used for any parameter of a remote message to pass that parameter by value rather than by reference. For example, instead of

  ```
  aRemoteObject message: localObject
  ```

  you can use

  ```
  aRemoteObject message: localObject asDsByValueObject
  ```

  to have *localObject* copied by value to the remote object space.

  For arrays, the corresponding method is *asDsByValueArray*.

  See the *VisualAge Distributed User's Guide* for a complete reference of the application programming interface.

Distributed FCE: In the third iteration of our residency project, we used *dsPerformWithLocalResult:* to get a copy of the complete currency list object structure from the server object space.

- ❑ Cluster related objects and classes together, that is, within the same object space.

  Each class can exist in one or more object spaces. An instance must be in the same object space as its class.

- ❑ When appropriate, choose *location-independent data types* for attributes and actions (of parts), as well as for parameters and return values (of methods) that are accessed over the network.[*] Location-independent means that instances of these types are always local, regardless of what object space refers to them. Instead of creating shadow objects, these objects are copied between object spaces. Location-independent data types are:

  - ➢ Numbers[†]
  - ➢ Strings
  - ➢ Symbols
  - ➢ Dates
  - ➢ Times
  - ➢ Boolean data (*true*, *false*)
  - ➢ UndefinedObject (*nil*).

  These objects are location-independent because they are immutable, that is, they are not capable of changing state. Therefore, the identity of a location-independent object is unimportant; any copy is valid.

  Because every reference to a remote location-independent object (such as an integer in a remote object space) is resolved automatically to a local object, the use of location-independent objects is an easy way of minimizing references to remote objects and network messaging.

  For example, instead of using an array of three strings as a result value, you could combine the strings into one large string with appropriate separators. Returning the large string creates a local copy in the client object space, so the access to each of the strings can be done locally.

  Distributed FCE: In the second iteration of our residency project, we used an integer representation of the exchange rate value instead of a float since that value is sent between the different object spaces.

[*] The terms *transportable* , *immutable* , and *manifest* data types are sometimes used as synonyms for location-independent data types.

[†] At the time this document was written, decimals, that is, instances of the *Decimal* class, were **not** location-independent. The problem has been reported to the product development team and should be fixed in a later release.

- ❑ Introduce new *light objects* to be used within the VisualAge Composition Editor when you notice heavy traffic between user interface models (views) and business domain models.

  Due to the architecture of VisualAge's event/notification mechanism, lots of messages are sent between a view and an underlying part to handle the connections. Let us look at two examples:

  - ➢ To show dynamic pop-up menus, the VisualAge Composition Editor asks each part for its public interface, its preferred connection features, and so on.
  - ➢ In the first iteration of our distributed FCE application, we defined an attribute-to-attribute connection between the items of a table and the collection of currencies of our currency list object.

    When we opened that view, that connection was resolved column by column, row by row, to get the actual values for the table cells. This meant that no more than about `2 x columns x rows` shadow objects were being created temporarily (one shadow for the currency object and the value of each cell). As you might expect, this could take some time, depending on the size of the table...

  To overcome the problem of many messages, you can implement local parts that interact as an interface between the local view and remote object. These kinds of technical parts we call *light objects*. They should provide a functional subset of their counterparts to handle requests regarding static information like attribute names and preferred connections.

  Of course, all operational functions must be routed to the real object; so, the light objects need a pointer to a shadow of the remote object.

Second Rule: Minimize Remote Messages

During code development, be aware that the *number of messages* is much more critical for good performance than the actual *amount of data* contained in a message (like parameters, return values).

Our second golden rule tells us to *Minimize remote messages!*. The event profiler and object visualizer, introduced in the section titled The IBM Smalltalk Distribution Toolkit on page 20, can be used to track the number of remote messages and to analyze the traffic between two or more object spaces. The Distributed feature API provides several methods to create different kinds of event profiles:

dtProfile (Object instance method)
Messages to an instance (This can be an instance of class *DsObjectSpace*; in this case, you are profiling the messages crossing the object space boundary.)

dtProfileNext (Object class method)
Messages to the next instance of a class

dtProfileNext: (Object class method)
Messages to the next n instances of a class

dtProfileAll (Object class method)
Messages to all instances of a class

To learn more about how to use the event profiler, see the *VisualAge Distributed User's Guide*. This guide also includes complete reference information on the application programming interface.

To adhere to the second rule, consider the following recommendations:

- Create special methods to return collections of results.

  For example, instead of using three different methods to get three attribute values of a remote instance, provide an additional instance method. In the method running in the remote object space, three local messages are used to get the values, and a temporary collection containing all values is passed back to the original sender.

- Create special methods to reduce the message count.

  For example, in the FCE application, we might want to get the exchange rate of a certain currency contained in a remote currency list. One way to achieve this is to code the following:

  ```
  ((aCurrencyList currencies) at: index) exchangeRate
  ```

  That code results in three messages being sent to the remote object space. Furthermore, as shown in Figure 79 on page 180, two additional temporary shadow objects are created in the local object space.

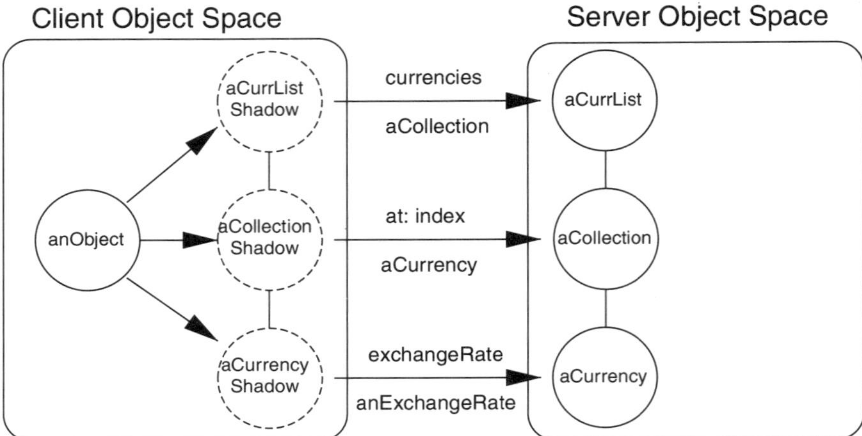

Figure 79. *Messages Example, Before*

By adding a new instance method to the *EmsCurrencyList* class, we can reduce the number of messages to one:

```
aCurrencyList exchangeRateAt: index
```

Figure 80 on page 180 shows the effect of that change.

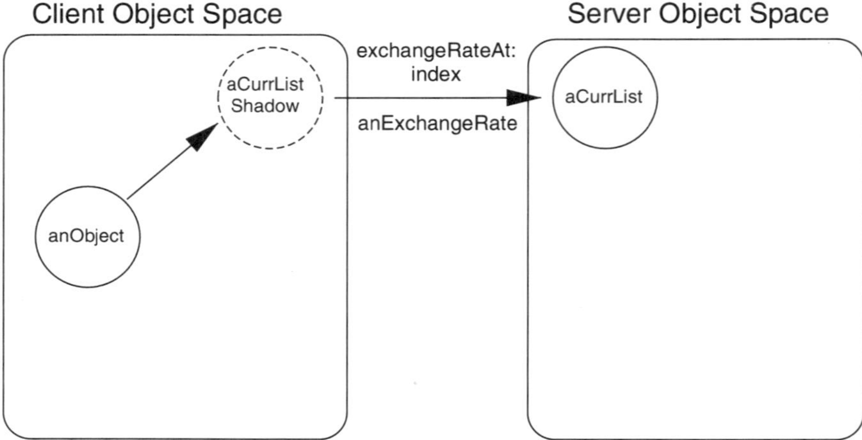

Figure 80. *Messages Example, After*

Distributed FCE: In the second iteration of our residency project, we added a class method *newFor:requester:currencyId:exchangeRate:* instead of using *newFor:* and sending several messages to the instance returned.

Third Rule: Do Not Wait Unless You Have To

Our third golden rule says: *Do not wait unless you have to!*. To adhere to the third rule, consider the following recommendations:

- Use parallel processing to minimize wait times.

  If target objects reside in different object spaces, messages can be processed in parallel on different machines, which usually makes processing even faster.

  The API provided by the Distributed feature toolkit offers extensions that simplify parallel processing:

  dtParallelDo:
  : For any collection, fork a process and evaluate the block for each item in the collection. Wait until all processes have completed.

  dtForkEachAndJoin
  : For a collection of blocks, fork a process for each item (block) and evaluate the block. Wait until all blocks have been completed.

  dtForkEachAndJoinWithMaximum:
  : This extension is like *dtForkEachAndJoin*, but it has a maximum number of processes being created.

  dtForkEachAndContinue
  : For a collection of blocks, fork a process for each item (block) and evaluate the block. Continue without waiting.

  dtForkEachAndContinueWithMaximum:
  : This extension is like *dtForkEachAndContinue*, but it has a maximum number of processes being created.

  to:by:dtParallelDo:, to:dtParallelDo:
  : Fork a process and evaluate the block for each element in the series. Wait until all blocks have completed.

  See the *VisualAge Distributed User's Guide* for complete reference information on the Application Programming Interface (API).

  Figure 81 on page 182 and Figure 82 on page 182 show how to achieve the same results using serial and parallel processing.

Serial

```
self labelForName     setString: aRemoteObject name.
self labelForAddress  setString: aRemoteObject address.
self labelForPhone    setString: aRemoteObject phone.
```

Figure 81. *Parallel Processing Support Example, Before*

Parallel

```
| parallelBlocks |
parallelBlocks := OrderedCollection new.
parallelBlocks
 add: [ self labelForName     setString: aRemoteObject name];
 add: [ self labelForAddress  setString: aRemoteObject address];
 add: [ self labelForPhone    setString: aRemoteObject phone].
parallelBlocks dtForkEachAndJoin.
```

Figure 82. *Parallel Processing Support Example, After*

Distributed FCE: In the second iteration of our residency project, we used *dtForkEachAndContinue* in our broadcast method to notify clients asynchronously when an exchange rate was modified.

- ❑ Be aware of the complexity of processes running in parallel.

  Parallelism cannot in all cases be added as simply as described above. Often, dependencies between different processing blocks require a more sophisticated approach.

Optimization Through Design

In addition to following the golden rules, you can achieve dramatic performance improvements with other changes in the application design.

In Chapter 18, "Lessons Learned, Hints, and Tips" we recommend that you *design in a natural way, then distribute*. However, if you keep distribution in mind during early design phases, you can save a lot of time at the end of a project. Decide whether to implement distribution in IBM Smalltalk or to use other services (for example, DB2/2 client services).

Iterations of Distribution Design

When you initially design an application, you usually divide the application into modules based on its logical or functional parts. However, after you distribute your application across different object spaces across a network, you might find that these *splits* are not optimal. As with everything else in developing OO applications, be prepared for several iterations until you find the optimal distribution design.

There is no rule of thumb. Try to anticipate object space boundaries. Minimize cross-space communication; in other words, avoid having every object communicate with every other object. But, do not go overboard. Designs tend to change during implementation. You can refactor and optimize after the infrastructure is complete.

Be confident! Gaining more experience with the Distributed feature will lead to fewer design mistakes and thus offset the degree of reengineering.

Object Copy Management

Use object mobility to select whether local or remote objects are sent or returned in remote messaging. Put the objects where they will be referenced the most.

Copy global objects that are used frequently. To get a local copy of a remote object, use one of the API methods described in First Rule: Maximize Local References on page 176:

- *asDsByValueObject*
- *asDsByValueArray*
- *dsPerformWithLocalResult:(...)*

If these objects are used as read-only objects, there is nothing more to do. If, however, these objects can be modified and the changes must be reflected at the same time in each client object space, we must implement additional logic to handle updates. In the second iteration of our residency project, we enhanced the basic dependency mechanism provided by the IBM Smalltalk Object class as follows:

1. Each local copy has a (shadow) pointer to the original (remote) object.
2. Each local copy adds itself as a dependent of the remote object.
3. Each local change is routed to the original object.
4. The remote object informs its dependents about any change. We used parallel blocks and the *dtForkEachAndContinue* method to send the update notification to dependents (see Third Rule: Do Not Wait Unless You Have To on page 181). When we use just the

default *broadcast:* or *changed:* methods provided by the object class, the notification process is delayed if one of the dependent object spaces is not available. For example, there might be an open modal dialog on the client system.

5. Local copies react on this notification by updating their local values.

Distributed FCE: In the third iteration of our residency project, the local currency list provides a shadow object of the (remote) server currency list. Local updates of an exchange rate are sent to the central currency list, which propagates this update to all of its dependents.

Object Space Layering

Our implementation of the distributed FCE application involves a client layer and server layer. This results in two kinds of object spaces, a client object space for all user workstations and a server object space on the central server machine.

In a real situation, every client (cashier machine) probably would not directly communicate to the center's computer, but with a local branch server machine. The latter would be the one that requests the list of currencies (including their exchange rates) from the center's computer. Figure 83 on page 185 illustrates the connection between these different object spaces.

Depending on the distances and kinds of connections between the branches and central site, the layering design results in improved performance on the client workstation. Besides, it enables the local branches to work autonomously for some time when the central server is not available.

Uniqueness of Instances

In Chapter 9, "An Approach to VisualAge Application Architecture", we introduced our UNI concept (uniqueness of instances) and described its implementation in our residency project. The intention of the UNI concept is to avoid multiple instances of holding the same information within the same object space. Obviously, this also adds some benefits related to an application's performance.

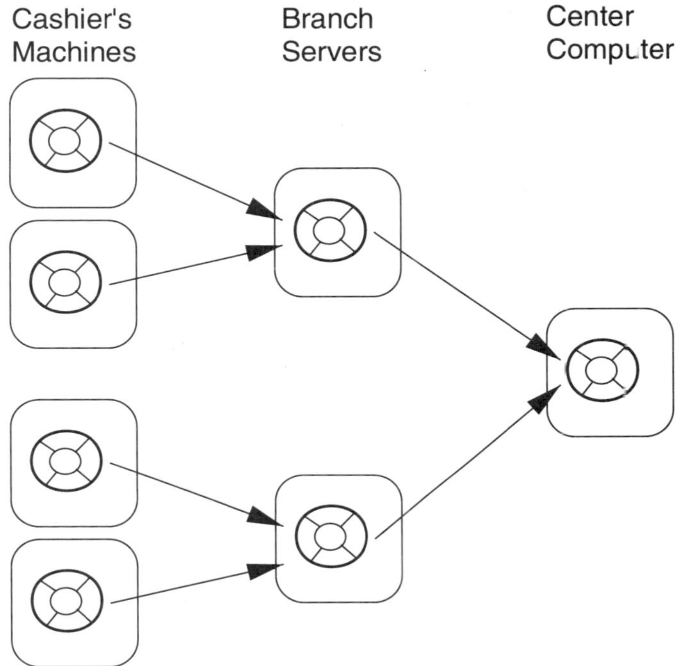

Figure 83. *Object Space Layering*

Preconnect Object Spaces

Preconnect object spaces if you suspect racing conditions will prevail at connection. For example, if client object spaces register themselves at a server object space and the server informs other already-registered clients, synchronization problems could occur.

To preconnect object spaces using name server location references, follow these steps:

1. Add a new name server and call it *Live Object Spaces*.
2. Add a reference to that name server in your *Default* name server. Call it *Link to Live Object Spaces*.
3. Install the reference in your name server chain somewhere as a next name server.
4. For each object space you will be working with, enter a location reference in the *Live Object Spaces* name server.
5. Make sure that the following code is executed during the startup of your application (during development, you might want to enter the code into a workspace and execute it):

```
| nameServer remoteObjSpace |
nameServer :=
  (NameServerList default
    referenceAtFirstIdentifier: 'Live Object Spaces') shadow.
nameServer localKeys do: [ :eachID |
  remoteObjSpace := (nameServer referenceAt: eachID) objectSpace.
  (Point dsInSpace: remoteObjSpace) new.
].
```

More information on how to use a common name server for all object spaces during application development can be found in Development and Setup on page 191 . For a detailed description of how to define name servers, see the *VisualAge Distributed User's Guide*.

Optimization Summary

The following list is a summary of all optimization steps mentioned above. You can use it for a quick reference during an actual project.

- ❑ Golden Rule 1: Maximize local references.
- ❑ Golden Rule 2: Minimize remote messages.
- ❑ Golden Rule 3: Do not wait unless you have to.
- ❑ Make temporary copies when needed.
- ❑ Cluster related objects and classes together.
- ❑ Use location-independent data types.
- ❑ Introduce light models.
- ❑ Create special methods to return collections of results.
- ❑ Create special methods to reduce the message count.
- ❑ Use parallel processing.
- ❑ Be aware of the complexity of processes running in parallel.
- ❑ Try to anticipate object space boundaries.
- ❑ Avoid having every object communicate with every other object.
- ❑ Be prepared for several iterations.
- ❑ Use object mobility.
- ❑ Copy global objects that are used frequently.
- ❑ Implement object space layers.
- ❑ Implement uniqueness of instances.
- ❑ Preconnect object spaces.

18 Lessons Learned, Hints, and Tips

General Advice

Design in a natural way, then distribute!

This chapter summarizes the lessons, hints, and tips from our residency project.* We also include valuable information from the developers and testers of the Distributed feature.

- "Experiences During the Quick Tour" recaps the experiences we had during our quick tour.
- "Modal Dialogs" describes what to attend to when using modal dialogs.

* Optimization and performance-related issues are covered in Chapter 17, "Optimization and Performance Tuning".

- "Explicit Notification Mechanisms" provides hints on how to implement your own notification mechanism.
- "Configuration Management" contains some recommendations on the management of distributed VisualAge applications.
- "Development and Setup" describes what to consider during application development using the Distributed feature.
- "Concurrency" provides some hints on how to handle concurrency conflicts.
- "Using Callbacks" describes the usage of callbacks on object space boundaries.
- "Further Hints and Tips" contains hints and tips that are not covered in previous sections.

Note: Paragraphs that begin with **Distributed FCE** contain comments on the lessons learned from our residency project, described in Introduction to the Distributed FCE Case Study on page 119.

Experiences During the Quick Tour

In A Quick Tour Through Distributed Object Land on page 57, we made the following observations based on our experiences during the quick tour:

- It is sometimes necessary to interrupt suspended operations or "frozen" user interfaces. There are four ways to break into a suspended process. (Be sure to try these methods in the order given!)

  1. Press the **Alt+SysRq** (System Request) keys simultaneously and hold them until a beep sounds. This usually brings up a debug window. Sometimes, a user break must be performed several times before a break occurs.
  2. Press and hold the **Ctrl** key, then press the **Esc** key once. Wait about 15 seconds. One of two things will happen:

  a. The OS/2 Window List will be displayed. Select the Transcript window from this list and press Delete. This will usually close the Smalltalk application. Doing so can cause the image to close without an option to save it. If this happens, you must recover all work since the last image save.

  b. Sometimes this will present a window that says a task is not responding and asks you to press Enter to close it. If you press Enter, you can often close the application. In IBM Smalltalk and VisualAge, using this technique to close any window will cause the image to be closed: consequently, all work since the last save must be recovered.

3. To execute system shutdown, press the **Ctrl+Alt+Delete** keys simultaneously or use the **Shut down** option in the OS/2 desktop context menu.
4. Turn the power off on your machine.

- To use the visual programming features provided by the Composition Editor, we must include all the necessary model classes in the client object spaces. This can be done with the **Local load** service of the configuration map.
- Distributed processing can be tested with the **Distributed load**; however, views must be opened explicitly from a Workspace window by executing the following:

  ```
  ViewClass newPart openWidget
  ```

  As an alternative, we can select the desired view in the VisualAge Organizer and press the **Test** button.
- The **Distributed load** will be unsuccessful if the image contains instances of local classes that are to be unloaded from the local object space (for example, because they will reside remotely). To get rid of these instances, enter and execute the following Smalltalk code:

  ```
  ClassToBeUnloaded allInstances do: [ :i | i become: nil ]
  ```
- Using the event mechanisms and connections provided by the VisualAge environment results in numerous messages being sent between objects during run-time, for example, to build and synchronize a connection. If you move objects to remote object spaces, this might seriously impact performance.

Modal Dialogs

As recommended in the CUA guidelines, avoid using modal user dialogs unless it is necessary. This guideline becomes even more important when using distributed applications. Keep in mind that a modal dialog on one object space also blocks other object spaces if they try to communicate with the blocked one at the same time.

If you use the Distributed feature to develop traditional client/server concepts (clients requesting services from server machines), there should be no problem. Usually, the server is an unattended machine so there must not be any modal dialogs.

If your application uses advanced client/server mechanisms like the *active server* or *peer-to-peer* (see Chapter 3, "Applications Suitable for the Distributed Feature"), you must take care of modal dialogs. Consider using asynchronous messages (provided by the *dtForkEachAndContinue* API method) to send information to a client that might be unavailable.

Distributed FCE: In the second iteration of our residency project, we had to use *dtForkEachAndContinue* to inform clients about an exchange rate object, otherwise the modal *CwMessagePrompter* we used on the clients to show a user message would have blocked the server from further processing.

Explicit Notification Mechanisms

In iteration two of our residency project, we modified our object model by moving the exchange rate attribute of the *EmsCurrency* class to a new *EmsExchangeRate* class that resided in the server object space only. A local currency instance held a pointer to its corresponding exchange rate object.

The reason for that iteration was that the exchange rate was the only attribute of the currency that could be modified in our application. To achieve better performance, we did not want to access all other (static) attributes remotely.

Using this approach, we had to provide an explicit dependency/notification mechanism to reflect updates of the exchange rate in every client view connected to a currency. In Applying the Event Services Framework on page 159 we discuss how to use the event services framework as an alternative to our approach.

Distributed FCE: The technique we used is the same as when implementing an object copy management and is therefore described in Object Copy Management on page 183.

Configuration Management

The following tips refer to the management of VisualAge classes, applications, and configuration maps:

- ❑ Design the system with distribution in mind.

  If you use the distribution matrix, the unit of distribution is the application, not the class. Try to anticipate the number of applications needed. For example, in the second iteration of our distributed FCE application, we had three different types of classes:

  - ➢ Classes that were used only in client object spaces

- Classes that were used only in server object spaces
- Classes that were used in both client and server object spaces.

Therefore, we had to define three different applications to be able to load only the necessary classes into each object space.

- Remember to release classes.

To test a distributed application on two or more machines using the distributed load feature, you must first assign a version to the classes and release them to be able to load the containing application into different object spaces.

- Distribute changes to *owned* object spaces only.

To test minor changes of one or more classes, you do not necessarily have to assign a version and release these classes. Instead, you can use the **Distribute changes** action. It is found in the pop-up menu of an application (with this method, you must specify the target object space) and in the pop-up menu of a location that is defined within a given distribution matrix.

Be careful when using the **Distribute changes** action! Only the developer of a class edition can load the edition into an object space. For example, when a VisualAge user *Sven* makes changes to a class and tries to distribute the changes into a remote object space *Matti*, the load will be unsuccessful unless the current user, that is, the image owner of object space *Matti*, is set to *Sven*.

To overcome this problem, either you must be the owner of all object spaces that you want to distribute changes into, or you must assign a version to the classes, release them, and use the distribution matrix.

- Minimize the number of object space configurations.

Do not define more object space configurations than are necessary. Sometimes it can be better to load classes into object spaces (even though they are not used there), as compared to defining and maintaining too many applications.

- Extensions to location-independent classes must be visible on both sides.

If you extend a location-independent class (see First Rule: Maximize Local References on page 176), remember to define the extensions in the application that will be loaded on the client and server side. Otherwise, these methods might be undefined in some object spaces.

Development and Setup

- Optimum distributed development includes team collaboration. Proximity of application developers influences code quality.

- ❑ Use similar VisualAge installations.

  On each development workstation, use the same drive and directory names to install the VisualAge client portions. This makes it easier to maintain common configurations.

- ❑ Use only one activator configuration file.

  Define the key entries for all object spaces in that configuration file and place the file in a shared directory somewhere in the development LAN.

- ❑ Minimize the number of images to load.

  If several clients have identical configurations, define a distribution matrix to load the image for one of them, save the image, and then copy it to a central distribution point. Start the other clients using the image.

  Loading every client using one distribution matrix takes more time, and, in addition, the distribution matrix is more difficult to maintain.

- ❑ Plan to re-enter TCP/IP addresses.

  If you do not have a TCP/IP name server that provides the mapping from host names to addresses, you must re-enter all object references if TCP/IP addresses change. Also, if you move a class to another object space during development, remember to change the corresponding object reference.

- ❑ Use a common name server.

  Define one name server in an appropriate object space to be used by all development object spaces. In the local name servers, add a reference to the name server and install this reference in the name server chain somewhere as a next name server.

  Define the references that are needed by all or most of the clients in the common name server.

- ❑ Use identical names for both the TCP/IP host name and corresponding object space name (object space keys).

- ❑ Use variables within the Composition Editor instead of parts.

  Use variables instead of parts for classes that might be remote. Otherwise, if you do not have the class in your local object space, you cannot open the Composition Editor. Provide scripts or connections to fill the variables with actual instances during runtime.

Concurrency

If you expect multiple clients to update the same remote object concurrently, you must provide mechanisms to overcome the problems of racing conditions and of blocking situations (see Accessing the Same Model Object from Two Clients on page 67). The Semaphore class contained in IBM Smalltalk can be used for these purposes.

new (class method)
: Create a new semaphore to use with the *wait* and *signal* instance methods.

forMutualExclusion (class method)
: Create a new semaphore that serves to ensure mutual exclusion of a resource using the *critical:* instance method. This type of semaphore is also called a *mutex semaphore*.

wait (instance method)
: Wait until the semaphore is signaled.

signal (instance method)
: Signal the semaphore, or allow the next waiting process to continue.

critical: aBlock (instance method)
: Get exclusive access to a resource controlled by a mutex semaphore, execute the block, and free the resource after completion.

Attention: To avoid lockups, do not allow a single process to recursively enter a critical block.

Using Callbacks

You can use callbacks to get a notification when communication between two object spaces occurs. Several class methods are provided in the *DsCallbackRec* class to create callbacks for different kinds of events such as:

dsSendOpInCallback
: Message received from an object space.

dsSendOpOutCallback
: Message sent to an object space.

dsResultOpInCallback
: Result received from an object space.

dsResultOpOutCallback
: Result sent to an object space.

dsObjectSpaceConnectCallback
Connected to an object space.

dsObjectSpaceConnectionFailedCallback
Failed to connect to an object space.

dsObjectSpaceDisconnectCallback
Disconnected from an object space.

The *VisualAge Distributed User's Guide* contains a complete reference on the application programming interface.

The following code provides an example how to add a callback for a specific event:

```
...
  anObject dsSpace addCallback:
    (DsCallbackRec dsObjectSpaceDisconnectCallback
      receiver: self
      selector: #disconnected:clientData:callData:
      clientData: 'disconnect').
...

disconnected: anObjectSpace clientData: text callData: aCallDataRec
  System prompt: 'The requested system has been disconnected'.
...
```

Figure 84 on page 194 shows the different events occurring during remote messaging.

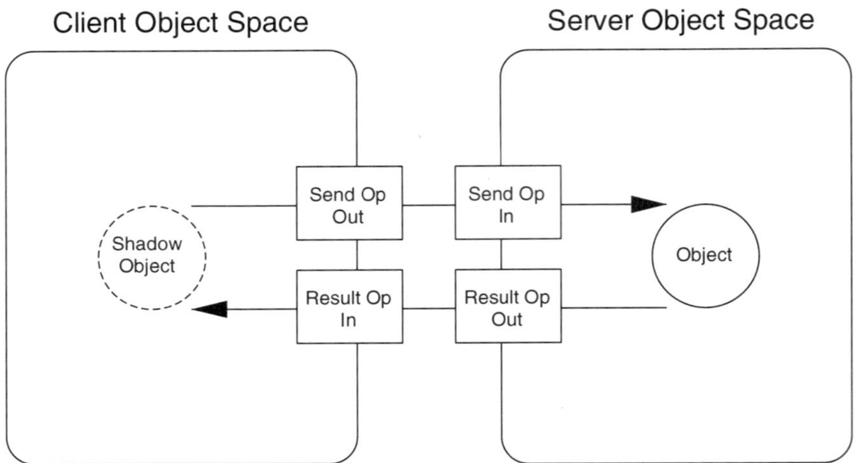

Figure 84. *Callbacks*

Further Hints and Tips

In this section we provide additional hints and tips which we did not cover in previous sections:

- ❑ Connected object spaces are saved with an image and reconnected at startup. The logical processes and remote objects on each object space will be accessible. However, if the connection states of the two object spaces do not match, both will be automatically reset to an initial connection state.

  To disable the reconnection feature, execute the following Smalltalk code:

  ```
  DsDistributedSystem saveConnectionState: false
  ```

- ❑ If you attempt to access an object that cannot be reached (the target object space cannot be found, the target machine is turned off, the activator on the target machine is not started, TCP/IP is not started, or other problems), you will get an *unavailable object exception* when you send the first message.

  There are two ways of avoiding walkbacks due to unavailable object exceptions:

  - ➢ You can wrap the code in exception handling, as shown in the following example:

    ```
    | objRef |
    objRef := NameServerList default
           referenceAtFirstIdentifier: 'Kitty Hawk Casino'.
    [ Transcript cr; show: 'The object is:',
                     (objRef shadow printString)
    ] when: (DsDistributedSystem unavailableObjectException)
      do: [ :signal |
        Transcript show: 'The object is not available'.
        signal exitWith: 'Bummer, dude!'
      ].
    ```

➢ You can use the *dtYourself* and *dtIsAvailable* messages. The *dtYourself* message will attempt to connect and answer the remote object from the shadow; the *dtIsAvailable* message will not send a message but will answer as to whether the answer from *dtYourself* is an available object.

Consider the following example:

```
| myShadow myObjRef |
myObjRef := NameServerList default
       referenceAtFirstIdentifier: 'Kitty Hawk Casino'.

myShadow := myObjRef shadow.  "No message sent"

(myShadow dtYourself dtIsAvailable) ifTrue: [
  Transcript cr; show: 'The Object is: ',myShadow print
String.
] ifFalse: [
  Transcript show: 'The object is not available'.
].
```

The *dtYourself* message will answer an instance of *DtUnavailableObject* if it encounters the unavailable object exception condition. If you fix the exception condition (usually, by starting the activator), you can send *dtYourself* to the *DtUnavailableObject* instance again and it will try to get the remote object.

❑ Shadow objects behave somewhat like global variables. They use an object reference to locate the remote object they represent. The shadows look for their remote object (using the address in the object reference) every time they relay a message. Thus, if a shadow references a global in another object space and the value of that global changes (for example, from 1 to 2), a second reference to it will answer its new value (for example, 2).

The side effect of this is that shadow objects do not adhere to the object identity rule. In other words, you may have two shadows that represent the same object, but for which the identity operator (==) will answer *false*. The equality operator (=) will answer the proper value.

Other remote objects that are not created directly from object references, such as objects that are created as answers to messages to other remote objects, still adhere to the object identity rule.

❑ The Smalltalk compiler will optimize out certain messages when a method is saved. This optimization introduces some complexity for distributed support, which relies on the fact that messages are sent, and are then forwarded to their remote counterparts. Two messages that are optimized out are *isNil* and *yourself*. In remote applications, use the *dtIsNil* and *dtYourself* messages instead. The *dtIsNil* and *dtYourself* messages work on local objects as well.

- Creating event profiles takes a few seconds and the performance of the messages being sent to the object (or objects) will be degraded as the messages are recorded. Thus, use profiling sparingly and turn profiling off (or delete the profile) when it is not needed.

  Some instances cannot be profiled and attempting to profile them will result in a walkback. These instances are all implementers of *dtCanBeProfiled* that answer *false*.

  Note also that when an instance is profiled, it becomes *monitored*. Packaged images should not include monitored objects. In case of error, or to remove monitors for other reasons, use the **Unlink** and **Delete All Profiles** actions under the **Repair** menu item in the **Profiles** menu of the profiles browser.

  When object profiles are created, mutual exclusion semaphores are used to avoid conflicts. If an error occurs, sometimes critical sections get interrupted, and processes begin to freeze. In these situations, use the **Signal All Waiting Processes** action under the **Repair** menu item in the **Profiles** menu of the profiles browser. You may have to interrupt a locked user interface process first.

Part 5

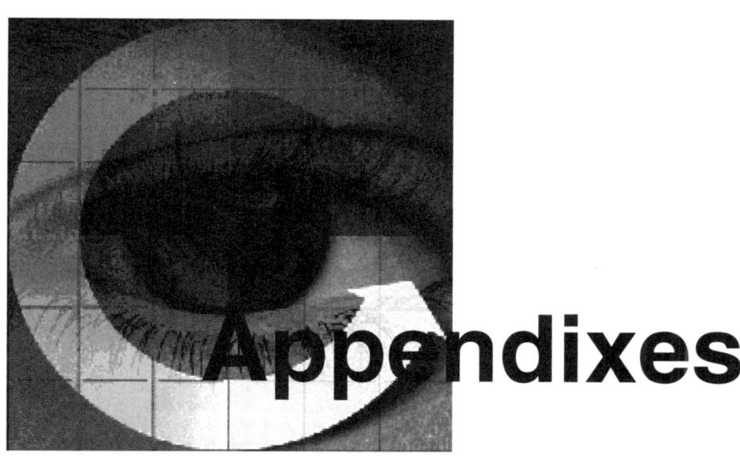

Appendixes

A Requirements Specifications

This section describes the specifications of the FCE application. It is important to understand the functional requirements for the branch and central bank and see how they differ from each other.

- "Branch Functions" summarizes the main functions performed at the branches.
- Central Bank Functions on page 203 lists the functions performed at the central site.

Branch Functions

The main functions performed at the branch regarding foreign currency are the following:

- Manage customer orders.

➢ Customer purchases from branch cashier.

This is the most frequently performed function of this subapplication.

- The usual activities of this function are:
- Check stock levels.
- Reduce branch stock level.
- Determine currency and/or check denominations.
- Obtain exchange rate.
- Print tab.
- Generate accounting entries.
- Handle multiple currencies and checks.
- Handle country restrictions, warnings, and general information.

➢ Customer sells to branch cashier.

Tourists and travelers returning with foreign currency or travel checks sell or cash in to the bank.

The usual activities of this function are:

- Obtain exchange rates.
- Increase branch stock level.
- Print tab.
- Generate accounting entries.
- Handle multiple currencies and checks.
- Handle country restrictions, warnings, and general information.

➢ Customer order form cannot be satisfied.

Not all branches stock currencies and checks. Very few branches stock the full range because it is not economical to do so. All orders that cannot be met by the branch are routed to the central bank.

- The usual activities of this function are:
- Handle country restrictions, warnings, and general information.
- Reduce branch stock level.
- Determine currency and/or check denominations.
- Obtain exchange rate.
- Print tab.
- Take deposit if non-customer.
- Generate accounting entries.
- Handle multiple currencies and checks.

- ❑ Manage the cashiers.
  - ➢ Reconcile cashier stock.

    At the end of each day, or more frequently, each cashier must verify that the checks and foreign currency in his/her cabinet are equal to the totals held in the system. This is done by viewing the values held for each denomination, within each currency or check.

    The usual activities of this function are:

    - Obtain exchange rate for each currency or check.
    - Display each currency or check totals and local currency equivalent.
    - Order replenishment stock if minimum stock quantity reached.
    - Send excess stock to the central bank if maximum stock quantity exceeded.
    - Raise or lower compensating accounting entries for small losses or gains.
    - Reconcile archives.
- ❑ Manage the branch.

  At the end of each day, the requests of the cashiers are consolidated.

  - ➢ Branch stock replenishment.
  - ➢ General inquiry of branch stocks.
  - ➢ General inquiry of central stock.
  - ➢ Forgery recognition (computer image).

Central Bank Functions

The central bank is responsible for supplying foreign currency and travelers checks to the branches and for selling off excess foreign currency received from the branches. The central bank does this by dealing on the foreign currency markets, arranging bulk shipments at favorable exchange rates.

The functions performed at the central bank include:

- ❑ Manage the bank.
  - ➢ Handle branch orders.

    Orders from branches are normally for several currencies and checks. All orders are processed in batch mode, bulk quantities are picked, delivery arrangements are made, postal charges are set, stock levels are reduced, and accounting entries are passed between branch and central accounts.

    - Branch order functions include:
    - Check currency and check denominations.
    - Check stock levels.
    - Print picking lists.
    - Reduce central bank stock level.
    - Obtain exchange rate.
    - Weigh packages and establish postal charges.
    - Print branch documents.
    - Pass accounting entries.
  - ➢ Handle customer orders.

    When a branch has been unable to satisfy any part of a customer order, the whole order is then supplied by the central bank.

    Customer order functions include:

    - Handle currency and check denominations.
    - Handle check stock levels.
    - Handle single and multiple currency and checks.
    - Print picking lists.
    - Reduce central bank stock level.
    - Obtain exchange rate.
    - Weigh packages and establish postal charges.
    - Print branch documents.
    - Pass accounting entries.
  - ➢ Handle branch excess.

    Excess foreign currency received from the branches is counted, reconciled with the branch delivery record, and added to central currency stocks.

    Branch excess functions include:

    - Handle currency and check denominations.
    - Handle check stock levels.
    - Handle single and multiple currency and checks.
    - Print picking lists.
    - Reduce central bank stock level.
    - Obtain exchange rate.
    - Weigh packages and establish postal charges.
    - Print branch documents.
    - Pass accounting entries.

➢ Reconcile central stock.

At the end of each day, or more frequently, the central bank verifies that the checks and foreign currency in its stocks are equal to the totals held in the system.

Central stock reconciliation functions include:

- Obtain exchange rate for each currency or check.
- Display each currency or check totals and local currency equivalent.
- Order replenishment stock if minimum stock quantity reached.
- Send excess, if maximum stock quantity exceeded, to other banks (U.S.A. and abroad) through foreign note dealers.
- Raise or lower compensating accounting entries for small losses or gains.
- Reconcile archives.

➢ Maintain branch stock limits.

Periodically, the stock held at each branch is reviewed to check whether the minimum and maximum stock levels are still appropriate.

Stock limit processing includes:

- See if the general inquiry stock levels are still valid.
- Change the stock level minimum or maximum.
- Add or remove stock type or denomination.

➢ Maintain central bank stock limits.

Similar to branch, but includes issues of bulk transport, international availability, and capacity.

➢ Maintain exchange rates.

Dealers maintain the rates for each currency and check by comparing with other banks' rates, general market rates from Reuters, telerate, and the like, and by checking general availability.

➢ Conduct miscellaneous transactions.

- Maintain forgery images.
- Create, amend, and delete currency images.
- Produce labels, envelopes, and documents.
- Produce branch sack labels and documents.

B

Database Definition

This appendix lists the data definition language for the two tables we used in our implementation. To build and populate the tables we recommend that you use the appropriate DB2/2 tools.

COUNTRY Table

```
CREATE TABLE COUNTRY
       (CNTY_NAME              CHAR(30)    NOT NULL,
        CNTY_ID                CHAR(3)     NOT NULL,
        PRIMARY KEY (CNTY_NAME)
```

CURRENCY Table

```
CREATE TABLE CURRENCY
       (CURR_ID                  CHAR(3)      NOT NULL,
        CURR_NAME                CHAR(16)     NOT NULL,
        CURR_CNTY                CHAR(30)     NOT NULL,
        CURR_XRATE_BUY           DEC(8,4)     NOT NULL,
        CURR_XRATE_SELL          DEC(8,4)     NOT NULL,
        CURR_FORG_INFO           CHAR(40),
        CURR_DESC                CHAR(80),
        PRIMARY KEY (CURR_ID),
        FOREIGN KEY CURRCNTY (CURR_CNTY)
            REFERENCES COUNTRY ON DELETE CASCADE)
```

C Sample Code

This appendix lists the applications and their classes for our three project iterations. For visual parts, the screen layouts are provided. For non-visual parts, we provided the public interface. For both visual and non-visual parts, we include listings of the methods (Smalltalk scripts).

This appendix consists of the following sections:

- "First Iteration" contains the applications, parts, and methods of the first version of our application.
- "Second Iteration" contains the changes from the first to the second version of our application.
- "Third Iteration" contains the changes from the second to the third version of our application.

First Iteration

The first iteration consists of two applications:

- *EmsAFceClientApp* as shown in Figure 85 on page 210 contains all classes for the client object space.
- *EmsAFceServerApp* as shown in Figure 86 on page 211 contains all classes for the server object space.

EmsAFceServerApp is a prerequisite application for *EmsAFceClientApp*.

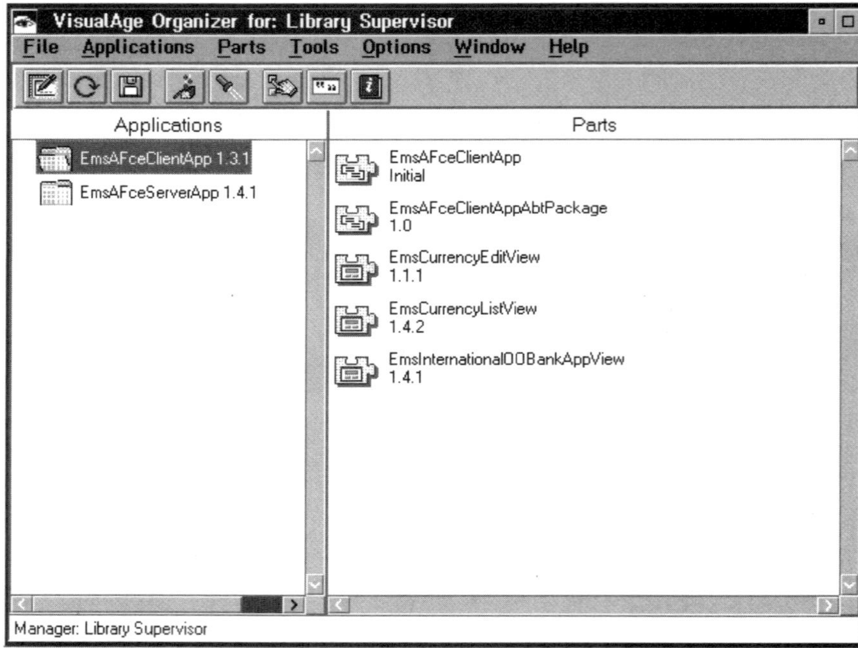

Figure 85. *EmsAFceClientApp Application, First Iteration*

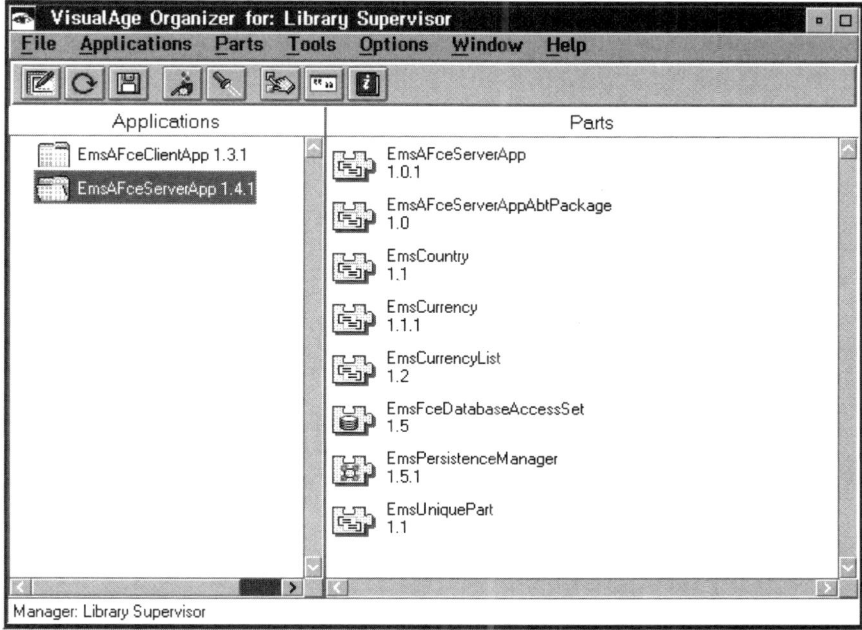

Figure 86. *EmsAFceServerApp Application, First Iteration*

EmsCurrencyEditView

Table 6 contains the public interface of an *EmsCurrencyEditView* part.

Table 6. EmsCurrencyEditView, Public Interface				
	Class: **Superclass:**	EmsCurrencyEditView AbtAppBldrView		
Promote	*Prom. feat. name* aCurrency	*Subpart name* aCurrency	*Feature type* attribute	*Promotable feature* self

Figure 87 shows the visual layout of an *EmsCurrencyEditView* part.

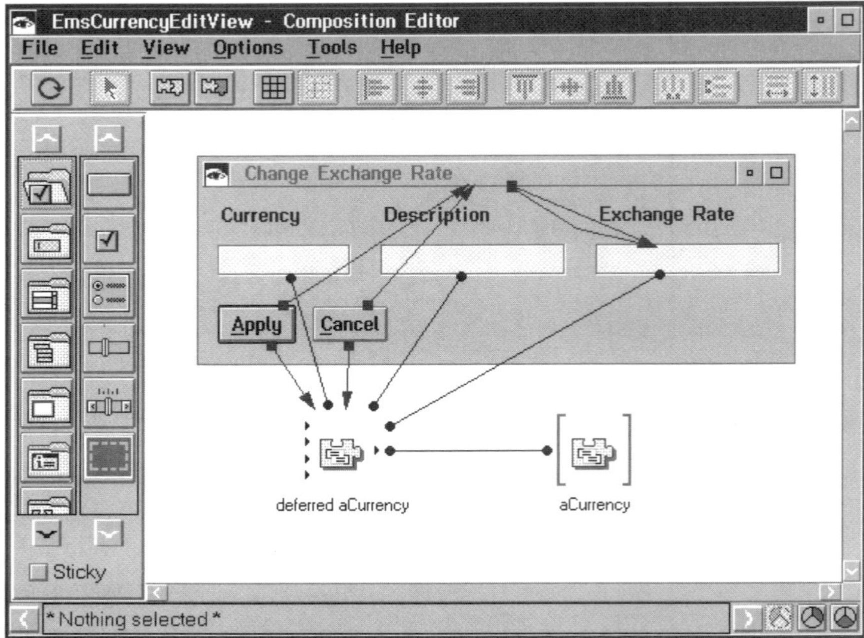

Figure 87. *EmsCurrencyEditView, Composition Editor*

EmsCurrencyListView

Figure 88 on page 213 shows the visual layout of an *EmsCurrencyList-View* part.

Instance Methods

```
getCurrencyList
  "Private -
Create a currency list instance and assign it to the variable."
  (self subpartNamed: 'aCurrencyList') value: EmsCurrencyList new.
```

EmsInternationalOOBankAppView

Figure 89 on page 218 shows the visual layout of an *EmsInternationa-lOOBankAppView* part.

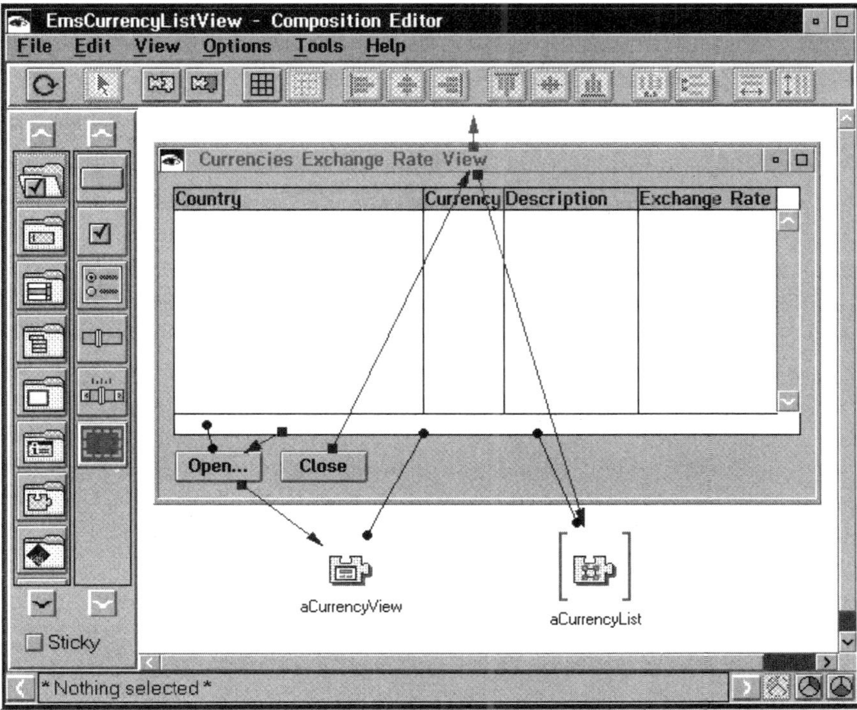

Figure 88. *EmsCurrencyListView, Composition Editor*

EmsCountry

Table 7 contains the public interface of an *EmsCountry* part.

Table 7. EmsCountry, Public Interface					
	Class: **Superclass:**	EmsCountry EmsU-niquePart			
Attribute	*Attribute name*	*Get selector*	*Set selector*	*Change event symbol*	*Instance variable class*
	currency	currency	currency:	currency	EmsCurrency
	name	name	name:	name	String

Class Definition

```
EmsUniquePart subclass: #EmsCountry
    instanceVariableNames: 'currency name '
    classVariableNames: ''
    poolDictionaries: ''
```

Instance Methods

```
currency
  "Return the value of currency."
  ^currency
currency: anEmsCurrency
  "Save the value of currency."
  currency := anEmsCurrency.
  self signalEvent: #currency
     with: anEmsCurrency.
name
  "Return the value of name."
  ^name
name: aString
  "Save the value of name."
  name := aString.
  self signalEvent: #name
     with: aString.
```

EmsCurrency

Table 8 contains the public interface of an *EmsCurrency* part.

Table 8. EmsCurrency, Public Interface

	Class:	EmsCurrency			
	Superclass:	EmsUniquePart			
Attribute	*Attribute name*	*Get selector*	*Set selector*	*Change event symbol*	*Instance variable class*
	country	country	country:	country	EmsCountry
	countryName	countryName		countryName	String
	denomination	denomination	denomination:	denomination	Set
	denominationList	denominationList		denominationList	OrderedCollection
	description	description	description	description	String
	exchangeRate	exchangeRate	exchangeRate:	exchangeRate	Float
	shortId	shortId	shortId:	shortId	String

Class Definition

```
EmsUniquePart subclass: #EmsCurrency
    instanceVariableNames: 'country denomination description
                            exchangeRate shortId '
    classVariableNames: ''
    poolDictionaries: ''
```

Instance Methods

```
country
  "Return the value of country."

  ^country

country: anEmsCountry
  "Save the value of country."

  country := anEmsCountry.
  self signalEvent: #country
     with: anEmsCountry.
  self signalEvent: #countryName.

countryName
  "Return the country name provided by my country object."

  self country isNil ifTrue: [^nil].
  ^self country name

denomination
  "Return the value of denomination."

  denomination isNil ifTrue: [ self denomination: Set new ].
  ^denomination

denomination: aSet
  "Save the value of denomination."

  denomination := aSet.
  self signalEvent: #denomination
     with: aSet.
  self signalEvent: #denominationList.

denominationList
  "Return the value of denominationList."

  ^self denomination asOrderedCollection

description
  "Return the value of description."

  ^description
```

```
description: aString
  "Save the value of description."

  description := aString.
  self signalEvent: #description
     with: aString.

exchangeRate
  "Return the value of exchangeRate."

  ^exchangeRate

exchangeRate: newRate
  "Save the value of exchangeRate."

  exchangeRate := newRate asFloat.
  self signalEvent: #exchangeRate
     with: exchangeRate.

releaseComponents
  "Release my collaborator (country) before I am released
   myself."

  self country notNil ifTrue: [ self country releaseRequester ].

shortId
  "Return the value of shortId."

  ^shortId

shortId: aString
  "Save the value of shortId."

  shortId := aString.
  self signalEvent: #shortId
     with: aString.
```

EmsCurrencyList

Table 9 contains the public interface of an *EmsCurrencyList* part.

Table 9. EmsCurrencyList, Public Interface

	Class:	EmsCurrencyList			
	Superclass:	EmsUniquePart			
Attribute	*Attribute name*	*Get selector*	*Set selector*	*Change event symbol*	*Instance variable class*
	currencies	currencies	currencies:	currencies	OrderedCollection

Class Definition

```
EmsUniquePart subclass: #EmsCurrencyList
    instanceVariableNames: 'currencies '
    classVariableNames: ''
    poolDictionaries: ''
```

Class Methods

```
new
    "Use the inherited #newFor: method. Provide an arbitrary but
     fixed id for the instance to ensure that there is one and
     only one instance created for all possible requests."

   ^self newFor: #CurrencyList.

persistenceManagerClass
"Return the class of my Persistence Manager."
^EmsPersistenceManager
```

Instance Methods

```
currencies
  "Return the value of currencies."

  currencies isNil ifTrue: [ self retrieve ].
  ^currencies

currencies: anOrderedCollection
  "Save the value of currencies."

  currencies := anOrderedCollection.
  self signalEvent: #currencies
     with: anOrderedCollection.

releaseComponents
  "Private - Release all of my currency objects before I'm being
released myself."

  self currencies do: [ :each | each releaseRequester ].
```

EmsFceDatabaseAccessSet

The database access set contains only one SQL query named *select-AllCurrencies* as follows:

```
SELECT [DB2 Qualifier].CURRENCY.CURR_CNTY,
       [DB2 Qualifier].CURRENCY.CURR_ID,
       [DB2 Qualifier].CURRENCY.CURR_NAME,
       [DB2 Qualifier].CURRENCY.CURR_XRATE_SELL
       FROM [DB2 Qualifier].CURRENCY ORDER BY 1 ASC'
```

EmsPersistenceManager

Table 10 contains the public interface of an *EmsPersistenceManager* part.

Table 10. EmsPersistenceManager, Public Interface				
	Class: **Superclass:**	EmsPersistenceManager AbtAppBldrPart		
Action	*Action name*	*Action symbol*	*Parameter name*	*Parameter class*
	retrieve	retrieve:	anInstance	Object

Figure 89 on page 218 shows the visual layout of an *EmsPersistenceManager* part.

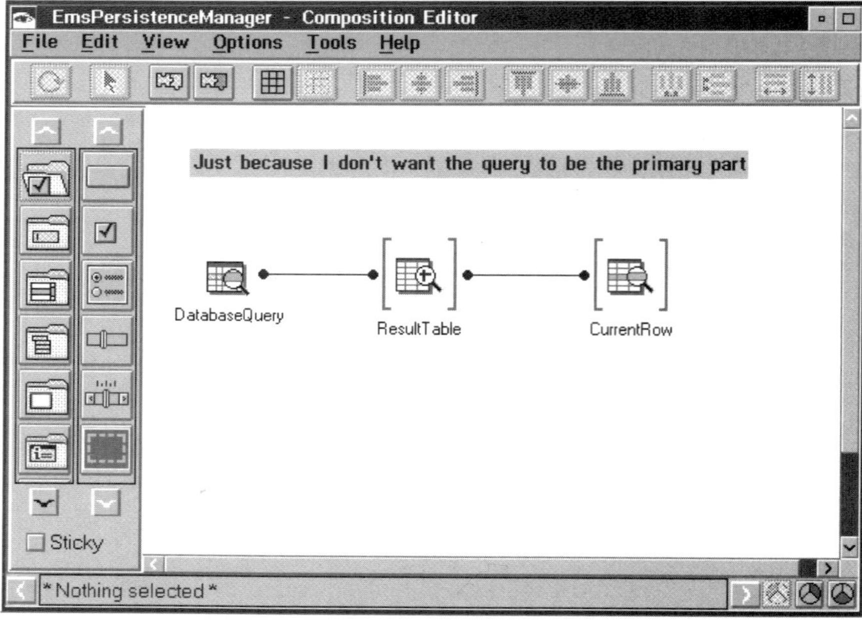

Figure 89. *EmsPersistenceManager, Composition Editor*

Using the multi-row database query, one SQL query named *selectAllCurrencies* is defined. For the corresponding SQL statement see EmsFceDatabaseAccessSet on page 217.

Class Definition

```
AbtAppBldrPart subclass: #EmsPersistenceManager
    instanceVariableNames: 'querySpecNames '
    classVariableNames: ''
    poolDictionaries: ''!
```

Instance Methods

```
allCurrencies: aCurrencyList
  "Private - Run the selectAllCurrencies query. Use the query
   result table to set the instance data for aCurrencyList."

   | aCollection |

  self dbQuery querySpecName: 'selectAllCurrencies';
    executeQuery.
  aCollection := OrderedCollection new.
  self resultTable rows do: [ :aRow |
    aCollection add: (self currencyFromRow: aRow).
  ].
  aCurrencyList currencies: aCollection.
  ^true

currencyFromRow: aRow
  "Private - Create and return a new Currency instance
   from given row."

  | aCountryObject aCurrencyObject |
  aCurrencyObject := EmsCurrency newFor: (aRow at: #CURR_ID).
  aCountryObject :=  EmsCountry newFor:  (aRow at: #CURR_CNTY).
  aCountryObject currency: aCurrencyObject;
                 name:     (aRow at: #CURR_CNTY).
  aCurrencyObject country:      aCountryObject;
                  description:  (aRow at: #CURR_NAME);
                  shortId:      (aRow at: #CURR_ID);
                exchangeRate: (aRow at: #CURR_XRATE_SELL) asFloat.
  ^aCurrencyObject

currentRow
  "Private - Return my current row part."
  ^(self subpartNamed: 'CurrentRow') value!

dbQuery
  "Private - Return my database query part."
  ^(self subpartNamed: 'DatabaseQuery') yourself!

resultTable
  "Private - Return my result table part."
  ^(self subpartNamed: 'ResultTable') value! !

retrieve: anInstance
  "Retrieve the persistent data for anInstance.
   At the moment, only CurrencyList instances are supported."
```

```
(anInstance isKindOf: EmsCurrencyList) ifTrue: [
  ^self allCurrencies: anInstance.
].
CwMessagePrompter
 error: 'Retrieving instances of class ', anInstance class name,
        ' not supported yet'.
^false
```

EmsUniquePart

Table 11 contains the public interface of an *EmsUniquePart* part.

Table 11. EmsUniquePart, Public Interface					
	Class: **Superclass:**	EmsU-niquePart AbtPart			
Attribute	*Attribute name*	*Get selector*	*Set selector*	*Change event symbol*	*Inst. variable class*
	id	id	id:	id	Object
Action	*Action name*	*Action symbol*	*Parameter name*	*Parameter class*	
	releaseRe-quester	releaseRe-quester			
	retrieve	retrieve			

Class Definition

```
AbtPart subclass: #EmsUniquePart
    classInstanceVariableNames: 'instances persistenceManager '
    instanceVariableNames: 'id numberOfRequesters '
    classVariableNames: ''
    poolDictionaries: ''
```

Class Methods

```
initialize
  "Remove all existing instances and initialize the class
   instance variable."

  Transcript cr; show: 'Initializing ', self name.
  self instances do: [ :each |
    Transcript show: '.'.
    each become: nil
```

```
    ].
    instances := nil.
    super initialize.
```

instances

```
    "Private - Return the value of instances."

    instances isNil ifTrue: [ instances := Dictionary new ].
    ^instances
```

newFor: anId

```
   "Create a new instance for anId, if it doesn't already exist.
     Return the instance."

    | anInstance |

    anInstance := self instances at: anId
                    ifAbsentPut: [ super new
                                    id: anId;
                                    yourself ].
    ^anInstance addRequester;
       yourself
```

persistenceManager

```
    "Return the value of persistenceManager."

    persistenceManager isNil ifTrue: [
      persistenceManager := self persistenceManagerClass new
    ].
    ^persistenceManager
```

persistenceManagerClass

```
    "Return the corresponding Persistence Manager class.
     This method is to be overwritten by subclasses."

    self subclassResponsibility
```

removeInstance: anInstance

```
    "Private - Remove anInstance from instances."

    self instances removeKey: anInstance id ifAbsent: [nil].
```

retrieve: anInstance

```
    "Ask my Persistence Manager to retrieve anInstance from
     the persistent storage."

    ^self persistenceManager retrieve: anInstance
```

Instance Methods

addRequester

```
    "Private - Increment the number of my requesters by 1."

    self numberOfRequesters: self numberOfRequesters + 1.
```

```
id
  "Return the value of id."

  ^id

id: anObject
  "Save the value of id."

  id := anObject.
  self signalEvent: #id
     with: anObject.

numberOfRequesters
  "Private - Return the value of numberOfRequesters."

  numberOfRequesters isNil ifTrue: [ self numberOfRequesters: 0 ].
  ^numberOfRequesters

numberOfRequesters: anInteger
  "Private - Save the value of numberOfRequesters."

  numberOfRequesters := anInteger.

releaseComponents
  "Private - This method has to be overwritten in any specific
   subclass that contains other unique parts created with a
   #newFor: class method. To all of these objects you should
   send #releaseRequester."

releaseRequester
  "Decrement the number of my requesters by 1.
   If no requesters are left, release my collaborators
   and ask my class to release myself."

  self numberOfRequesters: self numberOfRequesters - 1.
  self numberOfRequesters <= 0 ifTrue: [
    self releaseComponents.
    self class removeInstance: self
  ].

retrieve
  "Ask my class to retrieve me."

  ^self class retrieve: self
```

Second Iteration

The second iteration consists of three applications:

- *EmsAFceClientApp* as shown in Figure 90 on page 223 contains all classes for the client object space.
- *EmsAFceClientServerApp* as shown in Figure 91 on page 224 contains all classes that are needed both in the server and in the client object space.
- *EmsAFceServerApp* as shown in Figure 92 on page 224 contains all classes for the server object space.

EmsAFceClientServerApp is a prerequisite application for *EmsAFceServerApp*. *EmsAFceServerApp* is a prerequisite application for *EmsAFceClientApp*.

In the second iteration, we also moved some classes to a different application.

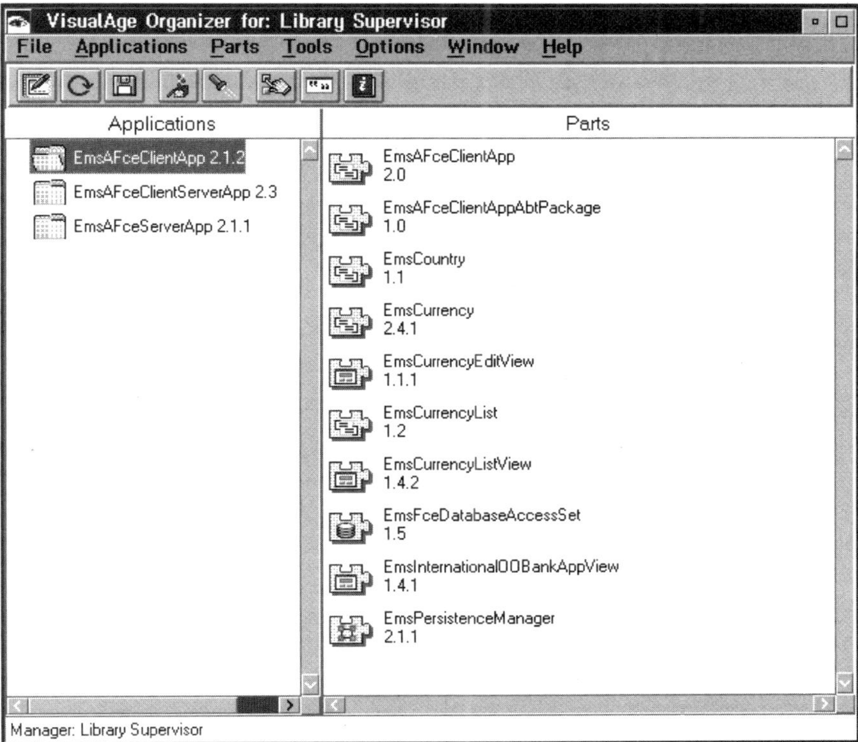

Figure 90. *EmsAFceClientApp Application, Second Iteration*

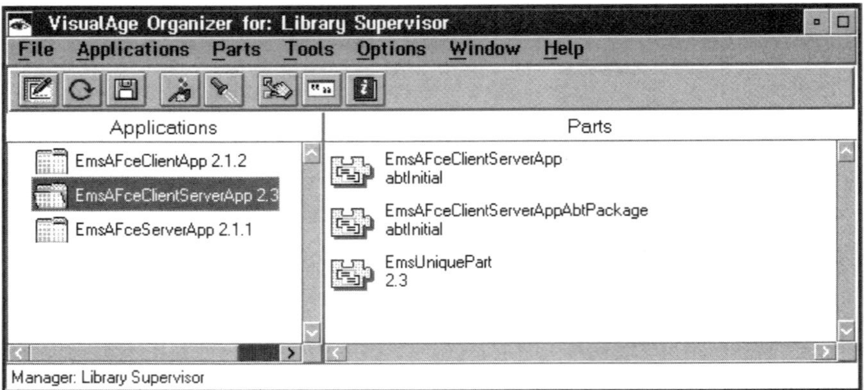

Figure 91. *EmsAFceClientServerApp Application, Second Iteration*

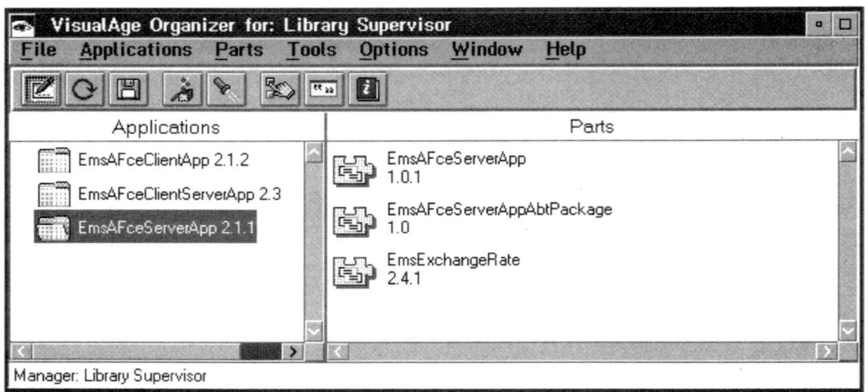

Figure 92. *EmsAFceServerApp Application, Second Iteration*

The following classes remained **unchanged** during the second iteration; to see their implementation, refer to First Iteration on page 210:

- *EmsCountry*
- *EmsCurrencyEditView*
- *EmsCurrencyList*
- *EmsCurrencyListView*
- *EmsFceDatabaseAccessSet*
- *EmsInternationalOOBankAppView*

The following class was **added** in the second iteration:

- *EmsExchangeRate*

The following classes were **changed** during the second iteration:

- ❑ *EmsCurrency*
- ❑ *EmsPersistenceManager*
- ❑ *EmsUniquePart*

EmsCurrency

The public interface was not changed; refer to EmsCurrency on page 214.

Class Definition

In the class definition, the instance variable *exchangeRate* was replaced by a new instance variable named *exchangeRateObject*.

```
EmsUniquePart subclass: #EmsCurrency
    instanceVariableNames: 'country exchangeRateObject description
                            shortId denomination '
    classVariableNames: ''
    poolDictionaries: 'CldtConstants '
```

Instance Methods

The following instance methods were changed as compared to the first iteration (see EmsCurrency on page 214):

```
exchangeRate
 "Use my exchange rate object to return the value of exchangeRate."

   self exchangeRateObject isNil ifTrue: [^nil].
   ^self exchangeRateObject exchangeRate

exchangeRate: newRate
   "Send the new exchangeRate value to my exchangeRate object."

   self exchangeRateObject isNil ifTrue: [^nil].
   self exchangeRateObject exchangeRate: newRate asFloat.
   self signalEvent: #exchangeRate
      with: newRate asFloat.

releaseComponents
   "Release all of my collaborators (country and exchange rate)
    before I'm released myself."

   self country notNil ifTrue: [ self country releaseRequester ].
   self exchangeRateObject notNil ifTrue: [
     self exchangeRateObject removeDependent: self;
       releaseRequester.
   ].
```

The following instance methods were added as compared to the first iteration (see EmsCurrency on page 214):

```
exchangeRateObject
  "Private - Return the value of exchangeRateObject."
  ^exchangeRateObject

exchangeRateObject: anEmsExchangeRate
  "Private - Set the exchangeRate object."

  exchangeRateObject := anEmsExchangeRate.
  self signalEvent: #exchangeRate
    with: self exchangeRate.

update: newRate
  "Process the information from the server exchangeRate object
   about the new exchangeRate value.
  Signal the corresponding event and also show a message box."

  self signalEvent: #exchangeRate with: newRate.
  CwMessagePrompter
    message: 'Attention:', LineDelimiter,
             'Exchange rate for ', self description trimBlanks,
             ' (', self shortId, ') has changed to ',
             newRate printString.
```

EmsPersistenceManager

The public interface, Composition Editor definitions, and class definition were not changed; refer to EmsPersistenceManager on page 218.

Instance Methods

The following instance method was changed as compared to the first iteration (see EmsPersistenceManager on page 218):

```
currencyFromRow: aRow
  "Private -
Create and return a new currency object from given row."

  | aCountryObject aCurrencyObject anExRateObject |

  aCurrencyObject := EmsCurrency newFor: (aRow at: #CURR_ID).
  aCountryObject :=  EmsCountry newFor:  (aRow at: #CURR_CNTY).
  anExRateObject := EmsExchangeRate newFor: (aRow at: #CURR_ID)
              requester:    aCurrencyObject
              currencyId:   (aRow at: #CURR_ID)
              exchangeRate: (aRow at: #CURR_XRATE_SELL) asFloat.
  aCountryObject currency: aCurrencyObject;
                 name:     (aRow at: #CURR_CNTY).
  aCurrencyObject country:            aCountryObject;
                  description:        (aRow at: #CURR_NAME);
                  shortId:            (aRow at: #CURR_ID);
                  exchangeRateObject: anExRateObject.
  ^aCurrencyObject
```

EmsUniquePart

The public interface, class definition, and class methods were not changed; refer to EmsUniquePart on page 220.

Instance Methods

The following instance methods were added as compared to the first iteration (see EmsUniquePart on page 220):

```
addDependent: anObject
  "Private - Overwrite the Smalltalk kernel method to make

   sure that there are no duplicates among the dependents."
  (self dependents includes: anObject) ifFalse: [
    ^super addDependent: anObject
  ].

dtBroadcast: aSymbol
  "Send the argument aSymbol as a unary message to all of the
   receiver's dependents. Use parallel blocks to send the
   messages.

   Fail if aSymbol does not represent a unary message."

  | aCollectionOfBlocks |

  self dependents notEmpty ifTrue: [
    aCollectionOfBlocks := OrderedCollection new.
    self dependents do: [ :dependent |
      aCollectionOfBlocks add:
        [ (dependent respondsTo: aSymbol) ifTrue: [
          dependent perform: aSymbol ]
        ]
    ].
    aCollectionOfBlocks dtForkEachAndContinue
  ].

dtBroadcast: aSymbol with: anObject
 "Send the argument aSymbol as a keyword message with argument
   anObject to all of the receiver's dependents. Use parallel
   blocks to send the messages.

  Fail if aSymbol is not a Symbol.
 Fail if the number of arguments expected by aSymbol is not 1.

"    | aCollectionOfBlocks |

  self dependents notEmpty ifTrue: [
    aCollectionOfBlocks := OrderedCollection new.
    self dependents do: [ :dependent |
      aCollectionOfBlocks add:
        [ (dependent respondsTo: aSymbol) ifTrue: [
```

```
                dependent perform: aSymbol with: anObject ]
            ]
        ].
        aCollectionOfBlocks dtForkEachAndContinue.
    ].
```

dtChanged

```
  "Inform all dependents that the receiver has changed."
  self dtChanged: self
```

dtChanged: anObject

```
  "Inform all dependents that the receiver has changed
   in an aspect represented by the argument anObject."

  self dtBroadcast: #update: with: anObject
```

EmsExchangeRate

Table 12 contains the public interface of an *EmsExchangeRate* part.

Table 12. EmsExchangeRate, Public Interface

	Class:	EmsExchangeRate			
	Superclass:	EmsUniquePart			
Attribute	*Attribute name*	*Get selector*	*Set selector*	*Change event symbol*	*Instance variable class*
	currencyId	currencyId	currencyId:	currencyId	String
	exchangeRate	exchangeRate	exchangeRate:	exchangeRate	Float

Class Definition

```
EmsUniquePart subclass: #EmsExchangeRate
    instanceVariableNames: 'currencyId exchangeRate '
    classVariableNames: ''
    poolDictionaries: ''
```

Class Methods

newFor: anId currencyId: aString exchangeRate: aFloat

```
 "Create a new instance for anId and provide its instance variable
   values. Return the instance."

  ^(self newFor: anId)
      currencyId: aString;
      exchangeRate: aFloat;
      yourself.
```

```
newFor: anId requester: anObject currencyId: aString
  exchangeRate: aFloat
 "Create a new instance for anId and provide its instance variable
   values. Return the instance."

  ^(self newFor: anId)
      currencyId: aString;
      exchangeRate: aFloat;
      addDependent: anObject;
      yourself.
```

Instance Methods

```
currencyId
  "Return the value of currencyId."

  ^currencyId
currencyId: aString
  "Save the value of currencyId."

  currencyId := aString.
  self signalEvent: #currencyId
     with: aString.

exchangeRate
  "Return the value of exchangeRate."

  ^exchangeRate

exchangeRate: newRate
 "Save the value of exchangeRate. If the value has not changed,
do nothing. Otherwise, signal an event and inform all dependents
using the asynchronous broadcast mechanism."

  | rate |

  rate := newRate asFloat.
  exchangeRate ~= rate ifTrue: [
    exchangeRate := rate.
    self signalEvent: #exchangeRate with: exchangeRate.
    Transcript cr;
      show: 'Exchange rate for ', self currencyId printString,
            ' changed to ', exchangeRate printString,
            ' - inform dependents ...'.
    self dtChanged: exchangeRate.
    Transcript show: ' done!'.
  ].
```

Third Iteration

The third iteration consists of the same three applications as the second iteration:

- *EmsAFceClientApp* as shown in Figure 93 on page 230 contains all classes for the client object space.
- *EmsAFceClientServerApp* as shown in Figure 94 on page 231 contains all classes that are needed both in the server and in the client object space.
- *EmsAFceServerApp* as shown in Figure 95 on page 231 contains all classes for the server object space.

EmsAFceClientServerApp is a prerequisite application for *EmsAFceServerApp*. *EmsAFceServerApp* is a prerequisite application for *EmsAFceClientApp*.

In the third iteration, some classes were moved again to a different application as compared to the second iteration.

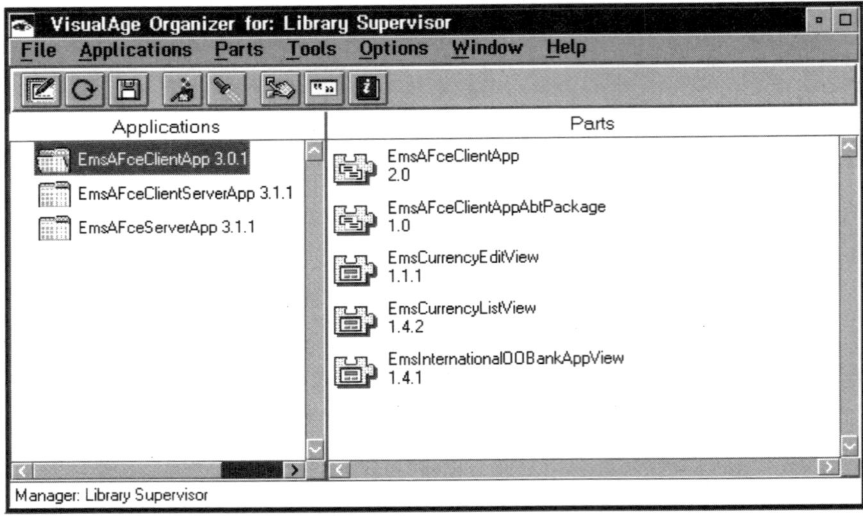

Figure 93. *EmsAFceClientApp Application, Third Iteration*

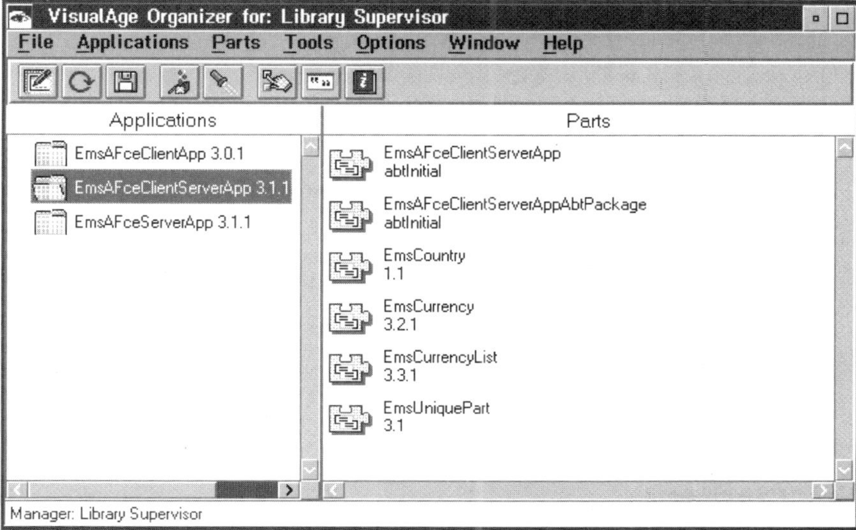

Figure 94. *EmsAFceClientServerApp Application, Third Iteration*

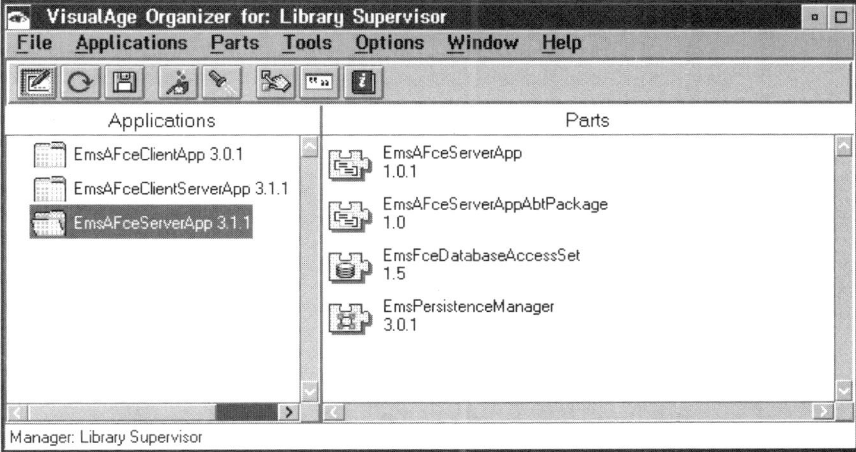

Figure 95. *EmsAFceServerApp Application, Third Iteration*

The following classes remained **unchanged** during the third iteration; to see their implementation, refer to First Iteration on page 210:

- *EmsCountry*
- *EmsFceDatabaseAccessSet*
- *EmsCurrencyEditView*
- *EmsCurrencyListView*
- *EmsInternationalOOBankAppView*

The following class was **removed** in the third iteration:

- *EmsExchangeRate*

The following classes were **changed** during the third iteration:

- *EmsCurrency*
- *EmsCurrencyList*
- *EmsPersistenceManager*
- *EmsUniquePart*

EmsCurrency

The public interface was not changed; refer to EmsCurrency on page 214.

Class Definition

In the class definition, the instance variable *exchangeRateObject* was replaced by *exchangeRate* so that the class definition actually looks the same as it did in the first iteration.

```
EmsUniquePart subclass: #EmsCurrency
    instanceVariableNames: 'country exchangeRate description
                            shortId denomination '
    classVariableNames: ''
    poolDictionaries: 'CldtConstants '
```

Instance Methods

The following instance methods were changed as compared to the second iteration (see EmsCurrency on page 225):

```
exchangeRate
  "Return the value of exchangeRate."

  ^exchangeRate

exchangeRate: newRate
  "Inform my dependents about the change. The actual instance
  variable value will be changed after the notification within
  the #localSetExchangeRate: method. The latter will be called
```

```
 by my CurrencyList.
| rate |
rate := newRate asFloat.
exchangeRate ~= rate ifTrue: [
  Transcript cr;
    show: 'Exchange rate for ', self shortId printString,
          ' locally changed to ', rate  printString,
          ' - inform dependents ...'.
  self dtBroadcast: #localRateUpdate:for:
    withArguments: (Array with: rate with: self shortId).
  Transcript show: ' done!'.
].
```

```
releaseComponents
  "Release my collaborator (country) before I'm being released
   myself."

  self country notNil ifTrue: [ self country releaseRequester ].
```

The following instance method was added as compared to the first and second iteration (see EmsCurrency on page 214 and EmsCurrency on page 225):

```
localSetExchangeRate: newRate
  "Private - Save the local value of exchangeRate.
   Signal a local event but don't inform dependents since that
   should have already been done before."

  exchangeRate := newRate asFloat.
  self signalEvent: #exchangeRate with: exchangeRate.
```

The following instance methods were removed as compared to the second iteration (see EmsCurrency on page 225):

- *exchangeRateObject*
- *exchangeRateObject:*

EmsCurrencyList

The public interface was not changed; refer to EmsCurrencyList on page 216.

Class Definition

The instance variable *serverCurrencyList* was added to the class definition.

```
EmsUniquePart subclass: #EmsCurrencyList
    instanceVariableNames: 'currencies serverCurrencyList '
    classVariableNames: ''
    poolDictionaries: 'CldtConstants '
```

Class Methods

The following class methods were added as compared to the first iteration (see EmsCurrencyList on page 216):

```
newFor: anId
 "Create a new instance for anId, if it doesn't already exist.
 Create also a 'master' currency list within the server object
   space. Return the instance."

  | anInstance localList remoteList oRef |

  anInstance := self instances at: anId ifAbsentPut: [
    localList := super new.

  "Use the global reference to get an object reference for the
   CurrencyList class within the server object space. Create a
     remote object by using a shadow, then store a pointer to
     that object in the local currency list."
    oRef := NameServerList default
          referenceAtFirstIdentifier: 'EmsServerCurrencyList'.
  remoteList := oRef shadow newFor: anId dependent: localList.

    localList id: anId;
      serverCurrencyList: remoteList;
      yourself
  ].
  ^anInstance addRequester;
     yourself

newFor: anId dependent: aDependent
 "Create a new instance for anId, if it doesn't already exist.
   Add aDependent to the instance's dependents.
   Return the instance."

  ^(super newFor: anId)
     addDependent: aDependent;
     yourself
```

Instance Methods

The following instance method was changed as compared to the first iteration (see EmsCurrencyList on page 216):

```
currencies: anOrderedCollection
  "Save the value of currencies."

  currencies notNil ifTrue: [
    currencies do: [ :each | each removeDependent: self ].
  ].
  currencies := anOrderedCollection.
  currencies do: [ :each | each addDependent: self ].
  self signalEvent: #currencies
     with: anOrderedCollection.
```

The following instance methods were added as compared to the first iteration (see EmsCurrencyList on page 216):

```
globalRateUpdate: newRate for: aCurrencyId
"Process the information from a remote currency list about the
   new exchangeRate value. Signal the corresponding event and also
   open a message box."

  | matchingCurrencies currency |

  "Find my currency object for aCurrencyId."
  matchingCurrencies := self currencies select: [ :each |
                          each shortId = aCurrencyId ].
  matchingCurrencies isEmpty ifTrue: [ ^nil ].
  currency := matchingCurrencies first.

  "Set the local exchange rate."
  currency exchangeRate = newRate ifTrue: [ ^nil ].
  currency localSetExchangeRate: newRate.

  self serverCurrencyList isNil ifTrue: [

    "No serverCurrencyList means I'm the server list.
     Therefore, I have to  broadcast the message to all
     client CurrencyList objects."
    Transcript cr;
      show: 'Exchange rate for ', aCurrencyId, ' changed to ',
            newRate printString, ' - inform dependents ...'.
    self dtBroadcast: #globalRateUpdate:for:
      withArguments: (Array with: newRate with: aCurrencyId).
    Transcript show: ' done!'.

  ] ifFalse: [

    "serverCurrencyList means, I'm in a client object space.
     Show a message box."
    CwMessagePrompter
      message: 'Attention:', LineDelimiter,
               'Exchange rate for ',
               currency description trimBlanks,
               ' (', currency shortId, ') has changed to ',
               newRate printString.
  ].

localRateUpdate: newRate for: aCurrencyId
  "Process the information from a local currency about the new
   exchangeRate value. Set the value in the server object."

  self serverCurrencyList notNil ifTrue: [
    self serverCurrencyList
      globalRateUpdate: newRate for: aCurrencyId
  ].
```

```
releaseComponents
  "Private - Release all of my currency objects and remove
   myself from the server object dependents list, before
   I'm released."

  self currencies do: [ :each | each releaseRequester ].
  self serverCurrencyList notNil ifTrue: [
    self serverCurrencyList removeDependent: self;
      releaseRequester.
  ].

retrieve
"If I have a serverCurrencyList, I'm in a client object space.
   Then I ask the server object to obtain the value.
   Otherwise, I'm the server list. Then default behavior."

  self serverCurrencyList notNil ifTrue: [
    self currencies:
      (self serverCurrencyList
         dsPerformWithLocalResult: #currencies).
  ] ifFalse: [
    super retrieve
  ].

serverCurrencyList
  "Return the value of serverCurrencyList."

  ^serverCurrencyList

serverCurrencyList: anEmsCurrencyList
  "Save the value of serverCurrencyList."

  serverCurrencyList := anEmsCurrencyList.
```

EmsPersistenceManager

The public interface, Composition Editor definitions, and class definition were not changed as compared to the first iteration; refer to EmsPersistenceManager on page 218.

Instance Methods

The following instance method was changed as compared to the second iteration (see EmsPersistenceManager on page 226):

```
currencyFromRow: aRow
  "Private -
Create and return a new currency object from given row."

  | aCountryObject aCurrencyObject |
  aCurrencyObject := EmsCurrency newFor: (aRow at: #CURR_ID).
  aCountryObject  := EmsCountry  newFor: (aRow at: #CURR_CNTY).
```

```
aCountryObject currency: aCurrencyObject;
               name:     (aRow at: #CURR_CNTY).
aCurrencyObject country:            aCountryObject;
      description:          (aRow at: #CURR_NAME);
      shortId:              (aRow at: #CURR_ID);
      localSetExchangeRate: (aRow at: #CURR_XRATE_SELL) asFloat.
^aCurrencyObject
```

EmsUniquePart

The public interface, class definition, and class methods were not changed compared to the first iteration; refer to EmsUniquePart on page 220.

Instance Methods

The following instance method was added as compared to the first and second iteration (see EmsUniquePart on page 220 and EmsUniquePart on page 227):

```
dtBroadcast: aSymbol withArguments: anArray
"Send the argument aSymbol as a keyword message with arguments
   anArray to all of the receiver's dependents. Use parallel
   blocks to send the messages. Answer self.

   Fail if aSymbol is not a Symbol.
   Fail if the number of arguments expected by aSymbol is not
   equal to the array's size."

  | aCollectionOfBlocks |

  self dependents notEmpty ifTrue: [
    aCollectionOfBlocks := OrderedCollection new.
    self dependents do: [ :dependent |
      aCollectionOfBlocks add:
        [ (dependent respondsTo: aSymbol) ifTrue: [
          dependent perform: aSymbol withArguments: anArray ]
        ]
    ].
    aCollectionOfBlocks dtForkEachAndContinue.
  ].
```

List of Abbreviations

API	Application Programming Interface
CRC	Class-Responsibility-Collaboration
CORBA	Common Object Request Broker Architecture
CUA	Common User Access
DCE	Distributed Computing Environment
DRDA	Distributed Relational Database Architecture
DSOM	Distributed System Object Model
DTP	Distributed Transaction Processing
FCE	Foreign Currency Exchange
GSS	Generic Security Services
GUI	Graphical User Interface
IBM	International Business Machines Corporation
IDL	Interface Definition Language
IP	Internet Protocol
IPMD	IBM Presentation Manager Debugger
ITSO	International Technical Support Organization
NetSP	Network Security Program
OMA	Object Management Architecture
OMG	Object Management Group
OMT	Object Modeling Technique
OOSE	Object-Oriented Software Engineering
ORB	Object Request Broker
OSF	Open Systems Foundation
OTS	Object Transaction Service
RDD	Responsibility-Driven Design
SOM	System Object Model
UNI	uniqueness of instances
VMT	Visual Modeling Technique

Bibliography

[Cupparo93] John A. Cupparo. "Iterate Applications not just Prototypes." *OOPSLA '93 Proceedings (Addendum)*, IBM, 1993.

[Jacob92] Ivar Jacobson, Magnus Christerson, Patrik Jonsson, and Gunnar Övergaard. *Object-Oriented Software Engineering: A Use Case Driven Approach*, Addison-Wesley Publishing Company, 1992.

[Orfali94] Robert Orfali, Dan Harkey. *Client/Server Survival Guide with OS/2*, Van Nostrand Reinhold, 1994.

[Rumba91] J. Rumbaugh, M. Blaha, W. Premerlani, F. Eddy, and W. Lorenson. *Object-Oriented Modeling and Design*, Prentice Hall, 1991.

[Tkach96] D. Tkach, W. Fang, and A. So. *Visual Modeling Technique: Object Technology with Visual Programming*, Addison–Wesley, 1996.

[Wirfs90] R. Wirfs-Brock, B. Wilkerson, and L. Wiener. *Designing Object-Oriented Software*, Prentice Hall, 1990.

Index

A

B

C

D

E

F

G

H

I

L

M

N

O

P

Q

R

S

T

U

V

W

X

Y

Z

LICENSE AGREEMENT AND LIMITED WARRANTY

READ THE FOLLOWING TERMS AND CONDITIONS CAREFULLY BEFORE OPENING THIS DISK PACKAGE. THIS LEGAL DOCUMENT IS AN AGREEMENT BETWEEN YOU AND PRENTICE-HALL, INC. (THE "COMPANY"). BY OPENING THIS SEALED DISK PACKAGE, YOU ARE AGREEING TO BE BOUND BY THESE TERMS AND CONDITIONS. IF YOU DO NOT AGREE WITH THESE TERMS AND CONDITIONS, DO NOT OPEN THE DISK PACKAGE. PROMPTLY RETURN THE UNOPENED DISK PACKAGE AND ALL ACCOMPANYING ITEMS TO THE PLACE YOU OBTAINED THEM FOR A FULL REFUND OF ANY SUMS YOU HAVE PAID.

1. **GRANT OF LICENSE:** In consideration of your payment of the license fee, which is part of the price you paid for this product, and your agreement to abide by the terms and conditions of this Agreement, the Company grants to you a nonexclusive right to use and display the copy of the enclosed software program (hereinafter the "SOFTWARE") on a single computer (i.e., with a single CPU) at a single location so long as you comply with the terms of this Agreement. The Company reserves all rights not expressly granted to you under this Agreement.

2. **OWNERSHIP OF SOFTWARE:** You own only the magnetic or physical media (the enclosed disks) on which the SOFTWARE is recorded or fixed, but the Company retains all the rights, title, and ownership to the SOFTWARE recorded on the original disk copy(ies) and all subsequent copies of the SOFTWARE, regardless of the form or media on which the original or other copies may exist. This license is not a sale of the original SOFTWARE or any copy to you.

3. **COPY RESTRICTIONS:** This SOFTWARE and the accompanying printed materials and user manual (the "Documentation") are the subject of copyright. You may not copy the Documentation or the SOFTWARE, except that you may make a single copy of the SOFTWARE for backup or archival purposes only. You may be held legally responsible for any copying or copyright infringement which is caused or encouraged by your failure to abide by the terms of this restriction.

4. **USE RESTRICTIONS:** You may not network the SOFTWARE or otherwise use it on more than one computer or computer terminal at the same time. You may physically transfer the SOFTWARE from one computer to another provided that the SOFTWARE is used on only one computer at a time. You may not distribute copies of the SOFTWARE or Documentation to others. You may not reverse engineer, disassemble, decompile, modify, adapt, translate, or create derivative works based on the SOFTWARE or the Documentation without the prior written consent of the Company.

5. **TRANSFER RESTRICTIONS:** The enclosed SOFTWARE is licensed only to you and may not be transferred to any one else without the prior written consent of the Company. Any unauthorized transfer of the SOFTWARE shall result in the immediate termination of this Agreement.

6. **TERMINATION:** This license is effective until terminated. This license will terminate automatically without notice from the Company and become null and void if you fail to comply with any provisions or limitations of this license. Upon termination, you shall destroy the Documentation and all copies of the SOFTWARE. All provisions of this Agreement as to warranties, limitation of liability, remedies or damages, and our ownership rights shall survive termination.

7. **MISCELLANEOUS:** This Agreement shall be construed in accordance with the laws of the United States of America and the State of New York and shall benefit the Company, its affiliates, and assignees.

8. **LIMITED WARRANTY AND DISCLAIMER OF WARRANTY:** The Company warrants that the SOFTWARE, when properly used in accordance with the Documentation, will operate in substantial conformity with the description of the SOFTWARE set forth in the Documentation. The Company does not warrant that the SOFTWARE will meet your requirements or that the operation of the SOFTWARE will be

uninterrupted or error-free. The Company warrants that the media on which the SOFTWARE is delivere shall be free from defects in materials and workmanship under normal use for a period of thirty (30) day from the date of your purchase. Your only remedy and the Company's only obligation under these limite warranties is, at the Company's option, return of the warranted item for a refund of any amounts paid by yo or replacement of the item. Any replacement of SOFTWARE or media under the warranties shall not exten the original warranty period. The limited warranty set forth above shall not apply to any SOFTWARE whic the Company determines in good faith has been subject to misuse, neglect, improper installation, repai alteration, or damage by you. EXCEPT FOR THE EXPRESSED WARRANTIES SET FORTH ABOVE THE COMPANY DISCLAIMS ALL WARRANTIES, EXPRESS OR IMPLIED, INCLUDING WITHOU LIMITATION, THE IMPLIED WARRANTIES OF MERCHANTABILITY AND FITNESS FOR A PAR TICULAR PURPOSE. EXCEPT FOR THE EXPRESS WARRANTY SET FORTH ABOVE, THE COM PANY DOES NOT WARRANT, GUARANTEE, OR MAKE ANY REPRESENTATION REGARDIN THE USE OR THE RESULTS OF THE USE OF THE SOFTWARE IN TERMS OF ITS CORRECTNESS ACCURACY, RELIABILITY, CURRENTNESS, OR OTHERWISE.

IN NO EVENT, SHALL THE COMPANY OR ITS EMPLOYEES, AGENTS, SUPPLIERS OR CONTRACTORS BE LIABLE FOR ANY INCIDENTAL, INDIRECT, SPECIAL, OR CONSEQUEN TIAL DAMAGES ARISING OUT OF OR IN CONNECTION WITH THE LICENSE GRANTED UNDE THIS AGREEMENT, OR FOR LOSS OF USE, LOSS OF DATA, LOSS OF INCOME OR PROFIT, O OTHER LOSSES, SUSTAINED AS A RESULT OF INJURY TO ANY PERSON, OR LOSS OF O DAMAGE TO PROPERTY, OR CLAIMS OF THIRD PARTIES, EVEN IF THE COMPANY OR A AUTHORIZED REPRESENTATIVE OF THE COMPANY HAS BEEN ADVISED OF THE POSSIBIL ITY OF SUCH DAMAGES. IN NO EVENT SHALL LIABILITY OF THE COMPANY FOR DAMAGE WITH RESPECT TO THE SOFTWARE EXCEED THE AMOUNTS ACTUALLY PAID BY YOU, I ANY, FOR THE SOFTWARE.

SOME JURISDICTIONS DO NOT ALLOW THE LIMITATION OF IMPLIED WARRAN TIES OR LIABILITY FOR INCIDENTAL, INDIRECT, SPECIAL, OR CONSEQUENTIAL DAMAGES SO THE ABOVE LIMITATIONS MAY NOT ALWAYS APPLY. THE WARRANTIES IN THIS AGREE MENT GIVE YOU SPECIFIC LEGAL RIGHTS AND YOU MAY ALSO HAVE OTHER RIGHT WHICH VARY IN ACCORDANCE WITH LOCAL LAW.

ACKNOWLEDGMENT

YOU ACKNOWLEDGE THAT YOU HAVE READ THIS AGREEMENT, UNDERSTAN IT, AND AGREE TO BE BOUND BY ITS TERMS AND CONDITIONS. YOU ALSO AGREE THA THIS AGREEMENT IS THE COMPLETE AND EXCLUSIVE STATEMENT OF THE AGREEMEN BETWEEN YOU AND THE COMPANY AND SUPERSEDES ALL PROPOSALS OR PRIOR AGREE MENTS, ORAL, OR WRITTEN, AND ANY OTHER COMMUNICATIONS BETWEEN YOU AND TH COMPANY OR ANY REPRESENTATIVE OF THE COMPANY RELATING TO THE SUBJECT MA TER OF THIS AGREEMENT.

Should you have any questions concerning this Agreement or if you wish to contact the Con pany for any reason, please contact in writing at the address below or call the at the telephone number pr vided.

PTR Customer Service
Prentice Hall PTR
One Lake Street
Upper Saddle River, New Jersey 07458
Telephone: 201-236-7105